'This timely and engaging contribution extends the metaphor approach, which has been used to great effect in economics, law and organizational theory, to the study of professional occupations. The results are extremely insightful as this book, through the visual power of metaphors, casts new light on a series of key debates within the sociology of the professions.'

Daniel Muzio, *Professor of Professions and Organization, University of Newcastle, UK*

'Liljegren and Saks are to be congratulated in bringing together a fine edited collection of new and published pieces on the role of metaphors in understanding professions. This novel focus should appeal to those interested in the professions generally and in particular professions such as medicine, education and social work.'

Jonathan Gabe, *Royal Holloway, University of London, UK*

Professions and Metaphors

Professions and Metaphors: Understanding Professions in Society explores the way that two traditions have contributed to our understanding of both theory and society over recent decades. In the first tradition, the growing literature on metaphors has helped to guide thinking, providing insights into such phenomena as the study of organizations. In the second, there has been an increased interest in professions, from lawyers and university academics to doctors and social workers.

This edited collection brings together these two traditions for the first time, providing a unique and systematic overview, at macro and micro level, of the use of metaphors in the sociology of professions. A range of professional fields are explored, from law and medicine to social work and teaching, showing how metaphors can enhance our understanding of the operation of professional groups.

By demonstrating how metaphors can add to our understanding of professions in society, as well as in professional practice, this ground-breaking book makes an invaluable contribution to advanced students and researchers in fields such as the sociology of professions and work and organization – as well as informing professionals and policy makers themselves.

Andreas Liljegren is Associate Professor in Social Work in the Department of Social Work at the University of Gothenburg, Sweden.

Mike Saks is Research Professor in Health Policy at University Campus Suffolk, UK, and holds Visiting Chairs at the University of Lincoln, UK, the Royal Veterinary College, University of London, UK, and the University of Toronto, Canada.

Routledge Studies in Management, Organizations and Society

This series presents innovative work grounded in new realities, addressing issues crucial to an understanding of the contemporary world. This is the world of organized societies, where boundaries between formal and informal, public and private, local and global organizations have been displaced or have vanished, along with other nineteenth century dichotomies and oppositions. Management, apart from becoming a specialized profession for a growing number of people, is an everyday activity for most members of modern societies.

Similarly, at the level of enquiry, culture and technology, and literature and economics, can no longer be conceived as isolated intellectual fields; conventional canons and established mainstreams are contested. **Management, Organizations and Society** addresses these contemporary dynamics of transformation in a manner that transcends disciplinary boundaries, with books that will appeal to researchers, student and practitioners alike.

Recent titles in this series include:

Untold Stories in Organizations
Edited by Michal Izak, Linda Hitchin, and David Anderson

Gender Equality in Public Services
Chasing the dream
Hazel Conley and Margaret Page

Sexual Orientation at Work
Contemporary issues and perspectives
Edited by Fiona Colgan and Nick Rumens

Organizations and the Media
Organizing in a mediatized world
Edited by Josef Pallas, Lars Strannegård and Stefan Jonsson

Management and Neoliberalism
Connecting policies and practices
Alexander Styhre

Professions and Metaphors

Understanding professions in society

Edited by Andreas Liljegren
and Mike Saks

Routledge
Taylor & Francis Group

LONDON AND NEW YORK

First published 2017 by Routledge

2 Park Square, Milton Park, Abingdon, Oxfordshire OX14 4RN
52 Vanderbilt Avenue, New York, NY 10017

*Routledge is an imprint of the Taylor & Francis Group,
an informa business*

First issued in paperback 2019

British Library Cataloguing in Publication Data
A catalogue record for this book is available from the British Library

Library of Congress Cataloging-in-Publication Data
A catalog record for this book has been requested

ISBN: 978-1-138-94418-3 (hbk)
ISBN: 978-0-367-87445-2 (pbk)

Typeset in Sabon
by ApexCovantage, LLC

Contents

Notes on contributors

Editors

Andreas Liljegren is Associate Professor in Social Work in the Department of Social Work at the University of Gothenburg in Sweden – having previously been employed professionally in social work. He has obtained undergraduate degrees in both Social Work and Practical Philosophy from the University of Gothenburg – where he also completed his PhD in Social Work. He has published several articles in English and Swedish on the professions and related themes in journals, ranging from *Comparative Sociology* and the *Journal of Professions and Organization* to the *European Journal of Social Work* and the *International Journal of Integrated Care*. Apart from book chapters, he has won major Swedish research grants on professions both as Principal and Co-investigator and has given a number of international conference papers associated with the theme of the book. He currently lectures on the key areas of professions, organizational theory and research methods.

Mike Saks is Research Professor in Health Policy at University Campus Suffolk (UCS), having previously been Provost at UCS, Deputy Vice Chancellor at the University of Lincoln and Dean of the Faculty of Health and Community Studies at De Montfort University. He studied Sociology at the University of Lancaster and the University of Kent – obtaining his PhD in this subject from the London School of Economics, where he also taught. He holds Visiting Professorships at the University of Lincoln, the Royal Veterinary College and the University of Toronto – having previously held a Visiting Chair in Sociology at the University of Essex – and is currently on the Board of Rose Bruford College of Theatre and Performance in London. He has published fifteen edited and sole-authored books on professions, health, regulation and research methods with leading publishers, and many articles and book chapters on these subjects. Aside from acting as an adviser to professions and governments nationally and internationally, he has won several major research grants and is on the editorial board of a number of international journals. He is the current Vice President and former President of the International Sociological Association Research Committee on Professional Groups.

Other contributors

Andrew Abbott has taught sociology in the United States at Rutgers University from 1978 to 1991 and the University of Chicago, where he has been Professor of Sociology since 1991. He has written books on professions, methodology, social theory and the sociology of modern academic knowledge, as well as texts on heuristics and library research. He is the current Editor of the *American Journal of Sociology*.

Ola Agevall is Professor of Sociology and Research Director for the Forum of Research on Professions at Linnaeus University in Sweden. He received his PhD from Uppsala University for a thesis on *A Science of Unique Events*. His research has since focused on sociological theory, sociology of knowledge and conceptual history, as well as the sociology of professions.

Martin Cortazzi is Visiting Professor in the Centre for Applied Linguistics at the University of Warwick in the United Kingdom. He has trained teachers at primary, secondary and university levels of education in the United Kingdom and internationally. His research publications develop qualitative methods of narrative and metaphor analysis, and investigate cultural aspects of language teaching.

Robert Dingwall is a consulting sociologist in private practice and part-time Professor of Sociology at Nottingham Trent University in the United Kingdom. His published work covers the interdisciplinary study of law, medicine, science and technology. Within these fields, he has focused particularly on topics related to professions, work and organizations.

Lixian Jin is Professor in Linguistics and Intercultural Learning at De Montfort University in the United Kingdom. She has taught linguistics, English language and clinical linguistics and led collaborative research teams internationally. She has over one hundred publications which focus on researching cultures of learning, metaphor and narrative analysis, and bilingual clinical assessments.

Vittorio Olgiati was Associate Professor of Law in the Faculty of Law, University of Macerata in Italy, where he taught the Sociology of Law. He has also been President of the International Sociological Association Research Committee in this area. His research interests lie in socio-legal changes, legal professions, legal culture and legal pluralism.

Inge Kryger Pedersen is Associate Professor of Sociology at the University of Copenhagen in Denmark, where she obtained her PhD in Sociology. Her teaching areas are social theory, methodology, sociology of health and medical technologies, and her research publications concentrate on expertise, embodiment and health-related issues. Currently, she is involved in a major cross-disciplinary research project on antibiotic resistance.

Rudolf Schmitt has been Professor in Counselling and Research Methods in the Faculty of Social Sciences at the University of Applied Sciences in Goerlitz in Germany since 1997. He initially studied Psychology and German Literature and received his PhD in Psychology. His present research focus is on metaphor analysis in social science.

Permissions

Grateful thanks are due to the following publishers for permission to reproduce the works cited below:

Brill:

Liljegren, A. (2012) Key metaphors in the sociology of profession: Occupations as hierarchies and landscapes, *Comparative Sociology* 11(1): 88–112.

Chicago University Press:

Abbott, A. (1995) Boundaries of social work or social work of boundaries? *The Social Service Review* 69(4): 545–62.

Oxford University Press:

Saks, M. (2014) Regulating the English health professions: Zoos, circuses or safari parks? *Journal of Professions and Organization* 1(1): 84–98.

The copyright of the other original publications contained in this volume lies with Routledge and the authors themselves.

1 Introducing professions and metaphors

Andreas Liljegren and Mike Saks

Introduction

During the last few decades, metaphors have increasingly been employed to aid academic understanding of theory and society in the modern Western world. The impact of metaphors is difficult to ignore in that, as Johnsson (2008:48) points out, "virtually all of our abstract concepts appear to be structured by multiple, typically inconsistent, conceptual metaphors". This general observation means that understanding metaphors is also pivotal to interpreting both the professions and the framework(s) that we use to understand them. As such, the contributors to this book seek to explore the range of key metaphors currently employed to understand professions and to look ahead and propose new ones. Their work is framed by a critical discussion by the editors of the strengths and limitations of using them in the context of analyzing professions in an area that has hitherto been largely uncharted in the academic literature. Metaphors, then, have guided our way of thinking by adding to our understanding of specific phenomena – from perspective, relationships, direction and distances to causality, features and principles. In sociology, organizational theory has probably come furthest in its use of metaphors (see, for instance, Morgan 2006), following on from earlier beliefs that metaphors were of limited value and were best left outside science (Cornelissen 2005). An increasing number of contributors now recognize the valuable employment of metaphors in organizational studies and think that our concern should be figuring out how they work best in order to facilitate their use by academic researchers.

This growing interest in metaphors in the UK, Western Europe and North America has been paralleled by an increased interest in professions as a social group, from university academics to doctors and social workers. It is now widely recognized that such professions are pivotal groups in society whose operation needs to be more fully understood both intellectually and in terms of future policy (see, for instance, Freidson 2001; Scott 2008). Their importance has been acknowledged in a wide range of social theorizing at a macro level, not least given their central role in problem solving. On the one hand, the more positive early work of trait, and especially functionalist, writers saw the significance of creating professional bodies with a privileged position in society as part of the assurance that they use their expertise in the interests of clients and the broader public (as exemplified by Goode 1960; Wilensky 1964). On the other hand, a less rosy view of the role of professions has been provided recently by the more critical Marxist, Foucauldian and now dominant neo-Weberian analyses of professional bodies, which see them as supporting the capitalist status quo, being absorbed in governmentality and acting as self-interest groups based on exclusionary social closure in the marketplace (as illustrated respectively by Esland 1980; Johnson 1995; Saks 2010). There is therefore a strong case for enhancing our understanding of the operation of professions using metaphors.

The main rationale for this edited book is therefore to combine these two areas because no systematic overview of metaphors has yet been provided in the sociology of professions. While metaphors have recently been comprehensively reviewed in other cognate fields, such as leadership (Alvesson and Spicer 2011), this is not yet true of professions. Metaphors have been employed by those studying the symbol of a profession as an honorific label at a micro level through interactionism and discourse analysis (see, for example, Fournier 2000; Hughes 1963), as well as at a macro level using such higher-level concepts as maps and landscapes (see, for instance, Becher and Trowler 2001; Gieryn 1999). Yet their use has not yet been applied and analyzed systematically, despite notable exceptions on which this collection draws – like the neo-Weberian study of shifting boundaries between professional jurisdictions (Abbott 1988) and approaches to the professions based on functionalist ecology (Dingwall and King 1995). As this aspect of the sociology of professions has been so heavily neglected, it is time to consider more fully the value of both existing and new metaphors in the analysis of professions – including in particular professional fields (see, for example, Pue and Sugarman 2003). The objective of this collection of readings, though, is not to describe and analyze every sort of metaphor in the study of professions and the wider occupational division of labour, but to focus mainly on key metaphors that have not been 'naturalized' and are easily identifiable, and potentially have a great impact on the understanding of professions. In this way, it is hoped that this volume will become a cornerstone in the sociological and broader social scientific literature on professions.

Conceptual metaphor theory

There are several ways to understand metaphors. In this book the focus is on the cognitive aspects of metaphors – in other words, on the understanding that metaphors provide. In conceptual metaphor theory, metaphors are considered to be conceptual by nature. In this perspective, an explanatory structure is transferred from a source domain to a target domain where it should shed new light on the phenomenon in focus. In the case of professions, such groups are portrayed in different ways – by, for example, being

situated in a landscape, a hierarchy or an organism. This approach to metaphors is seen as the 'two domain approach'. Here metaphors are viewed
as cognitive structures borrowed from one domain and applied in another,
with an explanatory structure typically transformed in a creative and often
complex manner (Andriessen 2011). As such, the structure should be related
closely enough to the target domain while being distant enough to challenge
conventional understanding. To define metaphors is not straightforward,
but in this context they involve the "use of language to refer to something
other than what it originally applied to, or what it 'literally' means, in order
to suggest some resemblance or make a connection between two things"
(Knowles and Moon 2006:3). This definition might not capture all phenomena that are seen as metaphors but should be viewed as sensitizing
and opening our eyes to important aspects of professions. In this sense, as
Ritchie (2013) notes, we can identify metaphors when we see them.

Metaphors can vary in many ways – with the less peripheral meriting
depiction as 'key metaphors'. There are also other terms that point to the
pivotal nature of a metaphor as root, profound, organizing or central.
Knowles and Moon (2006) too make a distinction between creative and
conventional metaphors. Creative metaphors are typically new and need to
be unpacked in order to understand them. Conventional metaphors are
found again and again. In this way some conventional metaphors might be
dead, which means that they are no longer perceived as metaphors, but others might be alive, which means that they are frequently used but are still
recognized as metaphors – as ascertained empirically. In addition, it is possible to separate out inductive and deductive approaches to metaphor analysis. The inductive approach does not assume that metaphors can be found
in a given text or narrative; instead researchers aim to find what is there. The
deductive approach, on the other hand, determines didactically what metaphors will be examined (Steen 2007). These distinctions relate to this book
in several ways – not least as it presents and analyzes some conventional
metaphors while being open to new and creative metaphors. In addition, it
focuses on living metaphors, as opposed to those not perceived as metaphors
anymore – even if these may still be interesting. Examples of both inductive
and deductive approaches to metaphor analysis are also given.

As Brown (1976) notes, any adequate philosophy must include an extensive inquiry into the workings of metaphor and how it shapes our most
important philosophical ideas. To understand the role and influence of metaphors in any branch of social science is therefore an important part of an
epistemic awareness (Boyd 1993). Although classical thinkers like Aristotle
and Nietzsche employed metaphors, there has now been a resurgence of
interest in them as a tool of 'great conceptual power' (Brown 2003). To some
extent metaphors are implicit knowledge, but their role in enhancing understanding is not explored sufficiently in general – and especially not in relation
to the particular case of the professions considered here. One of the earliest
attempts to employ metaphor theory to understand professions was that of

Hogan (1980), who listed a number of metaphors that can be used to describe professionalism – from a vocation for saints to a Trojan horse. He uses such metaphors to highlight the myths that are part of the ideology of profession. Meanwhile, Brown (1976) set out at an early stage the following more general criteria for gauging the adequacy of metaphors in sociology – isomorphism, originality, economy, cogency and range.

The uses of metaphors

But if metaphors are more or less important to our general and theoretical understanding of the world, there are at least two other benefits of using metaphors in the study of professions. First, they can be used to present and analyze actual empirical material. This can be done by examining the kind of metaphors used in text or talk, which can provide insight into the ideologies of professional groups. A previous study of how Swedish social workers relate to privatization found that they were negative towards private actors taking control of social work, but positive regarding social workers engaged in private social work (Liljegren, Dellgran and Höjer 2008). These findings were described and analyzed in terms of two discourses guided by different metaphors of privatization – the capitalist and the heroine. In the case of the capitalist, privatization was presented as a large-scale and profit-making enterprise where clients and staff were sacrificed for profit. The incentive for those involved was to make the highest profit in the shortest possible time. The heroine, on the other hand, was a female who – with some hesitation – opened up a small-scale business in social work to better help clients. The conclusion in terms of boundary work was that increased turf control was positive for the heroine and social work, while decreased turf control was negative for clients and social workers. The two metaphors also illustrate how to present discourses both as a construction and deconstruction of the metaphor.

Metaphor analysis can also be used to reflect on how empirical material should be perceived, as part of the wider consideration of the nature of research. There are several ways to view the gathering of empirical material. Kvale and Brinkmann (2009), for instance, separate out two ways of understanding interviews – either as the ore dug out of the ground or as the experiences of travel. In this terminology, conceptualizing data as ore is integral to a positivist and modernist approach where something solid is seen to be out there to be collected and worked on, while experiencing a journey is more phenomenological and post-modern – involving explorations of the landscape guided by the subjective and relativistic perceptions of the researcher. But whether the researcher is seen as mining data in classifying the objective world or as an active participant in the research itself, this debate clearly problematizes the exercise methodologically (Alvesson and Spicer 2011) and underlines its ideological dimensions from a metaphorical perspective (Olsson and Rombach 2015). Having importantly noted that approaches to metaphors can diverge, it is now time to turn to the more specific and varied contents of the book.

In this respect the volume contains a majority of newly commissioned and produced work, together with a handful of already published landmark contributions in which metaphors are explicitly used – including our own recent writing on professions and metaphors. The chapters cover professions generally, as well as particular professional groups, while the contributors are drawn from North America and a range of Western European societies – giving the book wider international appeal. As will be seen, this edited collection of papers is mainly aimed at students in higher level undergraduate and postgraduate courses examining professional behaviour in fields such as business studies, management, organizational analysis, public administration, political science, social policy and sociology – as well as those on focused programmes of professional study in fields such as education, health, law and social care. The use of professional metaphors included in the chapters here will also be of interest to those working in bodies in the public and private sector, including practising professionals, as well as university researchers in this field and the lay reader.

The chapters of the book

The substantive content of the book begins, though, with a generic reprinted chapter by Liljegren (2012) on key metaphors in the sociology of professions. Here two of the most profound metaphors in the study of professions are described and analyzed – those of hierarchies and landscapes. This chapter employs theory explicitly to examine the metaphors used to analyze professions, as classically illustrated by the notion of 'turf battles'. It is followed by an original chapter by Dingwall charting the influence of ecological and evolutionary metaphors derived from botany in the classic 'urban ecology' of the city – the implications of which have not yet been fully recognized. In so doing, he develops a more comprehensive account of occupations and their relationship to analyses of professions, providing a more fluid and productive direction for the sociology of professions, based on the ecological tradition. Saks then in another new contribution outlines his journey as a neo-Weberian sociologist actively to reform the professions in the public interest. He extensively uses Greek mythology to describe the processes involved, based on the slaying by Theseus in the labyrinth of the Minotaur – a cleft creature, like the professions, half human and half beast.

The next chapter, by Agevall, employs the metaphor of a boa constrictor to consider the neo-Weberian metaphor of social closure lying at the core of the sociology of professions – a metaphor that has been used to highlight the role of professions, upon which influential theories of professions have been built. In this novel piece he makes the case for reconsidering the spatial analogy underlying Weber's original concept of social closure, illustrating it with reference to the case of university teachers. The animal metaphor is taken further in a reprinted chapter by Saks (2014), who extends it to zoos, circuses and safari parks to accentuate the shifting forms of government regulation of the English health professions up to the period of Coalition government, before the Conservative election victory in 2015. In a further reprinted chapter, another well-known neo-Weberian contributor, Abbott (1995), considers in a special social services lecture the idea and use in social work of 'boundaries' and 'systems' as theoretical tools, metaphorical concepts to which several other authors in this volume refer. Olgiati meanwhile in a new chapter examines the position of women in the legal profession with reference to the historic institutional, cultural and political coupling between Law and Justice – in which the latter has for long been metaphorically identified and represented as a woman.

In the final set of more micro-oriented original chapters, Jin and Cortazzi discuss the 'engineers of the soul' by focusing on the teaching profession seen through metaphors in China and Iran. Public discourse metaphors for teachers as professionals are contrasted with insider metaphors of teachers themselves and their students – in an analysis in which, amongst other things, the implications of socio-cultural differences for teaching international students in European and American universities are highlighted. Schmitt then considers metaphors through the examination of the concepts used in the daily work of social workers with children, adults and psychiatric patients in the context of case work and family care. Several different metaphorical concepts are elaborated, largely based on aspects of bonding – none of which interestingly has a strong relation to theories learnt during the professional education of social workers. Pedersen finally notes that metaphors are a common way to describe life and death as well as symptoms of illness and health. While their employment by patients and clients is relatively well studied, this chapter explores the less well analyzed area of how doctors use mechanical metaphors to explain disease in their encounter with patients by employing a frame analysis to facilitate an understanding of authorized expertise and professional jurisdictions.

As such, the international set of chapters highlight that there are at least three different polar, but interrelated, types of ways in which writers approach metaphors and professions. First, on the one hand, they do so by analyzing metaphors in professional practice and, on the other, in theory. The second dichotomy is between the analysis of the actual use of metaphors and considering a more limited range of metaphors as ideal typical constructions. The third polar type of approach is between examining metaphors already employed as opposed to the important task of proposing new metaphors. In all this, as some of the contributors bring out, it is vital to understand the consequences of using particular metaphors, not least for professionals and their clients – whether the implications, for example, be social or cognitive. Whatever route is taken, though, it is clear that metaphors are an excellent means of gaining insights into professions and their operation in society, with much scope for further exploration both theoretically and practically. It is finally important by way of conclusion to stress the benefits of using metaphors in the sociology of professions – as highlighted by the work of contributors to this volume and that of writers in other areas and disciplines.

Conclusion

Although there are, as has been seen in this introductory chapter, many strengths in using metaphors, future directions for pragmatic work on the professions needs to be charted. Amongst these, their role in storytelling can be a very important force in consolidating existing operations or effecting change in professional domains. This has been interestingly explored in the organizations literature by authors such as Boje (2008), who sees the roots of storytelling in this context as lying in both collective memories and emergent tales that classically have a beginning, middle and end. These have yet to be mapped fully onto the professions field through metaphors – although there is a fertile literary base from Lewis Carroll's *Alice in Wonderland* to Franz Kafka's *Metamorphosis* that might readily be applied in this setting, without too much stretching of the imagination. In this vein, the prospect of seeing organizations in terms of science fiction has also not been lost on those working in this area (Smith et al. 2001). There therefore remains much catching up to be undertaken by both practitioners and theorists of the professions in relation to their counterparts working in, and on, organizational contexts – a gap that can and should be closed with positive effect.

This underlines the novelty of this particular volume on professions and metaphors, which is accentuated by the fact that there are no directly competing books in this field. To be sure, as previously indicated, there are books and articles about metaphors generally in organizational settings and elsewhere – both past (Boyd 1993; Grothe 2008; Kuhn 1993; Lakoff and Johnson 1980; Silber 1995) and present (Gibbs 2008; Inns 2002; Kövecses 2002; Landau, Meier and Robinson 2013; Schmitt 2005; Yablonsky and Baaquie 2007). There is also a range of specific publications on professions, of which some are more explicit in the use of metaphors (Becher and Trowler 2001; Gieryn 1999) while others employ them more implicitly (Evetts 2006; MacDonald 1995). It is hoped that this edited book systematically serves to combine these two fields of research in presenting an innovative overview of current work, thereby facilitating more reflective ways of using metaphors as an aid to understanding the sociology of professions. As such, it should provide a firmer platform to bring the study of professions closer to that of organizations where metaphors now form a staple part of the territory (see, for example, Grant and Oswick 1996; Morgan 2006).

References

Abbott, A. (1988) *The System of Professions: An Essay on the Division of Expert Labor*. Chicago: University of Chicago Press.
Abbott, A. (1995) Boundaries of social work or social work of boundaries? *Social Service Review* 69(4): 545–62.

Alvesson, M. and Spicer, A. (eds) (2011) *Metaphors We Lead By: Understanding Leadership in the Real World*. Abingdon: Routledge.

Andriessen, D. (2011) Metaphors in knowledge management, *Systems Research and Behavioural Management* 28(2): 133–37.

Becher, T. and Trowler, P. (2001) *Academic Tribes and Territories: Intellectual Enquiry and the Culture of Disciplines*, 2nd edition. Philadelphia: Open University Press.

Boje, D. M. (2008) *Storytelling Organizations*. London: Sage.

Boyd, R. (1993) Metaphor and theory change: What is 'metaphor' a metaphor for? In: A. Ortony (ed) *Metaphor and Thought*, 2nd edition. Cambridge: Cambridge University Press.

Brown, H. R. (1976) Social theory as metaphor: On the logic of discovery for the sciences of conduct, *Theory and Society* 3(2): 169–97.

Brown, T. L. (2003) *Making Truth: Metaphor in Science*. Urbana: University of Illinois Press.

Cornelissen, J. (2005) Beyond compare: Metaphors in organizational theory, *Academy of Management Review* 30(4): 751–64.

Dingwall, R. and King, M. (1995) Herbert Spencer and the professions: Occupational ecology, *Sociological Theory* 13(1): 14–24.

Esland, G. (1980) Diagnosis and therapy. In: G. Esland and G. Salaman (eds) *The Politics of Work and Occupations*. Milton Keynes: Open University Press.

Evetts, J. (2006) The sociology of professional groups, *Current Sociology* 54(1): 133–43.

Fournier, V. (2000) Boundary work and the (un)making of the professions. In: N. Malin (ed) *Professionalism, Boundaries and the Workplace*. London: Routledge.

Freidson, E. (2001) *Professionalism Reborn: The Third Logic*. Chicago: University of Chicago Press.

Gibbs, R. (ed) (2008) *The Cambridge Handbook of Metaphor and Thought*. Cambridge: Cambridge University Press.

Gieryn, T. F. (1999) *Cultural Boundaries of Science: Credibility on the Line*. Chicago: University of Chicago Press.

Goode, W. (1960) Encroachment, charlatanism and the emerging profession: Psychology, sociology and medicine, *American Sociological Review* 25: 902–14.

Grant, D. and Oswick, C. (1996) *Metaphor and Organizations*. London: Sage.

Grothe, M. (2008) *I Never Metaphor I Didn't Like: A Comprehensive Compilation of History's Greatest Analogies, Metaphors, and Simile*. New York: Harper Collins.

Hogan, H. W. (1980) Professionalism as metaphor, *Free Inquiry in Creative Sociology* 8(1): 41–42.

Hughes, E. C. (1963) Professions, *Daedalus* 92(4): 655–68.

Inns, D. (2002) Metaphor in the literature of organizational analysis: A preliminary taxonomy and a glimpse at a humanities-based perspective, *Organization* 9(2): 305–30.

Johnson, T. (1995) Governmentality and the institutionalization of expertise. In: T. Johnson, G. Larkin and M. Saks (eds) *Health Professions and the State in Europe*. London: Routledge.

Johnsson, M. (2008) Philosophy's debt to metaphor. In: R. Gibbs (ed) *The Cambridge Handbook of Metaphor and Thought*. Cambridge: Cambridge University Press.

Knowles, M. and Moon, R. (2006) *Introducing Metaphor*. Abingdon: Routledge.

Kövecses, Z. (2002) *Metaphor: A Practical Introduction*. New York: Oxford University Press.

Kuhn, T. (1993) Metaphor in science. In: A. Ortony (ed) *Metaphor and Thought*. New York: Cambridge University Press.

Kvale, S. and Brinkmann, S. (2009) *Interviews: Learning the Craft of Qualitative Research Interviewing*, 2nd edition. Thousand Oaks: Sage.

Lakoff, G. and Johnson, M. (1980) *Metaphors We Live By*. Chicago: University of Chicago Press.

Landau, M., Meier, B. and Robinson, M. (eds) (2013) *The Power of Metaphor: Examining Its Influence on Social Life*. Washington DC: American Psychological Association.

Liljegren, A. (2012) Key metaphors in the sociology of profession: Occupations as hierarchies and landscapes, *Comparative Sociology* 11(1): 88–112.

Liljegren, A., Dellgran, P. and Höjer, S. (2008) The heroine and the capitalist: The professions debate about privatization in Swedish social work, *European Journal of Social Work* 11(3): 195–208.

MacDonald, K. (1995) *The Sociology of the Professions*. London: Sage.

Morgan, G. (2006) *Images of Organization*. London: Sage.

Olsson, Ö. and Rombach, B. (2015) *The Tyranny of Metaphors*. Stockholm: Santerus Academic.

Pue, W. and Sugarman, D. (eds) (2003) *Lawyers and Vampires: Cultural Histories of Legal Professions*. Oxford: Hart Publishing.

Ritchie, D. L. (2013) *Metaphor*. Cambridge: Cambridge University Press.

Saks, M. (2010) Analyzing the professions: The case for the neo-Weberian approach, *Comparative Sociology* 9(6): 887–915.

Saks, M. (2014) Regulating the English health professions: Zoos, circuses or safari parks? *Journal of Professions and Organization* 1(1): 84–98.

Schmitt, R. (2005) Systematic metaphor analysis as a method of qualitative research, *Qualitative Report* 10(2): 358–94.

Scott, W. (2008) Lords of dance: Professionals as institutional agents, *Organization Studies* 29(2): 219–38.

Silber, I. F. (1995) Space, fields, boundaries: The rise of spatial metaphors in contemporary sociological theory, *Social Research* 62(2): 323–57.

Smith, W., Higgins, M., Parker, M. and Lightfoot, G. (eds) (2001) *Science Fiction and Organization*. Abingdon: Routledge.

Steen, G. (2007) *Finding Metaphor in Grammar and Usage*. Amsterdam: John Benjamin Publishing.

Wilensky, H. (1964) The professionalization of everyone? *American Journal of Sociology* 70(2): 137–58.

Yablonsky, G. and Baaquie, B. (2007) *Going Through the Mirror: Science for the 21st Century – Metaphors and Metonyms in Science*. Singapore: World Scientific.

2 Key metaphors in the sociology of professions

Occupations as hierarchies and landscapes

Andreas Liljegren

In some parts of the literature on the study of discourse, the advice given is to look for 'key metaphors' in a given set of text or talk (Wetherell and Potter 1988). Key metaphors guide our way of thinking in that, among other things, they provide perspective, relations, directions, distances, causality, features and principles. Metaphors are "a fundamental scheme by which people conceptualize the world" (Gibbs 2008:3). In other words, metaphors offer tools for understanding parts of reality. Some common metaphors used to describe society (or some part of it) include that of an organism, a system or a theatre. The metaphor chosen fundamentally affects how the reality is perceived and presented. If you see society as a system, for instance, you will see parts affecting other parts in an intricate relationship, but if you see society as a theatre you will see actors, stages and roles. As these metaphors are expressed in our language, it is also important to analyze how these cognitive devices are constructed. And since the metaphors are expressed in our language, we must also focus on language.

The literature on professions appears to encompass at least two overarching key metaphors, one that likens professional groups to a hierarchy, and another that describes them as a landscape. Since key metaphors mould our understanding, it is important to reflect on the ways in which metaphors affect our perceptions of professions. What, for example, do they highlight, and what do they conceal (Lakoff and Johnson 1980)? This chapter provides an analysis of two key metaphors in the literature on professions, the purpose being to outline, analyze and relate them to a number of other central concepts. In carrying out this analysis, questions relating to the similarities and differences between the two metaphors will be addressed. What, for example, are their epistemic virtues, and what are the consequences of privileging one metaphor over the other? The aim is to make a contribution to the sociology of professions in terms of an analysis of an important aspect of our understanding of professions. To my knowledge, no such attempt has, so far, been made to identify and analyze the use of metaphors in the sociology of professions, even though other fields of research, such as the sociology of organizations, have come further in the identification and analysis of central metaphors (Grant and Oswick 1996b; Inns 2002; Morgan 2006).

While others who write about the sociology of professions, such as Krause (1971), Macdonald (1995) and Pavalko (1971), map out the field, this chapter tries to take the analyses to the next analytical level and use a specific theory (about metaphors) to push our understanding of professions and the sociology of professions even further.

Doing metaphor analysis

As a way of making sense of the world, we use metaphors in most areas in life, and the social sciences are no exception (Kuhn 1993; Silber 1995). Even though there seems to be some agreement on the significance of metaphors, views differ in terms of their effect, with some scholars regarding them as liberating while others perceive them as constraining or even misleading (Grant and Oswick 1996a). On the one hand, it is argued, metaphors can be liberating, as they can stretch language beyond its elastic limits (Ortony 1993). On the other hand, metaphors have been claimed to be untestable and unfalsifiable and therefore undesirable in scientific study (Grant and Oswick 1996a). Irrespective of the stance one takes, the impact of metaphors is difficult to ignore in that, as Johnsson (2008:48) points out, "virtually all of our abstract concepts appear to be structured by multiple, typically inconsistent conceptual metaphors". A possible reason for this inconsistency is that, in practice, single metaphors are often blended into extended networks (Fouconnier and Turner 2008). In the sociology of professions, such a network could include other metaphors such as the market (Collins 1990), the system (Abbott 1988) and professions as negotiators (Kuhlmann 2008). Another consequence of Johnsson's insight is that metaphors play an important role in both the understanding of theory and the processes in which theory can change (Boyd 1993).

The study of metaphors includes several approaches, including biological (Lakoff 2008), linguistic (Glucksberg 2008) and cognitive (Johnsson 2008) aspects of narrative imagery. Since the focus of this chapter is on understanding how metaphors shape our perceptions of the world, a cognitive approach is adopted. From this perspective, metaphors are approached as a 'way of thinking' and the aim is to attempt to establish the strengths and weaknesses of particular metaphors (Thompson and Bunerson 2001; Tsoukas 1993). Regardless of the approach applied, research on metaphors can entail a focus on the process, the product, or both (Gibbs 2008; Steen 2007).

Commonly, metaphors are constructed conceptually in the form 'A is B', where one phenomenon or object is substituted by another (Kövecses 2002). In this case, occupations are likened to both hierarchies and landscapes. While conceptual metaphors often operate in the background, they are "typically manifested by dozens of linguistic expressions" (Steen 2007:50). In later sections I will give examples of these linguistic expressions as well as some arguments where they appear. One way of analyzing the function of a metaphor is in terms of analogies in that a metaphor involves a comparison between a 'base domain', where some aspect of a domain of knowledge is borrowed, and a 'target domain', where the knowledge is applied. In this perspective, knowledge is borrowed from the base domain that contains a more familiar and established knowledge, which is applied to the new and relatively unfamiliar target domain (Tsoukas 1993). However, it is not knowledge in general that is transferred but, rather, similarities between the base and the target, most often relational similarities, but also, to a lesser extent, attributes (Gentner 1983; Gentner and Bowdle 2008; Miller 1993; Ortony 1993). Through these analogues the metaphor constructs a model for understanding that exploits the similarities between the base and the target (Giere 2004). In this way, metaphors transfer an explanatory structure between the two arenas of use, something that is commonly known as the 'two-domain approach' (Steen 2007). Other approaches elaborate upon this by the addition of three or more domains. When it comes to the construction of theory, abstractions, as transferrals from the source to the target, are of importance in that they can be applied in an infinitely wider range of contexts (Tsoukas 1993).

Having sketched a number of theoretical ideas relating to the construction and operation of metaphors, attention now needs to be turned to the notion of 'key' metaphors. A number of categorizations have been made as a means of assessing the influence that metaphors have (Grant and Oswick 1996a). Influential metaphors have been variously labelled 'strong' (Black 1993), 'key' (Wetherell and Potter 1988) and 'deep' (Schön 1993), just to mention a few. Lakoff and Johnson (1980) use the term 'structural' and argue that metaphors can be evaluated on a scale on the basis of metaphorical systematicity. The most systematic metaphors are those that are structural in nature and that provide "highly structured and delineated concepts" (Lakoff and Johnson 1980:61). Less systematic metaphors can, for example, give direction to a phenomenon, such as emotion, where positive emotions can be perceived in terms of being 'up', while negative emotions can be seen as being 'down'.

Another clarification is also needed. The terminology of the analysis (key metaphor, metaphor and concepts) involves a certain degree of overlap, as some of the concepts belonging to key metaphors are also themselves metaphors, and, moreover, all metaphors are themselves concepts. However, in this chapter, the entities from which metaphors are constructed will be referred to as concepts. In other words, key metaphors are constructed out of a number of concepts.

Schmitt (2005) suggests that metaphor analysis should be conducted in five steps. The first of these involves an identification of a target area, the second an unsystematic, broad-based collection of metaphors, the third, an analysis of different subgroups, which, in the fourth stage, leads to a reconstruction of the metaphorical concepts. A fifth step involves the comparison of metaphors. It has, for some time, struck me in my research that two metaphors, the hierarchy and the landscape, operate concurrently in the sociology of professions, and therefore the first of Schmitt's phases, that is, the identification of metaphors, has been more of an implicit and a less conscious process than a strict application envisages. Thus, this chapter has emerged from a slightly different process than Schmitt's suggested procedure. The identification of the target area is not that clear-cut, as there are no easy ways of defining what should be included in the sociology of professions (or any other areas of research for that matter). This means that the selection of relevant references and the reconstructing of the metaphors is, to a certain extent, dependent on individual perspectives. Any demarcation of a research field is a construction; in this case the construction derives from my own knowledge of the field as a researcher with an active interest in the sociology of professions. The selection of references has been made on the basis of two criteria. First, the articles selected have been cognitively influential in the sociology of professions; second, they have made a contribution to theoretical development in the field.

With the exception of this initial phase, Schmitt's guidelines were followed more closely. In particular, a number of central elements of the literature on the sociology of professions were revisited and the metaphors were reconstructed separately in an attempt to unveil the underlying conceptual structure (Steen 2007). In addition to studying the usage of these metaphors in the sociology of professions, the analysis was about mapping out the concepts of each metaphor as a means of discerning similarities between the base and the target of each metaphor, and as a way of making comparisons between the two metaphors. Since its purpose is to discover the nature of the metaphors currently in use, the approach adopted in the study can be described as inductive (Grant and Oswick 1996a; Steen 2007).

Professions as hierarchies

In the hierarchy model, professional groups are seen as actors who manoeuvre in their context to ensure a position in society (Burrage, Jarausch and Siegrist 1990).[1] In the sociology of the professions, the hierarchy is often perceived as a pyramid where there are a few exclusive and strong 'top' occupations, namely the professions (for example, lawyers and physicians) with a broader base of semi-professions (for example, nurses and social workers) that are in turn separated from the lower, relatively weak and subordinated occupations (for example, plumbers and taxi drivers) (Etzioni 1969). In general, positions and directions in the hierarchy are important, as different actions, relations and definitions depend on what comes from where and from/by whom. Directions that can be found in the hierarchy model are, for example, downward, upward, sideways, from above and from within (more on this later). In this perspective, occupations interact through a social struggle of resources (Freidson 1975). The concepts of the 'professional project' and 'professionalization' became important in this tradition and have been, and still are, used to point at the perspective of social groups as actors striving to attain certain goals. Larson (1977:51) argues that:

> ... the professional project tends toward the monopolization of opportunities for income in a market of services or labor and toward the monopolization of status and work privileges in an occupational hierarchy.

The use of the hierarchy metaphor is in this case indicated by the use of the expression 'occupational hierarchy'. Larson also portrays the hierarchy as a 'pyramid of prestige', and by doing so she has shaped our perception toward seeing a few prestigious occupations at the top that stand over a broader base of occupations (Larson 1977).

While the professional project has been heavily criticized by some, it has been defended by others. According to Abbott (1988), Larson focuses too much on the associations that represent the professions and the internal professional activities that professions conduct in order to maintain a position in society. The sociology of professions should, he argues, focus instead on what professions actually do and on the interprofessional competition between different occupational groups. Nevertheless, it has also been argued that even if this criticism is right, it does not mean that the concepts themselves have to be abandoned (Macdonald 1995). It is possible to talk about a professional project and still be interested in the competition between professional groups and to analyze the negotiations on jurisdiction between professional groups as a part of the professional project.

One key argument in the hierarchy tradition is that professional groups conduct 'closure' strategies in order to maintain a position in the hierarchy. The terminology of closure, which, arguably, is one of sociology's best known concepts, was introduced by Weber (1978) and has been used frequently and in a variety of contexts. In the case of professions, closure operates on credentials and credentialism and is seen as a way of transforming one form of resources to another, where knowledge is turned into status and economic rewards (Collins 1979; Larson 1977). Collins (1990:25/36) claims that:

> ... the closure of occupations on the market is part of a larger structural pattern. There is a long-term dynamic consisting of endless conflict over market closure. .... What we mean by the 'professions' is a combination of market closure with high occupational status honour.

This can be seen as an example of the centrality of the closure terminology in the hierarchy; closure is both a fundamental mechanism in the shaping of a division of labour and an essential part of what we mean by 'profession'. Frequent use of the closure terminology was made during the 1960s and 1970s and became the dominant school of thought in approaches aimed at analyzing how professional groups act to ensure a (high) position in society

(Collins 1990; Larson 1977; Murphy 1983; 1988; Parkin 1979). There are at least two traditions in the actor-based hierarchy model: the neo-Marxist and the neo-Weberian. The neo-Marxists mainly see professions (and membership in them) as an upward movement in the class hierarchy and closure as the mechanism that creates the class stratification (Murphy 1988). A common discussion in the neo-Marxist hierarchy model of occupations is that professions lose their position in the hierarchy, or in other words, become proletarianized or deprofessionalized (Derber 1983; Derber and Schwartz 1991). The neo-Weberians, however, argue that professions struggle in a market trying to sell their services (as in Collins' discussion above). In the neo-Weberian version, professions mainly compete with other professions. It is not, in essence, a struggle between different classes, but rather an intra-class struggle that takes place inside the professional class.

In the hierarchical perception of professions, occupational groups seek to move upward in the hierarchy or to defend their current position in a 'hierarchy of closure' (Witz 1992). Losing prestige is perceived as a downward movement. Parkin (1979:45) distinguishes between two modes of closure, exclusion and usurpation, and argues that:

> . . . exclusionary closure represents the use of power in a 'downward' direction because it necessarily entails the creation of a group, class, or stratum of legally defined inferiors. Countervailing action by the 'negative privileged', on the other hand, represents the use of power in an upward direction in the sense that collective attempts by the excluded to win a greater share of resources always threaten to bite into the privileges of legally defined superiors.

The difference between the concepts is that they are aimed in different directions in the hierarchy. On the one hand, exclusion is directed downward against subordinated groups in order to maintain advantages and opportunities in the privileged group. Subordination is a key dimension in the hierarchy as occupations positioned above subordinate groups further down in the hierarchy. In contrast to strategies of exclusion, usurpation strategies are directed upward in order to gain advantages and opportunities. The purpose of strategies of exclusion is to gain a monopoly on the services provided by the profession. However, Freidson (1982) has argued against the concept of monopolization, claiming that there is no such thing as a monopoly for professions. Nevertheless, it is, he suggests, possible to create 'market shelters' that provide at least some protection from other groups.

Most frequently, exclusion and usurpation occur at the same time in a dynamic process, as exclusion tends to provoke usurpation. At times, a distinction is used between two kinds of usurpation: the inclusionary and revolutionary (Freidson 1977; Witz 1992). As the terms indicate, revolutionary usurpation is a more radical attempt to more fundamentally reconstruct power relations in the hierarchy. Inclusion is less radical and tries to modify opportunities without changing the fundamental order between professional groups.

So far, the discussion has been of different kinds of vertical strategies in the hierarchy. However, there are also strategies that are directed horizontally or sideways toward occupational groups on the same level. When closure is conducted sideways, the hierarchy model uses the concept of demarcation. Kreckel (1980:530–31) discusses Parkin's use of the concept of closure and:

> ... distinguishes between vertical and horizontal exclusion, the former term coinciding with Parkin's own notion of 'downward' exclusion or subordination, the latter referring to the possibility that the mutual differentiation and delimitation of special occupational competences may increase their respective bargaining strengths without their subordinating each other.

Kreckel regards 'demarcation' as a better term than 'exclusion', since occupations on the same level can have mutual interests and thus do not have the aim of attempting the subordination of another group. The notion of demarcation is used to identify a negotiated division of labour between occupational groups of equal strength. A slightly more intricate concept in the hierarchy metaphor is that of 'dual closure', which involves the simultaneous use of both exclusion and usurpation. Witz (1990:679) argues in relation to exclusion:

> Dual closure strategies are conceptually and empirically far more complex than this. They entail the upwards countervailing exercise of power in the form of resistance on the part of subordinate occupational groups to the demarcationary strategies of dominant groups, but who also in their turn seek to consolidate their own position within a division of labour by employing exclusionary strategies.

An example of dual closure would be gendered professional projects where, on the one hand, women strive for equality with their male colleagues while, on the other, they try to exclude other groups (Witz 1992).

Actions taken by occupations are not always conducted alone, and not infrequently strategies are formulated by several occupations collectively within broader occupational groups. These can include imperialistic strategies toward other occupational groups, which is seen as a way of organizing a division of labour in the mutual interest of several groups (Larkin 1983). Imperialistic strategies are directed toward groups on the same level and can be seen as the collective equivalent to demarcation (Witz 1992). In addition, subordinated groups have the option of activating strategies of solidarity in a joint venture as a response to the subordinating groups (Kreckel 1980).

It should be noted that the different forms of closure have a distinctly normative connotation that exemplifies a rather negative view of the oppressive nature of professions that was widely held from the 1960s to the 1980s. In the notion of 'the imperialism of occupations', the negative view is rather obvious. However, exclusion also has a somewhat cynical tone from which the sociology of professions has tried to distance itself in recent years. The work of Freidson (1975, 1977, 1982, 2001) can be seen as an example of the shift from an early negative 'power approach' to a much more positive stance, when he argues that compared with the logic of bureaucracy or the market, professionalism has a number of distinct advantages.

A more recent contribution that can be fitted into the hierarchy model is the idea that occupational groups can be professionalized from different directions. Evetts (2003:30–31) argues:

> Thus the appeal to professionalism is made and used by occupational groups [themselves], 'from within', then the returns to the group can be substantial. In the case of most contemporary service and knowledge based occupations, however, professionalism is imposed 'from above' and for the most part this means the employers and the managers of the service organizations in which these 'professionals' work.

Professionalization can be initiated from above, indicating that actors other than the occupational groups themselves take the initiative to professionalize. In the context of European countries, it has been suggested that the state pushes occupations toward realizing certain ideal typical images of professions. Occupations can also change on their own initiative, and this is perceived as professionalization from within, which was the case in the USA, where the professional associations have been more influential than in continental Europe and Scandinavia (McClelland 1990). In organizational contexts, such as welfare bureaucracies, it has been suggested that managers induce managerialism from above in order to control professional groups from a distance (Evetts 2007).[2]

Professions as landscapes

Another way of perceiving professions is in terms of the metaphor of a landscape. There are several important concepts in this tradition, such as social space, fields, territories, turf, land, landmarks, frontiers, gates, gatekeepers, and maps and mappings, just to mention a few. In this perception of professions, occupations have a territory that is sealed off from others by borders. Gieryn (1999:x) argues that science:

> . . . becomes a space on maps of culture, bounded off from other territories, labelled with landmarks showing travellers how and why it is different from regions of common sense, politics, or mysticism.

Even though all of these concepts are important, the most important concept in the landscape metaphor is arguably the notion of the boundary. Boundaries separate and create professional groups by means of dividing social space, or 'turf', into sections, over which different groups struggle to establish and maintain control (Fournier 2000). In essence, control over a piece of turf means, axiomatically, that you also have to control the boundaries that encompass the turf. If closure was the central concept in the hierarchy metaphor, boundaries play a similar role in the landscape model.

There are at least two ways of perceiving the landscape metaphor – either as a map where our mental images of a social landscape are manifested as in Gieryn's discussion above, or as a geographical landscape. Gieryn (1999) is primarily interested in the maps that guide us through the landscape, the cartographic tools that help us to get around in social space. The landscape metaphor as a map operates on two different levels: the social level and the symbolic/cognitive level. On the social level there are occupational groups performing different tasks. These groups have different educations and they demonstrate differences and similarities in an infinite number of ways. On the symbolic level are the maps that represent how we make sense of the world, our 'webs of significance' (Geertz 1973).

Becher and Trowler (2001), who represent the geographical view, analyze the cultures of different academic tribes and territories in a landscape of knowledge. They argue that:

> . . . the process of locating a discipline in relation to its neighbours is in itself of limited interest, and should be seen as no more than a preliminary to other more fundamental ones. Boundaries, after all, do not exist merely as lines on a map: they denote territorial possession that can be encroached on, colonized and reallocated.
>
> (Becher and Trowler 2001:58–59)

In this case the authors use such concepts as neighbours, lines, maps, territories, and boundaries to position themselves in the landscape metaphor. Different words are used to explain how groups arrange mutual boundaries. Strauss (1982) uses 'negotiations', Bourdieu (1985, 1989) 'struggles' and Light (1988) 'battles'. The concepts say something about the nature of the climate in which the boundaries have been delineated, whether friendly or hostile. Whatever word is used, all of these concepts point in the direction that, at various times, boundaries and turf have been contested. This process of the active construction and deconstruction of boundaries is often, in the landscape metaphoric tradition, called 'boundary work', although at times the concept of demarcation has also been used (Gieryn 1983). Gieryn (1983:781) claims:

> Construction of boundary between science and varieties of non-science is useful for scientists' pursuit of professional goals; acquisition of intellectual authority and career opportunities; denial of these resources

to 'pseudo-sciences'; and protection of the autonomy of scientific research from political interference.

Different actors make claims on a specific set of boundaries and, in that way, boundary work can be described as an implicit or explicit claim-making activity. Boundaries change for a number of reasons, such as, for example, when groups encounter other ways of perceiving reality, when other groups impose new boundaries, or when new boundaries better serve the interests of a particular group (Tilly 2004). However, one strong reason to create, maintain, break down, activate and deactivate boundaries is to serve the occupational groups as a part of a group's ideology.

Boundaries and boundary work operate on differences, as it is the construction of differences that results in the separation of insiders from outsiders, our work from theirs, and desirable tasks from those that are undesirable. While the conduct of boundary work is a continual and ongoing process, boundaries do not always become an established part of an arena. The creation of cognitive boundaries involves a dimension of descriptive characterization of what the differences are about, and a normative dimension is most often added implicitly or explicitly, indicating that some groups, working tasks or identities are better or worse than others. Perhaps the primary purpose of boundary work, however, is to achieve the 'naturalization' of the boundaries set by different groups. Put another way, the aim is that such lines of delineation should be seen as the most reasonable, and indeed unquestioned, set of boundaries. It is also important to emphasize that the cognitive aspect of boundary work should not be interpreted as a denial of the importance of rhetoric; on the contrary, it is an essential part of the boundary work (Holmquest 1990; Watson 1984). While the term 'boundary work' was coined by Woolgar and Gieryn (see Gieryn 1983), it was the latter who first put it to use (Gieryn 1999). Having said this, the intellectual roots of boundaries can be traced back at least as far as the work of both Weber and Durkheim (Lamont 2001).

Boundaries are not only important when understanding the ongoing relations between established occupations and professions, but also in the understanding of how occupations are created. Abbott (1995a:555) argues:

> In short, I am proposing that social entities come into existence when social agents tie social boundaries together in certain ways. The first things are the boundaries. The second are the entities.

He presumes "a kind of spatial structure to these contested boundaries, implicit in the phrase 'at the core of a profession' " (Abbott 1995a:554). The creation of occupational groups starts with the construction of differences in local workplaces which turn to proto-boundaries and which, over time, develop into more established boundaries. In this process, Abbott argues, it should be possible to observe how cognitive differences are transformed into social boundaries in the form of an occupation. Further, as Abbott makes clear, these occupational boundaries include "a particular group of people, a particular type of work, and an organized body or structure, other than the workplace itself, capable of some kind of reproduction" (Abbott 1995b:873–74).

It should be noted that the concept of boundaries is complex in that boundaries can vary in any number of ways, including, for instance, the ways in which they are constructed. Boundaries should not be perceived in any specific way in that, for example, they can be robust, strong, weak, shifting, rigid, flexible, passable, and/or impassable. Not only do boundaries vary in terms of how they are constructed, but also in terms of what they contain. While professional life contains a multitude of boundaries to relate to, one important set of boundaries is the jurisdictional boundaries that separate the working tasks of different groups. Abbott uses the landscape metaphor when he criticizes earlier research on professions, which he regards as overly simplistic in claiming that "there is a map of tasks to be done and an isomorphic map of people doing them" (Abbott 1988:35). For Abbott, the relations are much more complex than this. The concept of jurisdiction has two dimensions: the working tasks and the control an occupation has over those working tasks. Abbott makes a distinction between three aspects of work, namely diagnosis, inference, and treatment, arguing that, respectively, these refer to processes "to classify problems, to reason about them and to take action on it" (Abbott 1988:40). In terms of boundary work, this means that professional groups make claims on a desired part of the diagnosis, the inference and the treatment. Whereas, for example, social scientists seem most interested in keeping the cognitive/epistemic authority that enables them to dismiss a treatment as being 'normative', other groups, such as doctors, nurses, and social workers seem to be more interested in the actual treatment. Abbott argues that jurisdictional boundary disputes are conducted in three arenas: the media, the legal system and the workplace.[3] However, the jurisdictional boundaries are not the only lines of demarcation that are of importance for professional groups. Other types of boundaries with relevance to professions concern, among other things, identity, knowledge, autonomy, discretion and valued objects (Åkerström 2002; Bechky 2003; MacLure 1996; Norris 2001). While, for the purposes of analysis, these boundaries can be separated, in reality they are immanently intertwined. For instance, professionals, among other things, construct identities for themselves that are prefaced on doing the right type of working tasks, achieving a high level of discretion, and being rewarded by generous salaries.

Lamont and Molnár (2002) make a distinction between two types of boundaries: the symbolic and the social. While symbolic boundaries concern 'conceptual distinctions', social boundaries are objectified differences that are manifested in differing distributions of discretion, jurisdiction and other professional goods. Although symbolic boundaries are, primarily, identifiable in the eyes of the beholder, they can nevertheless sometimes also be shared by members of groups. However, symbolic boundaries can only turn (or be turned) into social boundaries when there is a certain amount of agreement as to the nature of such boundaries. Lamont and Molnár (2002) conclude that previous neo-Weberian research in sociology has focused, in general, on the study of social boundaries. However, there has been a recent shift toward symbolic boundaries in studies that focus on language and discourse. The same seems to be the case in the sociology of professions. The linguistic turn has meant that researchers in the sociology of professions are now more interested in what language does, especially with a focus on claim-making and the ways in which such claims are made, and, among other things, their effect on the nature and extent of jurisdictional boundaries (Allen 2000, 2001). The symbolic and the social boundaries have a dynamic and a dyadic relationship, and, conceptually, seem to correspond well with the ideas of van Dijk (1997, 1998) on the study of discourse in the sense that the cognitive dimensions support their social counterparts in ideologies.

There are several ways to define boundary work. Gieryn (1983:782) defines boundary work in relation to the study of science and technology as the:

> . . . attribution of selected characteristics to the institution of science for purposes of constructing a social boundary that distinguishes some intellectual activity as 'non-science'.

Even though Gieryn's interest lies in how scientists defend their cognitive authority in different credibility contests, there is no reason to believe that the same processes do not also occur in other professions. Fisher (1990) provides a more general description and defines boundary work as those acts and processes that create, maintain, and break down boundaries between knowledge units. However, both definitions highlight the fact that boundaries can be seen as a toolbox which can be used pragmatically (DiMaggio 1997).

Several different kinds of boundary work have been identified. Gieryn (1999) makes a distinction between three different genres of boundary work: expulsion, expansion, and autonomy.[4] Expulsion means boundary work between two groups that both claim to be scientific – for instance, between orthodox and heterodox, or mainstream and fringe segments of science – whereas expansion is a form of boundary work conducted toward other epistemic authorities, such as religion, politics or, indeed, common sense. If science is regarded as a profession, expulsion can be seen as a form of intraprofessional boundary work. In that case, expulsion would be interprofessional or even a form of boundary work directed toward nonprofessional actors. Indeed, these two genres seem to be located together on an internal/external dimension. The autonomy genre is, however, slightly different in that it tries neither to gain nor maintain epistemic authority, but, rather, to exploit the authority to secure material or symbolic resources. Gieryn also makes a distinction between first- and second-order boundary work. He argues that while first-order boundary work involves the creation of new maps and boundaries, in second-order boundary work, old maps are recycled.

In Gieryn's research on boundary work, the focus has been on situations of conflict when the cognitive boundaries of science have been in dispute. Mellor (2003) has instead focused on a more routinely conducted form of boundary work deriving from popular science. However, both authors have one thing in common: the fact that boundary work is directed toward a specific and visible opponent. Others have instead directed attention to another form of boundary work, that is, a form of general maintenance boundary work without specified opponents (Liljegren, Dellgran and Höjer 2008). Thus, while Abbott, Gieryn and others have mainly focused on how boundaries are constructed, Star and Griesemer (1989) have tried to explain how boundaries are overcome in the process of facilitating intergroup communication. They claim that communication is in fact made possible through different kinds of boundary objects, which are plastic enough to mean something in many social worlds, yet sufficiently rigid to carry meaning across boundaries.

Conclusion

The hierarchy metaphor functions to explain the directional focus of the closure strategies conducted by professional groups, some of which are vertical while others are horizontal. Here, while the vertical dimension implies a degree of subordination, horizontally directed closure can be equated with equality and the consolidation of mutual interests. The other metaphor, that of the landscape, uses boundaries and boundary work as theoretical tools to highlight how distinctions are used to create legitimacy in, among other things, jurisdiction and identity in the lengthy process from the creation to the maintenance of occupations. Importantly, professions do not consist of one solitary boundary; more often the map of any professional landscape may encompass several boundaries and, indeed, there may be several maps that can be used for different purposes.

Before moving on to the differences inherent in the two metaphors studied, it should be noted that there are at least two areas of overlap. One can be found in the concept of demarcation, which can be found in both the hierarchical and landscape constructions. In the former, demarcations are made at the same level of the hierarchy and do not involve groups either above or below. Thus, in a way, the hierarchy becomes almost as flat as the map, and arguably, it is for this reason that the concept of demarcation is inherent in both metaphors. The other area of crossover is that even though boundaries are a central concept in the landscape metaphor, hierarchical conceptions also encompass the notion of different kinds of borders. However, boundaries in the hierarchical model are not as explicitly used or as central a concept as they are in the landscape model.

Despite these overlaps, the differences implied by the use of the metaphors as cognitive tools are important. First, even though both metaphors are conceptual abstractions providing 'highly structured and delineated concepts', they nonetheless differ in terms of the amount of information they comprise. The landscape metaphor is significantly more complex with regard to the amount of systematic information that is borrowed from the base analogue. In contrast, while in some respects the notion of the boundary is a simple and easily grasped concept, in others, it is highly complex in its potential of functioning as a finely tuned theoretical tool in the analysis of professions that is comprised of numerous different types of boundaries and maps. The hierarchy does not borrow as much information from the base to the target analogue. Instead, it focuses on relatively few dimensions, such as strategies, the hierarchical direction of such strategies (that is, up or down), and the issue of subordination in terms of the position. This discrepancy in how much information is applied from the base to the target makes it possible for the landscape metaphor to provide a deeper understanding of the entirety of the process from creation to maintenance of professions. However, from another perspective, the gains to be made in using the finely tuned concept of boundaries and boundary work can be lost in terms of rhetorical clarity. In this sense, the concepts of exclusion and inclusion provide a much clearer understanding of what is going on than boundaries and boundary work. While exclusion tells a story of how someone (individual or group) has been denied opportunities, when an entity is said to be engaged in boundary work, it becomes more problematic to grasp the nature of what is taking place. In other words, it seems that while the landscape metaphor can explain more things in a more sophisticated manner, it lacks the rhetorical punch packed by the more readily accessible concepts of inclusion and exclusion.

A second difference has to do with some of the other relational attributes that come from the base. The landscape model implicitly portrays the relations between professional groups as equal. Professional groups negotiate or cooperate on (roughly) the same terms. The hierarchy model does the opposite, as it borrows a dimension of subordination from the base. Given that groups do not share the same level, subordination stands out in much sharper relief. With these differences come a number of attendant risks. There is, for example, a risk of perceiving subordination using the hierarchy model when, in fact, there is none. Similarly, using the landscape metaphor can instead imply negotiations between equal agents when equality does not exist. One conclusion might thus be that the hierarchy model fits better in situations (other advantages being equal) where there are clear cases of subordination, or where a professional group clearly dominates the arena.

Third, as mentioned above, there are different traditions underlying each metaphor. The hierarchy metaphor is shared by neo-Weberians and neo-Marxists, among others. The difference between them is that, in the neo-Marxist case, the entirety of society is included in the hierarchy, while for the functionalists and neo-Weberians it is only occupational groups that are included. McClelland (1990) also seems to include society in his discussion on professionalization from above. However, when Evetts (2007) borrows the concept of professionalism induced from above and claims that managers play an important role in the process, it seems as if the professional hierarchy has been exchanged for the hierarchy of the organization. Despite having different opinions on what should be included in the target domain (society, occupations or the organization) they share what is borrowed from the base, and that is the hierarchy.

Turning once again to the landscape metaphor, the difference between the versions is not located in the target but in the base domain, and the target remains the same. Occupations are seen as a landscape and in the different versions a map is used to emphasize the social constructivism of boundary work. The role of the landscape in relation to the map version is to provide the social dimension in relation to which the symbolic world is constructed. Thus a fourth conclusion is that maps more clearly indicate the analytical division between the social and the symbolic/cognitive dimension and, therefore, more clearly highlight the claim-making dimension of professional life.

Fifth, even though the question as to whether the normative dimension of the hierarchy metaphor is an advantage or a disadvantage is open to debate, it is nevertheless important to be aware that the vocabulary used affects the understanding of the material that is analyzed. At times, studies of professional controversies attempt to maintain a symmetrical approach, adopting a neutral stance in the presentation of alternatives and seeking to avoid taking a stand in the conflict (Hallberg and Bragesjö 2003). In such cases the use of concepts that are inherently normative can be problematic. As another comparison, it should also be noted that in regard to a number of issues that have occupied the sociology of professions – for example, a pragmatic vs. an essentialist definition of professions (compare Abbott 1988; Sciulli 2005a), an egoistic or altruistic set of motives (compare Collins 1990; Saks 1995) or the monolithic vs. the systemic view of professions (compare Abbott 1988; Larson 1977) – both metaphors are neutral. In the case of professions as systems or as monolithic projects, both metaphors seem to presume that there are others who should be excluded or against whom boundaries should be constructed. However, the level of engagement in other groups can vary in both models. Nevertheless, by tradition it seems as if landscape theorists have been more inclined to follow Abbott in the study of fields of groups and their relations. Neither does the way of describing the relations between professional groups seem to be affected by the two differing metaphors. Should the relations be described as if there were mainly hostile activities going on, or are the relations mainly friendly (compare Abbott 1988; Dingwall and King 1995)?

One quality that both metaphors seem to share is that they both involve an illumination of the acts and the actors of occupations. However, at the same time as they highlight the acts and actors, they provide much less help in the understanding of the context(s) of professional groups. This might be the reason that processes such as the influence of the organizations have been neglected to some extent. Since the sociology of professions has, in recent years, moved closer to the organizational context, a justifiable speculation might be that the theoretical influence of the hierarchy metaphor will increase in that the hierarchy is such an influential metaphor in the theorizing of organizations. In this sense, Evetts' (2007) discussions on professionalization from above can be seen as a step in that direction. Consequently, this could mean that following a period of waning importance in comparison with closure terminology, the hierarchy might, once again, return to a position of prominence.

Finally, an important question in relation to these metaphors is which one offers the greatest analytical promise and why. To a certain extent the appropriateness of a theory must be determined in relation to the empirical material. In that way it is difficult to say something final on which one seems most promising. Having made that disclaimer, it could still be argued that the hierarchy metaphor is less open, as it focuses on fewer aspects of professions, the main dimensions being subordination and closure. For that reason I would argue that the landscape metaphor provides a greater analytical promise, as it can do greater justice to our complicated world. However, my suggestion for the future would be to search for new metaphors that can more radically renew our perception of professions. These could either highlight few but completely new dimensions of professions or be more open and integrate more of the complexities of professional life. Before these are at hand, a first step is to be more conscious about the metaphors that we use, and how they shape our understanding of professions.

Notes

1 Before the advent of the hierarchy metaphor and the focus on professional groups as actors, a functionalist perspective was dominant and, in this paradigm, other metaphors were used. Durkheim (1964), for example, uses the metaphor of an organism to analyze how professions contribute to an 'organic solidarity' in society. The functionalists were also interested in determining the types of traits that could be used in order to identify genuine professions (therefore at times referred to as the trait view approach to professions (Brante 1990)). Suggestions as to the indicators of professional groups are numerous, and there is no broad agreement as to which should be used. However, the definitions often contain traits such as abstract knowledge, academic education, prestige, mandate, identity and autonomy (Flexner 1915; Greenwood 1957). Such traits can be seen as both means and goals for professional groups. Indeed, the call for a common definition has, on several occasions, been ruled out as an impossibility (Brante 1990). Nevertheless, debates regarding the proper definition of professions do still occur (see Evetts 2006; Malatesta 2005; Sciulli 2005a, 2005b, 2009; Torstendahl 2005).
2 The sociology of professions is by no means exclusive in its use of the hierarchy as a base domain. It should be noted that the metaphor of professions as a hierarchy shares its base with a way of regarding the workplaces and bureaucratic structures common to many professional groups. Just to give a few examples, Weber saw bureaucracy as a hierarchy, and this is possibly where the hierarchy

model emanates from. He saw advantages in having a clear chain of command and responsibility between different levels of the organization. Mintzberg (1999) differentiated between mechanical and professional bureaucracies depending, among other things, on the base of the hierarchy, while in organizational theory it is not unusual to encounter discussions about the advantages of implementing 'top-down' or 'bottom-up' strategies (Pressman and Wildavsky 1984).

3 For an overview of boundaries in the study of organization, see Heracleous (2004).
4 See Gieryn (1995) for a slightly different taxonomy.

References

Abbott, A. (1988) *The System of Professions: An Essay on the Division of Expert Labor*. Chicago: University of Chicago Press.

Abbott, A. (1995a) Boundaries of social work or social work of boundaries? *The Social Service Review* 69(4): 545–62.

Abbott, A. (1995b) Things of boundaries, *Social Research* 62(4): 857–85.

Åkerström, M. (2002) Slaps, punches, pinches – but not violence: Boundary-work in nursing homes for the elderly, *Symbolic Interaction* 25(4): 515–36.

Allen, D. (2000) Doing occupational demarcation: The 'boundary-work' of nurse managers in a district general hospital, *Journal of Contemporary Ethnography* 29(3): 326–56.

Allen, D. (2001) Narrating nursing jurisdiction: 'Atrocity stories' and 'boundary-work', *Symbolic Interaction* 24(1): 75–103.

Becher, T. and Trowler, P. R. (2001) *Academic Tribes and Territories: Intellectual Enquiry and the Culture of Disciplines*. Philadelphia: Open University Press.

Bechky, B. A. (2003) Object lessons: Workplace artefacts as representations of occupational jurisdiction, *American Journal of Sociology* 109(3): 720–52.

Black, M. (1993) More about metaphor. In: A. Ortony (ed) *Metaphor and Thought*, 2nd edition. Cambridge: Cambridge University Press.

Bourdieu, P. (1985) The social space and the genesis of groups, *Theory and Society* 14(6): 723–44.

Bourdieu, P. (1989) Social space and symbolic power, *Sociological Theory* 7(1): 14–25.

Boyd, R. (1993) Metaphor and theory change: What is 'metaphor' a metaphor for? In: A. Ortony (ed) *Metaphor and Thought*, 2nd edition. Cambridge: Cambridge University Press.

Brante, T. (1990) Professional types as a strategy of analysis. In: M. Burrage and R. Torstendahl (eds) *Professions in Theory and History: Rethinking the Study of the Professions*. London: Sage.

Burrage, M., Jarausch, K. and Siegrist, H. (1990) An actor-based framework for the study of the professions. In: M. Burrage and R. Torstendahl (eds) *Professions in Theory and History: Rethinking the Study of the Professions*. London: Sage.

Collins, R. (1979) *The Credential Society: An Historical Sociology of Education and Stratification*. New York: Academic Press.

Collins, R. (1990) Market closure and the conflict theory of the professions. In: M. Burrage and R. Torstendahl (eds) *Professions in Theory and History: Rethinking the Study of the Professions*. London: Sage.

Derber, C. (1983) Managing professionals: Ideological proletarianization and post-industrial labor, *Theory and Society* 12(3): 309–41.

Derber, C. and Schwartz, W. A. (1991) New mandarins or new proletariat?: Professional powers at work, *Research in the Sociology of Organizations* 8: 71–96.

DiMaggio, P. (1997) Culture and cognition, *Annual Review of Sociology* 23: 263–87.

Dingwall, R. and King, M. D. (1995) Herbert Spencer and the professions: Occupational ecology reconsidered, *Sociological Theory* 13(1): 14–24.

Durkheim, E. (1964) *The Division of Labor in Society*. New York: Free Press.

Etzioni, A. (ed) (1969) *The Semi-professions and Their Organization: Teachers, Nurses, Social Workers*. New York: Free Press.

Evetts, J. (2003) Reinterpreting professionalism: As discourse of social control and occupational change. In: L. G. Svensson and J. Evetts (eds) *Conceptual and Comparative Studies of Continental and Anglo-American Professions*. Södertälje: Almqvist & Wiksell International.

Evetts, J. (2006) Trust and professionalism: Challenges and occupational changes, *Current Sociology* 54(4): 515–31.

Evetts, J. (2007) Professionalism and managerialism: Organizational control 'from a distance'. Paper presented at the European Sociological Association Conference on Conflict, Citizenship and Civic Society, Glasgow.

Fisher, D. (1990) Boundary work and science: The relation between power and knowledge. In: S. E. Cozzen and T. F. Gieryn (eds) *Theories of Science in Society*. Bloomington: Indiana University Press.

Flexner, A. (1915) Is social work a profession? *School and Society* 1(26): 901–11.

Fouconnier, G. and Turner, M. (2008) Rethinking metaphor. In: R. W. J. Gibbs (ed) *The Cambridge Handbook of Metaphor and Thought*. Cambridge: Cambridge University Press.

Fournier, V. (2000) Boundary work and the (un)making of the professions. In: N. Malin (ed) *Professionalism, Boundaries and the Workplace*. London: Routledge.

Freidson, E. (1975) The division of labor as social interaction, *Social Problems* 23(1): 305–13.

Freidson, E. (1977) The futures of professionalization. In: M. Stacey, M. Reid, C. Heath and R. Dingwall (eds) *Health and the Division of Labour*. London: Croom Helm.

Freidson, E. (1982) Occupational autonomy and labor market shelters. In: P. L. Steward and M. G. Cantor (eds) *Varieties of Work*. Beverly Hills: Sage.

Freidson, E. (2001) *Professionalism: The Third Logic*. Chicago: University of Chicago.

Geertz, C. (1973) Thick description: Toward an interpretive theory of culture. In: C. Geertz (ed) *The Interpretation of Cultures*. New York: Basic Books.

Gentner, D. (1983) Structure-mapping: A theoretical framework for analogy, *Cognitive Science* 7(2): 155–70.

Gentner, D. and Bowdle, B. (2008) Metaphor as structure-mapping. In: R. W. J. Gibbs (ed) *The Cambridge Handbook of Metaphor and Thought*. Cambridge: Cambridge University Press.

Gibbs, R.W.J. (2008) Metaphor and thought: State of the art. In: R. W. J. Gibbs (ed) *The Cambridge Handbook of Metaphor and Thought*. Cambridge: Cambridge University Press.

Giere, R. N. (2004) How models are used to represent reality, *Philosophy of Science* 71: 742–52.

Gieryn, T. F. (1983) Boundary-work and the demarcation of science from non-science: Strains and interests in professional ideologies of scientists, *American Sociological Review* 48(6): 781–95.

Gieryn, T. F. (1995) Boundaries of science. In: S. Jasanoff, G. E. Markle, J. C. Peterson and T. Pinch (eds) *Handbook of Science and Technology Studies*, revised edition. London: Sage.

Gieryn, T. F. (1999) *Cultural Boundaries of Science: Credibility on the Line*. Chicago: University of Chicago Press.

Glucksberg, S. (2008) How metaphors create categories – Quickly. In: R. W. J. Gibbs (ed) *The Cambridge Handbook of Metaphor and Thought*. Cambridge: Cambridge University Press.

Grant, D. and Oswick, C. (1996a) Getting the measure of metaphors. In: D. Grant and C. Oswick (eds) *Metaphor and Organizations*. London: Sage.

Grant, D. and Oswick, C. (1996b) *Metaphor and Organizations*. London: Sage.

Greenwood, E. (1957) Attributes of a profession, *Social Work* 2: 45–55.

Hallberg, M. and Bragesjö, F. (2003) *Konflikt eller Konsensus?: Om Kontroversstudier som Forskningsfält*. Stockholm: Forskningsrådet för Arbetsliv och Socialvetenskap (FAS).

Heracleous, L. (2004) Boundaries in the study of organizations, *Human Relations* 57(1): 95–103.

Holmquest, A. (1990) The rhetorical strategy of boundary-work, *Argumentation* 4(3): 235–58.

Inns, D. (2002) Metaphor in the literature of organizational analysis: A preliminary taxonomy and a glimpse at a humanities-based perspective, *Organization* 9(2): 305–30.

Johnsson, M. (2008) Philosophy's debt to metaphor. In: R. W. J. Gibbs (ed) *The Cambridge Handbook of Metaphor and Thought*. Cambridge: Cambridge University Press.

Kövecses, Z. (2002) *Metaphor: A Practical Introduction*. New York: Oxford University Press.

Krause, E. A. (1971) *The Sociology of Professions*. Boston, MA: Little, Brown & Co.

Kreckel, R. (1980) Unequal opportunity structure and labour market segmentation, *Sociology* 14(4): 525–50.

Kuhlmann, E. (2008) Governing beyond markets and managerialism: Professions as mediators. In: E. Kuhlmann and M. Saks (eds) *Rethinking Professional Governance: International Directions in Healthcare*. Bristol: Policy Press.

Kuhn, T. S. (1993) Metaphor in science. In: A. Ortony (ed) *Metaphor and Thought*, 2nd edition. Cambridge: Cambridge University Press.

Lakoff, G. (2008) The neural theory of metaphor. In: R. W. J. Gibbs (ed) *The Cambridge Handbook of Metaphor and Thought*. Cambridge: Cambridge University Press.

Lakoff, G. and Johnson, M. (1980) *Metaphors We Live By*. Chicago: University of Chicago Press.

Lamont, M. (2001) Symbolic boundaries. Available at: http://www.people.virginia.edu/~bb3v/symbound/papers2001/LamontEncyclo.html

Lamont, M. and Molnár, V. (2002) The study of boundaries in the social sciences, *Annual Review of Sociology* 28: 167–95.

Larkin, G. (1983) *Occupational Monopoly and Modern Medicine*. London: Tavistock.

Larson, M. S. (1977) *The Rise of Professionalism: A Sociological Analysis*. Berkeley: University of California Press.

Light, D. W. (1988) Turf battles and the theory of professional dominance, *Research in the Sociology of Health Care* 7: 203–25.

Liljegren, A., Dellgran, P. and Höjer, S. (2008) The heroine and the capitalist: The professions debate about privatization in Swedish social work, *European Journal of Social Work* 11(3): 195–208.

Macdonald, K. (1995) *The Sociology of the Professions*. London: Sage.

MacLure, M. (1996) Telling transitions: Boundary work in narratives of becoming an action researcher, *British Educational Research Journal* 22(3): 273–87.

Malatesta, M. (2005) Comments on Sciulli, *Current Sociology* 53(6): 943–46.

McClelland, C. E. (1990) Escape from freedom? Reflections on German profession-alization, 1870–1933. In: R. Torstendahl and M. Burrage (eds) *The Formation of Professions: Knowledge, State and Strategy*. London: Sage.

Mellor, F. (2003) Between fact and fiction: Demarcating science from non-science in popular physics books, *Social Studies of Science* 33(4): 509–38.

Miller, G. A. (1993) Images and models, similes and metaphors. In: A. Ortony (ed) *Metaphor and Thought*, 2nd edition. Cambridge: Cambridge University Press.

Mintzberg, H. (1999) *Structure in Fives: Designing Effective Organizations*. Engle-wood Cliffs: Prentice-Hall.

Morgan, G. (2006) *Images of Organization*. Thousand Oaks: Sage.

Murphy, R. (1983) The struggle for scholarly recognition: The development of the closure problematic in sociology, *Theory and Society* 12(5): 631–58.

Murphy, R. (1988) *Social Closure: The Theory of Monopolization and Exclusion*. Oxford: Clarendon Press.

Norris, P. (2001) How 'we' are different from 'them': Occupational boundary main-tenance in the treatment of musculo-skeletal problems, *Sociology of Health and Illness* 23(1): 24–43.

Ortony, A. (1993) The role of similarities in similes and metaphors. In: A. Ortony (ed) *Metaphor and Thought*, 2nd edition. Cambridge: Cambridge University.

Parkin, F. (1979) *Marxism and Class Theory: A Bourgeois Critique*. London: Tavistock.

Pavalko, R. M. (1971) *Sociology of Occupations and Professions*. Itasca: Peacock.

Pressman, J. L. and Wildavsky, A. B. (1984) *Implementation: How Great Expecta-tions in Washington Are Dashed in Oakland: Or, Why It's Amazing that Federal Programs Work at All, This Being a Saga of the Economic Development Admin-istration as Told by Two Sympathetic Observers Who Seek to Build Morals on a Foundation of Ruined Hopes*. Berkeley: University of California Press.

Saks, M. (1995) *Professions and the Public Interest: Medical Power, Altruism and Alternative Medicine*. London: Routledge.

Schmitt, R. (2005) Systematic metaphor analysis as a method of qualitative research, *Qualitative Report* 10(2): 358–94.

Schön, D. A. (1993) Generative metaphor: A perspective on problem-setting in social policy. In: A. Ortony (ed) *Metaphor and Thought*, 2nd edition. Cambridge: Cam-bridge University Press.

Sciulli, D. (2005a) Continental sociology of the professions today: Conceptual con-tributions, *Current Sociology* 53(6): 915–42.

Sciulli, D. (2005b) Escaping without eliding an Atlantic divide, etymological and conceptual, *Current Sociology* 53(6): 952–58.

Sciulli, D. (2009) *Professions in Civil Society and the State: Invariant Foundations and Consequences*. Boston: Brill.

Silber, I. F. (1995) Space, fields, boundaries: The rise of spatial metaphors in contem-porary sociological theory, *Social Research* 62(2): 323–57.

Star, S. and Griesemer, J. (1989) Institutional ecology, 'transitions' and boundary objects: Amateurs and professionals in Berkeley's museum of vertebrate zoology, 1907–39, *Social Studies of Science* 19(3): 387–420.

Steen, G. J. (2007) *Finding Metaphor in Grammar and Usage: A Methodological Analysis of Theory and Research*. Amsterdam: John Benjamin Publishing.

Strauss, A. L. (1982) Social worlds and legitimation processes. In: N. K. Denzin (ed) *Studies in Symbolic Interaction*. London: Jai Press.

Thompson, J. A. and Bunerson, S. J. (2001) Work-Non-work conflict and the phenomenon of time: Beyond the balance metaphor, *Work and Occupations* 28(1): 17–39.

Tilly, C. (2004) Social boundary mechanisms, *Philosophy of the Social Sciences* 34(2): 211–36.

Torstendahl, R. (2005) The need for a definition of 'professions', *Current Sociology* 53(6): 947–51.

Tsoukas, H. (1993) Analogical reasoning and knowledge generation in organization theory, *Organization Studies* 14(3): 323–46.

van Dijk, T. A. (1997) Discourse as interaction in society. In: T. A. Van Dijk (ed) *Discourse as Social Interaction*. London: Sage.

van Dijk, T. A. (1998) *Ideology: A Multidisciplinary Approach*. London: Sage.

Watson, G. (1984) Social construction of boundaries between social and cultural anthropology in Britain and North America, *Journal of Anthropological Research* 40(3): 351–66.

Weber, M. (1978) *Economy and Society: An Outline of Interpretive Sociology*. Berkeley: University of California Press.

Wetherell, M. and Potter, J. (1988) Discourse analysis and the identification of interpretative repertoires. In: C. Antaki (ed) *Analysing Everyday Explanation: A Casebook of Methods*. London: Sage.

Witz, A. (1990) Patriarchy and professions: The gendered politics of occupational closure, *Sociology* 24(4): 675–90.

Witz, A. (1992) *Professions and Patriarchy*. London: Routledge.

3 The ecological metaphor in the sociology of occupations and professions

Robert Dingwall

This chapter explores some aspects of the history of one of the key metaphors in sociology, that of ecology, which identifies human societies with the processes of interaction between biological systems and their environment. This metaphor is particularly associated with the approach to sociology developed at the University of Chicago from the early years of the twentieth century onwards. The chapter will look first at the origins of the metaphor and its introduction to sociology through the urban and community studies carried out in Chicago during the 1920s. It will then examine the transfer of the metaphor to the study of work and occupations from the late 1930s onwards, particularly in the work of Everett Hughes and his students. Although this approach became less fashionable during the 1970s, it continued to develop in important ways. These developments will be traced before the chapter concludes with an argument for the continuing relevance of ecological studies in addressing fundamental sociological questions about the social organization of occupations and the subset that are described as professions.

'Ecology' now tends to be reserved as a label for an academic discipline, or an approach within a number of disciplines, with 'ecosystems' as the object of inquiry. For much of this metaphor's life within sociology, however, the term has been employed more generically, to cover both an approach and a topic of study, and that usage will be followed here. It is also important to note the difference between the ecological metaphor and sociology's other main borrowing from biology, the organismic metaphor. The latter identifies human societies with the processes that go on within a biological organism rather than the interactions between organisms and between organisms and their environment. Of course, these are not fully separable, in the sense that all organisms at all levels, from single cells to whole animals, constitute environments for each other and depend on interactions for key resources. Nevertheless, the difference in focus is important in the practice of the biological sciences and certainly in the metaphor's transfer to the social sciences.

The topic of metaphor has a long history in studies of language and rhetoric. Aristotle discussed the term as a dimension of the aesthetics of poetry and of the persuasiveness of argument. By asserting an identity, not merely a resemblance, between one thing and another, the author of a poem, a speech or a text might produce an effect on its hearers that was at once harmonious and disruptive. A pleasing image might attract the attention of its audience, while the unexpected identification preserved it in their memory (Levin 1982). These are features of value in a culture that is only just completing the transition from oracy to literacy, where utterances or texts need to be designed to be memorable (Ong 2002). More recently, however, attention has turned to the cognitive properties of metaphor and its use as a tool in thinking (Lakoff and Johnson 1980). Metaphors are seen to be ways of shaping or framing thought: a new metaphor may be the key to a new understanding of the world. This phenomenon has attracted the interest of researchers in science and technology studies (Brown 2003; Hellsten and Nerlich 2011; Hoffman 1980), who have noted how innovations are frequently accompanied, or preceded, by metaphorical shifts. In this chapter, we shall be concerned with this more recent sense in trying to understand how several generations of sociologists have thought with, and through, the metaphor of ecology.

Evolution, ecology and sociology

In a study of the early development of social science in Canada, Marlene Shore (1987) examines the establishment of ecological thinking within the sociology department at the University of Chicago. This defined the context within which key Canadian figures, such as Carl Dawson, the first sociologist at McGill University, were trained. Shore (1987) outlines the emergence of what came to be known as 'human ecology' through the work of Robert Park, Ernest Burgess and their students, particularly Roderick McKenzie and Louis Wirth, and their engagements with the biological thinking of the time. The paper by Park (1915) laying out a research programme on 'the city', refers to contemporary work on chemical communication between ants, and the introductory textbook in sociology by Park and Burgess (1969), first published in 1921, includes an extract from the influential book *Plant Succession*, published in 1916 by the plant ecologist Frederic Clements. In a memoir of Park, Winifred Raushenbush (1979), one of his early research assistants, lists a number of other ecological texts with which he was familiar. She also quotes Park's youngest son as recalling that his father tried to encourage him to study plant and insect ecology while visiting him at college in 1915 or 1917.

Why was Park so interested in ecology? Shore notes the strategic advantages of adopting ecological approaches within the University of Chicago at that time. This perspective was already well established in the university's biology department, which was a leading international centre and a major influence on other life science departments. When establishing a discipline – and Chicago had only created the world's first sociology department in

1892 – it makes sense to seek allies in powerful and longer-established fields. Park, together with his son-in-law, the anthropologist Robert Redfield, and another prominent anthropologist, Alfred Kroeber, regularly attended seminars on ecology with a core group of biologists from Chicago and Northwestern, the other major private university in the city (Shore 1987). However, as Shore observes, the attractions of the ecological metaphor were more profound. In effect, it provided a new way for sociologists to think systematically about social processes.

Just as with the leading European sociologists of the previous generation, like Emile Durkheim and Max Weber, Park and his colleagues were living in a rapidly changing urban environment. The central areas of Chicago had been devastated by a fire in 1871 that destroyed 9 square kilometres and left one hundred thousand people homeless. One tenancy of the underlying landform was eradicated, and the city rapidly rebuilt in a completely different shape. Early twentieth century sociology seemed to have a limited set of tools with which to understand this process and its outcomes. Park rejected the legacy of August Comte, with his emphasis on the inherent orderliness of society, derived from an internalized consensus on customs, language and institutions. In contrast, Park acknowledged the dynamic model offered by Herbert Spencer, where order was the spontaneous outcome of the division of labour: humans both competed to achieve their own goals and were obliged to co-operate because of their interdependence (Park 1952). Because the Chicago sociologists did not adopt Spencer's scepticism about the likely outcome of attempts to influence social organization, his influence on their work has often gone unrecognized, although, as Raushenbush (1979) points out, Spencer and Darwin are two of the ten most frequently cited writers in the Park and Burgess introductory textbook.

Herbert Spencer is little read by modern sociologists, partly because of the extent to which his reputation has been clouded by the legacy of Social Darwinism, a precursor to neo-liberal nihilism about the potential for collective action to ameliorate poverty and other social ills. In its own time, his work had a very wide intellectual impact: a good deal of early European and American sociology can only properly be understood as a response to his arguments. Spencer wrote extensively about biology before turning to sociology: he was one of the people most responsible for popularizing Charles Darwin's synthesis of the emerging thought about evolution. What excited his contemporaries, however, was the way in which he took as a model for sociology the evolutionists' dismantling of a natural universe fixed by God at the moment of Creation. If species and their order were not immutable, then neither were social institutions: they were human inventions that survived only as long as they were successful in maintaining their fitness in an environment that was made up of other institutions which were also seeking to change and adapt. This, incidentally, is why it is wrong to regard Spencer as a conservative: he does not accept that there is a divine order in human affairs any more than there is in nature. Social organization, in his thinking, is contingent, emergent and transient (Dingwall and King 1995).

One way of understanding the rise of ecological thinking in biology is as an attempt to verify and extend the Darwinian synthesis through specific and local studies of individual cases. Plant succession, then, is evolution at work. The mechanisms by which species occupy new niches, and the ways in which both niches and species change as a result, are fundamental evolutionary processes. When taken into a city like Chicago, where the spatial niches were completely reset by the Great Fire, the attractions of ecological thinking are clear. The city is a natural experiment in evolution. In its account of the development of plant formations, Clements' work set out much of the terminology that would later be used metaphorically by the Chicago studies of the city. Plant systems began with the colonization of a site by simple life-forms, which changed the space in ways that allowed the influx of more complex forms. As this happened, the original colonizing species were forced to the margins. This process was repeated, creating successive zones and spaces of transition, until a dominant life-form, fully adapted to the climate and soil, established itself, creating a stable system that could only be disrupted by external factors. This language – zones, succession, transition – was taken over by Park and Burgess (Park, Burgess and McKenzie 1925), in creating the research programme that produced many of the classic Chicago urban sociology monographs of the 1920s and 1930s.

The metaphor is spelt out most clearly by their student, McKenzie:

> The plant ecologist is aware of the effect of the struggle for space, food and light upon the nature of a plant formation, but the sociologist has failed to recognize that the same processes of competition and accommodation are at work determining the size and ecological organization of the human community.
>
> (Park, Burgess and McKenzie 1925:64)

Citing Clements, McKenzie argues that:

> The structural growth of community takes place in successional sequence not unlike the successional stages in the development of the plant formation. . . . [J]ust as in plant communities, successions are the products of invasion, so also in the human community the formations, segregations and associations that appear constitute the outcome of a series of invasions.
>
> (Park, Burgess and McKenzie 1925:74)

To be sure, McKenzie also acknowledges differences in the greater human capacity for mobility and for purposive interventions in their environment, the ability to select and control a habitat rather than to take what is given.

Nevertheless, these are layered on top of the basic model, tweaks to the metaphor rather than intrinsic properties.

The 1871 Chicago fire had cleared space for colonization, much as a forest or prairie fire might do. The flat, open landform on which the city was built presented few physical barriers to the processes of colonization and differentiation. In contrast, New York, for example, has always been shaped by the constraints of the islands and estuary where it developed. At most, the shoreline of Lake Michigan cut across the circular models of urban zoning that Burgess developed (Park, Burgess and McKenzie 1925). However, this very lack of physical constraint underlined the limitations of regarding the ecological processes as entirely natural and spontaneous. Zorbaugh (1929), for example, noted that planning or, as the Americans have it, zoning laws may be equivalent to natural barriers like cliffs or great rivers in shaping the spaces available for colonization. Everett Hughes' 1928 PhD dissertation explored the impact of the personnel of the Chicago Real Estate Board in shaping land use and zoning controls after the 1871 fire (Burns 1980). Zones and transitions were not the result of spontaneous evolutionary processes but of human interventions that shaped the processes of competition, succession and accommodation.

If the Park and Burgess research programme on the city concentrated largely on understanding the different characters of neighbourhoods, and the localized social pathologies which concerned the various individuals and organizations that funded their studies, the fundamental economic processes involved were clearly still in their thoughts. The women who danced with single men in taxi-dance halls were the product of economic circumstances that left men unable to marry and women lacking in alternative employment that paid a living wage (Cressey 2008). Taxi-dancing was not an indication of the loss of moral sensibilities under the conditions of urban life but a response to conventional processes of supply and demand. Zorbaugh (1929:250) comments on the way in which the zones he studied were the product of the advance of the division of labour:

> The economic differentiation of the city, with its attendant segregation of commerce and industry, has taken out of local areas many of the activities which formerly gave rise to a common body of experience among those who live in these areas. The ever more minute division of labour, with differentiation of occupations and professions, has resulted in an organization of sentiment and interest upon occupational lines rather than upon contiguity of residence.

While Zorbaugh, like most other sociologists of his time, almost certainly exaggerates the homogeneity of pre-industrial communities, comments like this point to the way in which Chicago thinking was moving towards a shift in focus from the neighbourhood to the workplace as the basis for understanding social organization. The echoes of the analysis by Durkheim

(1964) of the division of labour half a century earlier are not coincidental: the key passage of Durkheim's text was included in Park and Burgess' Introduction a decade before a full English translation was available. By 1929, when Zorbaugh first published *The Gold Coast and the Slum*, the limits of the spatially led approach to urban ecology outlined by McKenzie (Park, Burgess and McKenzie 1925) were evident.

Darwin's embarrassment and the economic metaphor in biology

Shore's focus on the intellectual environment at Chicago in the years after World War I and through the 1920s may obscure the extent to which the ecological metaphor was founded on social scientific thinking in the first place. Its ready adoption by sociologists is, arguably, less a case of the incorporation of biology than a return to its source, albeit with a greatly expanded analytic language. The paper by Park (1915) also quotes from Adam Smith, who was the subject of a major study by the Department of Sociology's founding chair, Albion Small (1972), first published in 1907. Charles Darwin was certainly familiar with Smith's work, although he may have taken more from Thomas Malthus, who places greater emphasis on the competitive nature of the struggle for existence (Schweber 1977). Nevertheless, Smith (1976b:87) in his first great work, *The Theory of Moral Sentiments*, anticipates the Darwinian synthesis in enjoining readers: "in the mechanism of a plant, or animal body, admire how everything is contrived for advancing the two great purposes of nature, the support of the individual and the propagation of the species". Perhaps more important, though, is his analysis of the division of labour in *Wealth of Nations* (Smith 1976a). Here, Smith, almost in passing, introduces the idea that occupational structures are not fixed but constantly in process. In some places, trades are combined, while in others they are separated, depending on the environmental conditions set by the available markets. Occupations change because of the development of new technologies or shifts in the demands and boundaries of markets according to Smith (1976a:19):

> In a tribe of hunters or shepherds a particular person makes bows and arrows, for example, with more readiness and dexterity than any other. He frequently exchanges them for cattle or for venison with his companions; and he finds at last that he can in this manner get more cattle and venison than if he himself went to the field to catch them. From a regard to his own interest, therefore, the making of bows and arrows grows to be his chief business, and he becomes a sort of armourer. Another excels in making the frames and covers of their little huts or movable houses. He is accustomed to be of use in this way to his neighbours, who reward him in the same manner with cattle and with venison, till at last he finds

it his interest to dedicate himself entirely to this employment, and to become a sort of house-carpenter. In the same manner a third becomes a smith or a brazier, a fourth a tanner or dresser of hides or skins, the principal part of the nothing of savages.

Although Smith rejects any comparison with the natural world – noting that the diversity among breeds of dog does not constitute a basis for the interdependence that is produced by the division of labour – his analysis provides a metaphor for challenging the fixity of species, which was the core obstacle to evolutionary thinking in the early nineteenth century. If Darwin had been less embarrassed about acknowledging the degree to which his synthesis was inspired by social scientists (Schweber 1980), we might be discussing the metaphors of political economy in biology rather than the ecological metaphor in sociology.

Everett Hughes and the ecology of work

Everett Hughes was not the first Chicago sociologist to write about work and occupations. His wife and fellow graduate student, Helen MacGill Hughes (1980),[1] recalls the participation of Frances Donovan in seminars. Donovan completed a BA degree at Chicago and mostly followed a career as a schoolteacher (Celarent 2009). However, she published three books in 1919, 1928 and 1938, the first two based on participant observation of waitresses – developed from coursework for her degree – and sales clerks and the third on her own life history as a teacher. Donovan was probably supervised for the work on waitresses by Annie Marion Maclean, who was the second woman to receive a PhD in sociology at Chicago, in 1900 (Deegan 2014). Maclean had also written a number of studies of women's occupations based on a mixture of participant observation and life history interviewing.

Writing in 1971, Hughes (1984) recalls his fascination with Park's ecological thinking. This is reflected in his first published paper, 'Personality types and the division of labour', which explicitly links human ecology and the division of labour in discussing the relationship between personality and occupation. Do occupations select for personality or do people with particular kinds of personality select particular occupations? (Donovan's work on waitresses is cited as one of the case studies.) Hughes (1984:328), however, is already beginning to invert the relationship between ecology and the division of labour:

As the division of labour proceeds, the life of each social organ is more conditioned by the others; the forces that hold it in place come to include neighbors as well as the soil beneath one's feet. It is this pattern of social organs, treated spatially, with which human ecology concerns itself.

The term 'social organ' is taken from Durkheim, who locates it much more firmly within an organismic metaphor. For Hughes, though, it is simply a way to describe a unit in a system that remains consistent with the ecological metaphor, while apparently relegating this to a concern with spatial organization rather than social organization. Nevertheless, the approach taken by Hughes (1984:329) retains the dynamism of ecological thinking:

> New occupations are created every day, and the concatenations of functions of old ones are subject to change. The industrial revolutions of every day mean to the individual that he is not sure of his job; or, at least, that one is not sure of one's son's job. . . . Occupational selection . . . becomes a fierce process which begins anew each day, atomizing families and tearing them loose from their soil.

Hughes sets out the challenge of devising a taxonomy of occupations, much like the taxonomy of the botanist, in order to understand the workings of this system. It is the system that interests him rather than the case studies offered by people like Maclean or Donovan (Simpson 1972). He proposes three dimensions of classification: how do people join the occupation; what is their attitude towards the occupation; how does the community evaluate the occupation? This is his equivalent of Linnaeus' classification of species.

At this point the taxonomy is not highly developed and Hughes simply presents a list of possible types without attempting to specify their relationships. The list is, however, of interest as the first point at which Hughes (1984:329) discusses 'professions and near-professions'. This is worth quoting in full:

> The professions are entered by long training, ordinarily in a manner prescribed by the profession itself and sanctioned by the state. The training is assumed to be necessary to learning the science and technique essential to practice of the function of the profession. The training, however, carries with it as a by-product assimilation of the candidate to a set of professional attitudes and controls, a professional conscience and solidarity. The profession claims and aims to become a moral unit. It is a phenomenon of the modern city that an increasing number of occupations are attempting to gain for themselves the characteristics and status of professions.

This one paragraph from 1927 effectively sets out Hughes' programme for work on professions by himself and his students. It defined professions as a distinctive subset of occupations, a unit within the taxonomy. This unit has certain properties. There is a special relationship with the state, which allows the occupation to control its own entry. Lengthy training is assumed to be necessary – note the way in which this is treated as an assumption or a claim rather than a proven fact. This allows graduates to perform a function, to move into a niche created for them by the division of labour. In the process, they acquire distinctive attitudes, values and a sense of mutual solidarity. These may appear as personal traits but are actually generated by the experience of group membership. This is not just a group of experts but people who claim a distinctive role in the moral ordering of a society. Finally, in the modern world, many occupations want to gain this privileged status. Competition works here just as much as in the spatial ecology of the city: professional status is residence in the Gold Coast neighbourhood of Chicago.

Hughes did not return to these interests until 1938: the intervening years were spent in a faculty position at McGill, where he worked mainly on issues of industrial development and intergroup relations between the Francophone and Anglophone communities in Quebec (Hughes 1984; Shore 1987). On his return to Chicago, however, he was asked to teach both an introductory course and a course on 'The Sociology of the Professions'. The first-year course seems to have been a scaled-down version of the graduate programme he had followed in the 1920s, with students going out to small areas of the city to carry out observations and report on them (Hughes 1980). The second course was soon retitled 'The Sociology of Work and Occupations'. Hughes (1984) gives two reasons for this: avoiding the preoccupation with upward mobility and encompassing a wider range of occupations. This underlines the focus of Hughes (1984:292) on the system of occupations, and the place of professions within this, rather than on professions *per se*:

> [A]n occupation is a more-or-less standardized one-man's part in some operating system [which] cannot be described apart from the whole. A study of occupations, then, becomes in part a study of the allocation of functions and the consequent composition of any given occupation.

His students followed the same approach as in the first year course, providing a large number of case studies as Hughes (1984:419) documents:

> A good many students wrote papers on the occupations of their fathers, their kin, and even on their own. Some of the papers were developed into more systematic studies and were presented as theses. The occupations considered included – I write them down as they come to me – janitors, junk dealers (and how they come to engage in the recovery industry), furriers, funeral directors, taxi drivers, rabbis, school teachers, jazz musicians, mental hospital attendants, osteopaths, city managers, pharmacists, and YMCA secretaries. Others studied lawyers, physicians, and the clergy, as well as the newer professions or the newer specialities in these older professions.

The core topics for these case studies were outlined in an unpublished memorandum, 'An Outline for the Sociological Study of an Occupation' (Hughes

2010). Again, we can see the concern for comparative analysis, with information collected in a form that might allow different cases to be classified in ways meaningful for sociological analysis.

From the published text, it is not clear when that manuscript took its present form. However, it seems to be the point at which Hughes first introduces two key terms: 'licence' and 'mandate'. He defines an occupation by: "the implied or explicit license that some people claim and are given to carry out certain activities rather different from those of other people and to do so in exchange for money, goods, or services" (Hughes 1984:287). It is important to note here that Hughes is engaging in metaphorical thinking of another kind: "License, as an attribute of an occupation, is usually thought of as specific legal permission to pursue the occupation. I am thinking of something broader" (Hughes 1984:287). The concept of a licence to practise a profession seems to go back to Tudor England. Religious dissent was controlled by restricting the right to preach and perform certain other religious functions to those clergy formally licenced by a bishop, by the Crown or by the ancient universities. The term 'licence' already had a number of other legal uses in granting permission to carry out certain activities, some of which it retains to the present day. In opening it up to all occupations, Hughes is asserting an identity between the formal legal recognition of professions and the social recognition accorded to anyone carrying out certain activities different from those of other people. An occupation may not have a statutory basis – but its claim to distinctiveness must still be treated as legitimate. The licence must be supplied to the occupation by the actions of those engaging with it, much as Adam Smith described in his suppositions about the origins of the division of labour. It is not purely a matter for members themselves. In this respect, Hughes' positioning within the broad interactionist tradition is evident: the meaning of acts is to be found in the responses of observers, not the intentions of actors. Anticipating a later discussion of the work of Eliot Freidson, one of Hughes' students, we should also note that Hughes emphasizes that occupations operate in a market where their activities are rewarded by 'money, goods or services'.

In some cases, however, occupation members may also claim a mandate, "to define – not merely for themselves, but for others as well – proper conduct with respect to the matters concerned in their work" (Hughes 1984:287). The mandate represents the occupation's self-justification. This is why it deserves to have the licence to perform those distinctive activities. The nature and extent of the mandate depends to some extent on the degree to which the occupation's members form a definite community that promotes some sense of solidarity. In the 1927 paper, Hughes (1984:333) acknowledged that some units in the division of labour were simply jobs where all that was required was "to present one's self at the proper time and place when manpower of a certain age, sex and perhaps a certain grade of intelligence, is wanted." Note the phrasing here: even for a mere job, it is the presentation of 'one's self' not 'oneself' that is demanded. Engagement goes beyond simple physical presence.

Subsequent usage rather blurred the distinction between these terms, and it is arguable that Hughes did not sufficiently clarify the difference between what an occupation claimed and what it was granted. He describes 'licence' as both a claim and a grant, for example, while 'mandate' is quite clearly only a claim. This is a point to which we shall return. In practice, although Hughes supervised students studying a wide range of occupations, much of his own work was on the professions, particularly in health and education. This was partly a matter of funding: Hughes was involved in two major projects on health professions in the early 1950s, studying changes in nursing (Hughes, Hughes and Deutscher 1958) and in medical education (Becker et al. 1961). It should, though, also be recognized that the health care system of the 1950s was a good proxy for 1920s Chicago, as social and technological change dramatically reconfigured hospitals, rendering some occupations and specialties obsolete, sometimes almost overnight, and creating new niches for colonization. The dynamism of the health sector continues to attract sociologists of occupations and professions, much as it did in the early post-war period (Heath 1984). Nevertheless, this empirical concentration on professions may have distracted attention from Hughes' more fundamental concern to understand the system of occupations. The desire of students "to write about the efforts of their own occupation to be recognized as a profession" (Hughes 1984:418) was no less marked after World War II than before and continues to the present day. The peculiarities of US health care also skewed the development of this approach: Hughes' early acknowledgement of the role of the state, for example, rather dropped out of subsequent work in this tradition. As more recent work has shown, the American medical profession was created in a fragmentary way at state level and often in the teeth of political opposition (Whooley 2013). In Europe, by contrast, national medical professions have been more typically created through state sponsorship, and analyses of professional work find it much harder to neglect this dimension.

Ecological thinking in the sociology of occupations since Everett Hughes

Hughes' project for a systematic, comparative study of occupations was taken forward by a number of his students, most notably Howard Becker and Eliot Freidson. Both struggled with the questions of definition, much as urban sociologists came to struggle with identifying the boundaries of zones or communities: what were viable principles of classification that would produce analytically useful categories. Some of this, as both acknowledged, came from the elision of folk classifications with those useful to sociologists. 'Profession' then had both a lay sense of an honorific title to describe a group of workers carrying out a particular set of tasks and a sociological sense, of a group of workers that belonged to a defined category that marked their set of tasks as sharing certain properties with other groups performing other sets – and distinguished them from groups that did not share these properties. Becker (1970) suggested that the problem might be addressed by developing two different research agendas: one would continue Hughes' programme of trying to classify workers and the other would look at the folk ascription of titles and status (Dingwall 2007). Freidson (1983) argued that, at the very least, writers in the field should be clear about which agenda they were pursuing: to the extent that they were trying to classify workers, they should set out the criteria that they were using so that it was clear that like was being compared with like.

Freidson, himself, explored three rather different ways of constructing useful categories for the comparison of occupations. The first of these, in his best-known work, *Profession of Medicine* (Freidson 1970), focused on expert or esoteric knowledge. In some ways, this returned to ideas developed by Adam Smith (Dingwall 2007) about the problem presented by occupations performing tasks that had high stakes for their clients, but which the clients were ill-equipped to evaluate. Lawyers lose trials, patients die on doctors, priests fail to reform sinners: in any given case was this the result of incompetence or some natural cause? Should we blame the experts or their materials? In the second phase, Freidson (1994) responded to some of the Marxist work on professions by writers like Johnson (1972, 1977) and Larson (1977) by exploring the professions as occupations that had successfully created 'market shelters'. These ecological niches were protected by various means, particularly regulation, but also potentially by industrial action. While physicians or lawyers might create a monopoly based on law, craft workers in traditional manual occupations might achieve the same result by threatening to disrupt production. A third phase is marked more by an exploration of relations between professions and the state (Freidson 1986, 2001). This pursues themes also identified with the work by Terence Halliday (1987) on lawyers and Donald Light (1995), Hughes' last student, on countervailing powers. Professions are now occupations that have a special relationship to the management of order in societies. This is also a theme hinted at by Adam Smith but much extended into an argument that Spencer would have recognized, namely that it is undesirable in democratic societies for states to concentrate too much power in their own apparatus. The health of those societies depends upon a decentralization and dispersion of power among a loosely coupled group of institutions, some of which might be occupations called professions.

Less well known is the sketch by Freidson (1978) of a wider understanding of the relationship between occupations and the organization of society. (This paper does not seem to have been published and is not available online: an accessible summary can be found in Dingwall 2007.) In this paper, Freidson considers the way in which tasks are distributed between the official market economy, measured by definitions of the workforce for various public policy purposes; the criminal economy, those occupations that are defined as illegal; the informal economy, those occupations that contribute to economic activity but are not counted in public measures; and the subjective economy, of volunteers, hobbyists and creatives:

> I shall suggest that the universe of work may be represented as a series of different but overlapping and interacting economies in which various kinds of work are organized in various ways. Some kinds of work may be generic to their particular economies, while others may shift from one economy to another as circumstances change. Occupations themselves can be delineated by the economies, or markets, in which they are practiced rather than by the kinds of tasks they perform, for while the same tasks can be performed in different economies, their social and economic organization is likely to vary with the characteristics of the economy in which they are performed.

Freidson is returning here to Hughes' original programme by insisting on decoupling the work or the tasks performed in a society, some of which may be necessary for survival and some for enhancing the quality of life, from the occupational structure that breaks up this work into units for analysis. At the highest level, we have the four economies, which are, in some sense analogous to the kingdoms recognized by Linnaeus. Below these, we still await the equivalents of class, order, genus and species, let alone the more modern refinements to this scheme. This is an agenda for the sociology of occupations. Tasks are its equivalent of landforms. What are the processes by which these metaphorical landforms are colonized and with what consequences?

The boundaries between economies are fluid and historically contingent. Prohibition in the USA saw a range of occupations in the liquor trade move from official to criminal and back again. The subjective economy may be the cradle and grave of many occupations: health visiting began in the subjective economy for middle class women and migrated into the official economy of state employees in the early twentieth century (Dingwall 2007). Ostlers just disappeared with the arrival of the automobile. The study by Becker (1982:227–28) of art worlds explores how works of art are constructed out of the interactions between different occupations in different relationships to the official economy:

> The work people do varies with the nature of their participation in an art world. But that does not mean that the character of their participation can be seen directly in the work itself. I will talk about integrated professionals, mavericks, folk artists, and naïve artists. These relational terms do not describe people, but rather how people stand in relationship to an organized art world.

Individuals may move between these economies without changing their work: the contested status of the Scottish artist Jack Vettriano is an interesting example. Entirely self-taught, Vettriano's work is hugely popular and has made him very wealthy but widely denigrated by art critics. Vettriano began painting for his own pleasure in the subjective economy, continued successfully in the official economy but has encountered continual questioning of the legitimacy of his claim to be a considered a member of the occupation 'artist'. The work does not change but its place within a system of social relations has varied considerably over the last forty years.

The social construction of occupations

A good deal of recent writing on professions has focused on second-order questions about public policy, about the translation of an Anglo-American folk label into the different historical experiences of other countries and about the continuing efforts of some occupations to be recognized as worthy bearers of that title. In doing so, as Freidson observed, we are still losing sight of the fundamental sociological questions: How is the world of work socially organized? What kinds of occupations are there? How do they relate to each other in a division of labour that goes beyond official categories of measurement? How do they maintain boundaries, compete and contest for ownership of tasks – and discard those that they do not want to retain? What are the drivers for this – social, cultural or technological? The ecological metaphor still helps us to identify these questions, as in this study of the emergence of bioethics as a recognized occupation in the USA – but not in France.

> Think of all the work that has to get done in a society as the landform upon which a city is based. The division of labor is the street grid that defines this landform: some areas are zoned for manufacturing, others for services, some for respectable tasks, others for deviant ones; some areas are identified for the market, others for domestic labor. Each zone, or jurisdiction (Abbott 1988), is a site for potential ecological struggle. Some are securely occupied by well-entrenched occupations. Others are scrapped over: some want to annex new areas to territory they already control; some wish to abandon a declining area in order to colonize a more desirable one; others desire to take over a neglected patch and displace or organize the existing occupants to improve it. This metaphor has its limits – landforms are less easily altered than material technology – nevertheless, it introduces a way to think sociologically about occupations.
>
> (DeVries, Dingwall and Orfali 2009:556)

Various tools already exist to undertake this task. We have already discussed 'licence' and 'mandate'. Although Abbott (1988) has resisted the suggestion that his *System of Professions* is really a basis for the study of occupations, his concept of jurisdiction is useful in disentangling Hughes' ambiguity as to whether licence is claimed or granted. We might see jurisdiction as a claim made by any occupational group and restrict licence to the response, which may be more or less formalized in law and regulation. There is, then, a set of occupations in any particular society that has a system of law which share the characteristic of being explicitly recognized by that system, whereas others may simply be the subject of fairly generic duties to carry out their work with a proper degree of care. This category, of 'regulated occupations', overlaps somewhat with the folk category of 'professions' in Anglo-American usage but is not identical to it. The tradesmen who maintain the gas appliances in my home are quite strictly regulated – but this does not make their social status equivalent to that of physicians. We may also identify a group of occupations based around expertise – but not all of these are regulated by law: for example, Microsoft runs a private scheme of accreditation for computer technicians.

Occupations have careers, just as much as individuals. If we are interested in regulated occupations, for instance, there are stories to be told as to how they came to be regulated, to create market shelters. How do myths concerning an occupation's origin compare with the versions a more disinterested historian might tell (Dingwall 2016)? Many more occupations seek market shelters than are granted them (Dingwall 2007). How do we understand the demand for regulated licences that guarantee ownership of a block of tasks and protect that jurisdictional claim from the encroachments of competitors and the supply of licences by legislators and executives that are reluctant to create monopolies? The idea of a social scheme of classification of work also implies the maintenance of that scheme. What are the dynamics of inclusion, acknowledging individuals and tasks as members of the occupation, and exclusion, defining other individuals and tasks as not fit and proper (Dingwall 2007)? How does this get accomplished through what Freidson's student, Thomas Gieryn (1983), called 'boundary work'?

The ecological metaphor need not distract attention from other questions that sociologists may be interested in, about the place of professions within class structures, about their engagements with the state and citizens, and about their modes of governance. However, if we neglect the agenda set out by Hughes we risk falling into the errors identified by Becker and Freidson that arise from confusing folk categories and analytic categories. Ecological and evolutionary thought is helpful in this process. To recall McKenzie's words, quoted earlier:

> [T]he same processes of competition and accommodation are at work determining the size and ecological organization of the human community . . . the formations, segregations and associations that appear.

> (Park, Burgess and McKenzie 1925:64/74)

At the same time, we need to be clear that this is no more than a metaphor. Evolution in human societies has Lamarckian as well as Darwinian features, being shaped by purposeful interventions as well as by random shocks. We can acquire characteristics, and transmit them, as well as inherit them. The social construction of occupations is the product of both the impersonal forces of markets and the deliberate choices and strategies of occupation members and those with whom they interact.

Note

1 A number of the sources consulted for this chapter have her – wrongly – as Helen McGill Hughes.

References

Abbott, A. (1988) *The System of Professions: An Essay on the Division of Expert Labor*. Chicago: University of Chicago Press.

Becker, H. S. (1970) *Sociological Work*. Chicago: Aldine.

Becker, H. S. (1982) *Art Worlds*. Berkeley: University of California Press.

Becker, H. S., Geer, B., Hughes, E. C. and Strauss, A. (1961) *Boys in White: Student Culture in Medical School*. Chicago: University of Chicago Press.

Brown, T. L. (2003) *Making Truth: Metaphor in Science*. Urbana: University of Illinois Press.

Burns, L. R. (1980) The Chicago School and the study of organization-environment relations, *Journal of the History of the Behavioral Sciences* 16: 342–58.

Celarent, B. (2009) Review of *The Woman Who Waits* by Frances Donovan, *The Saleslady* by Frances Donovan, *The Schoolma'am* by Frances Donovan, *American Journal of Sociology* 115(3): 984–90.

Cressey, P. G. (2008) *The Taxi-Dance Hall: A Sociological Study in Commercialized Recreation and City Life*, new edition. Chicago: University of Chicago Press.

Deegan, M. J. (2014) *Annie Marion Maclean and the Chicago Schools of Sociology 1894–1934*. New Brunswick, NJ: Transaction Publishers.

DeVries, R. G., Dingwall, R. and Orfali, K. (2009) The moral organization of the professions: Bioethics in the United States and France, *Current Sociology* 57(4): 555–80.

Dingwall, R. (2007) *Essays on Professions*. Aldershot: Ashgate.

Dingwall, R. (2016) Why are doctors dissatisfied? The role of origin myths, *Journal of Health Services Research and Policy* 21(1): 67–70.

Dingwall, R. and King, M. D. (1995) Herbert Spencer and the professions: Occupational ecology reconsidered, *Sociological Theory* 13(1): 14–24.

Durkheim, E. (1964) *The Division of Labor in Society*. New York: Free Press.

Freidson, E. (1970) *Profession of Medicine: A Study of the Sociology of Applied Knowledge*. New York: Dodd, Mead & Co.

Freidson, E. (1978) The official construction of occupations: An essay on the practical epistemology of work (unpublished).

Freidson, E. (1983) The theory of professions: State of the art. In: R. Dingwall and P. Lewis (eds) *The Sociology of the Professions: Lawyers, Doctors and Others*. London: Macmillan.

Freidson, E. (1986) *Professional Powers: A Study of the Institutionalization of Formal Knowlege*. Chicago: University of Chicago Press.

Freidson, E. (1994) *Professionalism Reborn: Theory, Prophecy and Policy*. Cambridge: Polity Press.

Freidson, E. (2001) *Professionalism: The Third Logic*. Chicago: University of Chicago Press.

Gieryn, T. F. (1983) Boundary-work and the demarcation of science from non-science: Strains and interests in professional ideologies of scientists, *American Sociological Review* 48(6): 781.

Halliday, T. C. (1987) *Beyond Monopoly: Lawyers, State Crises and Professional Empowerment*. Chicago: University of Chicago Press.

Heath, C. (1984) Review essay: Everett Cherrington Hughes (1897–1983): A note on his approach and influence 1, *Sociology of Health and Illness* 6(2): 218–37.

Hellsten, I. and Nerlich, B. (2011) Synthetic biology: Building the language for a new science brick by metaphorical brick, *New Genetics and Society* 30(4): 375–97.

Hoffman, R. R. (1980) Metaphor in science. In: R. P. Honeck and R. R. Hoffman (eds) *Cognition and Figurative Language*. Hillsdale: Lawrence Erlbaum Associates.

Hughes, E. C. (1984) *The Sociological Eye: Selected Papers*. New Brunswick: Transaction Books.

Hughes, E. C. (2010) Outline for the sociological study of an occupation, *Sociologica* 2 (October).

Hughes, E. C., Hughes, H. M. and Deutscher, I. (1958) *Twenty Thousand Nurses Tell Their Story: A Report on Studies of Nursing Functions Sponsored by the American Nurses' Association*. Philadelphia: JB Lippincott.

Hughes, H. M. (1980) On becoming a sociologist, *Journal of the History of Sociology* 3(1): 27–39.

Johnson, T. (1972) *Professions and Power*. London: Macmillan.

Johnson, T. (1977) Professions in the class structure. In: R. Scase (ed) *Industrial Society: Class, Cleavage and Control*. London: Allen & Unwin.

Lakoff, G. and Johnson, M. (1980) *Metaphors We Live By*. Chicago: University of Chicago Press.

Larson, M. S. (1977) *The Rise of Professionalism: A Sociological Analysis*. Berkeley: University of California Press.

Levin, S. R. (1982) Aristotle's theory of metaphor, *Philosophy and Rhetoric* 15(1): 24–46.

Light, D. (1995) Countervailing powers: A framework for professions in transition. In: T. Johnson, G. Larkin and M. Saks (eds) *Health Professions and the State in Europe*. London: Routledge.

Ong, W. J. (2002) *Orality and Literacy*. London: Routledge.

Park, R. E. (1915) The city: Suggestions for the investigation of human behavior in the city environment, *American Journal of Sociology* 20(5): 577–612.

Park, R. E. (1952) *Human Communities: The City and Human Ecology*. Glencoe: Free Press.

Park, R. E. and Burgess, E. W. (1969) *Introduction to the Science of Sociology*. Chicago: University of Chicago Press.

Park, R. E., Burgess, E. W. and McKenzie, R. D. (1925) *The City – Suggestions for Investigation of Human Behaviour in the Urban Environment*. Chicago: University of Chicago Press.

Raushenbush, W. (1979) *Robert E. Park: Biography of a Sociologist*. Durham: Duke University Press.

Schweber, S. S. (1977) The origin of the origin revisited, *Journal of the History of Biology* 10(2): 229–316.

Schweber, S. S. (1980) Darwin and the political economists: Divergence of character, *Journal of the History of Biology* 13(2): 195–289.

Shore, M. (1987) *The Science of Social Redemption: McGill, the Chicago School and the Origins of Social Research in Canada*. Toronto: University of Toronto Press.

Simpson, I. H. (1972) Continuities in the sociology of Everett C. Hughes, *Sociological Quarterly* 13(4): 547–59.

Small, A. W. (1972) *Adam Smith and Modern Sociology*. Clifton: Augustus M. Kelley.

Smith, A. (1976a) *An Inquiry Into the Nature and Causes of the Wealth of Nations*. Edited by Edwin Cannan. Chicago: University of Chicago Press.

Smith, A. (1976b) *The Theory of Moral Sentiments*. Oxford: Clarendon Press.

Whooley, O. (2013) *Knowledge in the Time of Cholera: The Struggle over American Medicine in the Nineteenth Century*. Chicago: University of Chicago Press.

Zorbaugh, H. W. (1929) *The Gold Coast and the Slum: A Sociological Study of Chicago's Near North Side*. Chicago: University of Chicago Press.

4 Slaying the Minotaur
Reflections on the sociology of professions

Mike Saks

The slaying of the professional Minotaur

In this chapter, the author sees the slaying of the Minotaur by Theseus in Greek mythology as emblematic of his own complex personal intellectual journey to understand, and contribute to the reform of, the professions – which variously appear in sociological work on professional groups like the Minotaur as half human, half beast. The golden thread charting a path out of the labyrinth is viewed as conceptual, leading to a more generic agenda for sociology – grasping the limits of the discipline in terms of the pursuit of value freedom while appreciating that understanding its value relevance enables it to be applied even more productively. Building on this and other aspects of a neo-Weberian approach, it is argued that sociologists can with integrity make a more positive contribution to the wider society in terms of both impact and social change. In so doing, this chapter seeks to underline the value of metaphors in illuminating the sociological enterprise – not least in relation to the study of professions as undertaken by the author and as a clarion call for future enquiry and action in this and other associated fields.

According to the Greek legend, when Theseus slayed the Minotaur he first made his way to the heart of the labyrinth to discover the creature – which reputedly had the head of a bull and the body of a man with a tail. Having disposed of the Minotaur, who was serially consuming human sacrifices, Theseus found his way out of the labyrinth by following a golden thread that he had laid on entering the labyrinth (Gide 2002). This is seen as metaphorically symbolic of the author's own journey through the intellectual labyrinth of the sociology of professional groups in modern societies, to understand and contribute as appropriate to the reform of the professions – which variously appear in sociological work on professions like that cleft creature, the Minotaur. The spin in the tale about the range of professions from accountants to lawyers and doctors is that the thread leading out of the labyrinth provides a path for sociologists in a far broader range of fields to make a positive wider impact on society. The chapter, though, first outlines the dualism associated with theoretical conceptualizations of the professions – as both being intensely human and bearing the characteristics of a beast.

Two sides of the professions: the human and the beast

The human side of the professions is most distinctly drawn out by taxonomic writers on the professions, whose work was particularly in the ascendance in the 1950s and 1960s, when – building on more sporadic but influential earlier work (such as Carr-Saunders and Wilson 1933) – it constituted the first serious attempt in sociology to study the professions. Professional groups were seen by such contributors as intrinsically different from other occupations (Millerson 1964). Their distinctive characteristics were centrally tinged with humanity – spanning from the possession of high level knowledge of public benefit to playing a positive part in society. Of the two types of taxonomic approach, trait writers produced a range of lists of attributes of professions including such items as esoteric knowledge, codes of ethics, altruism, rationality and high level educational credentials (for example, Greenwood 1957; Wilensky 1964). Functionalists, however, presented more theoretically coherent accounts, arguing that there was a functional relationship between professions and society (for instance, Barber 1963; Goode 1960). On this perspective, occupations with greatly important knowledge for society were viewed as being given a highly rewarded position in the social structure in return for protecting the public and/or clients.

However, the taxonomic perspective that was so prominent in Anglo-American sociology has been attacked for being ahistorical and uncritical. This was highlighted by the focus of the trait approach on constructing league tables glorifying one or other professions (usually that related to the occupational background of the contributor), based on the relatively arbitrary range and weighting of the elements included. Such characteristics were also often assumed to exist rather than necessarily being established – with trait and functionalist writers typically presenting professional ideologies as reality. This critique was initially underlined by interactionist contributors in the 1950s and 1960s who drew parallels between 'top dog' professions and less highly flung and marginal occupations such as janitors and prostitutes (as illustrated by Becker 1962; Hughes 1963). Failing to see significant differences between them, they regarded professions simply as honorific symbols in the politics of work – viewing the taxonomic writers as being hoodwinked by them into legitimating their powerful position in society (Roth 1974). As such, interactionism pointed the way to more beast-like interpretations of the professional Minotaur that were powerfully to emerge in the next half century of writing on professional groups.

Marxism certainly strongly emerged in the 1970s and 1980s as an antidote to taxonomic views of professions that presented them as fundamentally contributing to the cause of humanity. Proponents of this perspective took a macro structural approach to the interpretation of professions based on the relations of production under capitalism that contrasted with the micro-perspective of interactionism. Professional groups are variously interpreted by Marxist accounts, including as being agents of surveillance or control for a dominant class or part of this class itself, maintaining the capitalist status quo (as highlighted by Ehrenreich and Ehrenreich 1979; Navarro 1986). This is usually seen as having negative implications for the public – not least through individualizing pathology and deflecting attention away from wider patterns of class inequality despite professional ideologies of public service (Esland 1980). A different, but also primarily negative, contemporaneous stance on professions is provided by the Foucauldians, who question the rationality of scientific progress associated with professions in such areas as schools, prisons and health care (see, for instance, Foucault 1979; Nettleton 1992). This critique is centred on 'governmentality' through the 'institutionalization of expertise' in modern societies, which involves the political incorporation of professional expertise into state formation as part of the structure of governance (Johnson 1995).

The broader negative, helicopter views of professions in Marxist and Foucauldian approaches have their own difficulties – including that they do not usually provide sufficiently robust evidence for their interpretations. However, a more recent perspective offering an alternative to the taxonomic approach, employed in the analysis of occupations spanning from advertising to architecture, centres on the discourse of professionalism (see, for example, Cohen et al. 2005; Fournier 1999). This again offers critical insight into the culture of professionalism, in widening the range of occupations open to the lens of the sociology of professions by analyzing the role of professional ideologies in occupational discourse. This, and the foregoing more challenging perspectives on the professions, therefore provide a counterbalance to the trait and functionalist notion that professions are a positive, humanizing force in society; in not accepting professional ideologies on trust, they bring out more the beast side of professions resonant with the symbolic imagery of the Minotaur. For this author, though, the analytically most helpful perspective going beyond taxonomy and its critics in examining the balance of humanity and beast-like qualities of the professions is the neo-Weberian approach – which has for long driven my personal research in this area (see, for instance, Saks 1983, 2010).

Confronting the Minotaur: the neo-Weberian approach to professions

Professions are defined by neo-Weberian writers as a form of exclusionary social closure in the marketplace sanctioned by the state. In this sense, professions are simply seen as being based on the formation of legal monopolies with registers of insiders with defined credentials, which typically enhance the income, status and power of members against outsiders (as illustrated by Parkin 1979). The main benefit of a neo-Weberian approach is that it avoids, through the use of a definition centred on social closure, making unnecessarily positive assumptions of the taxonomic approach about the human face of the professions. At the same time, it acknowledges that professions can act in the manner of a beast in relation to the public – not least through the operation of group self-interests in a competitive marketplace. As such, unlike interactionism, it considers macro structural and historical processes; sidesteps the limiting assumptions embedded in a Marxist perspective about the role of professions under capitalism; finesses the shaky evidence base of Foucauldianism; and provides greater clarity and policy leverage than discourse analysis.

However, in terms of the role of neo-Weberianism in confronting the Minotaur, it must be said that in practice neo-Weberians have frequently been guilty of being unduly critical of professions – focusing on their group self-interests as opposed to their orientation to the public. Elliott (1972), for instance, too readily accepts without evidence that professional self-interests prevail over the public welfare when the two conflict, while Beattie (1995) makes similarly unsubstantiated claims about the tribal warfare driven by self-interests between health professional groups in the UK. Nonetheless, there is nothing intrinsic in the neo-Weberian approach that leads it in this direction. This is well exemplified by the neo-Weberian analysis by Halliday (1987) based on detailed evidence which concludes that the American legal profession can be seen to be public interest oriented because of its unique links to the state that encourage it to move beyond a simple preoccupation with the defence of its own domain. As such, as both Benoit (1994) and Porter (1996) demonstrate in the cases of midwifery and nursing respectively, professions can be assessed as much as a positive as a negative force in society through the theoretical lens of neo-Weberianism.

Having negotiated the intellectual labyrinth occupied by the range of theories of professions, the neo-Weberian approach, if appropriately applied, therefore provides an ideal base for empirically assessing the professions – in which they may variously appear, depending on circumstance, as intensely human or bearing the characteristics of a beast or some combination of the two. As such, neo-Weberianism has also been able to act as a driving force for my own long-standing engagement with research into the professions, which has been motivated by a desire to review the operation of professional groups and to seek to reform them wherever they manifestly fall short of advancing the public interest. This approach – which has also been taken up by certain other sociological researchers – involves using the neo-Weberian approach to the professions to confront the Minotaur, the creature which was the progeny of a human mother and the Cretan Bull, at the heart of the labyrinth. My personal research work on the professions throughout my career has been oriented in its own way towards overcoming the professional Minotaur by conducting rigorous analyses of professions and considering the implications for moving professions forward in a more humane approach. Such research on professions has been focused on health and social care, which has helped to advance a positive professional reform agenda both in the UK and internationally in slaying the Minotaur.

Slaying the Minotaur: reforming work on the professions in the UK

In the UK my long-standing interest in tackling the professional Minotaur was marked by the publication of my work on professions and the public interest (Saks 1995), following twenty years of research beginning with my doctoral work at the London School of Economics. In this work I discuss the relationship between professions, self-interest and the public interest both theoretically and operationally. This culminates in the application of the resulting conceptual and methodological framework to a detailed empirical case study that shows that the medical profession has obstructed the development of acupuncture as a complementary and alternative medicine in Britain over the past two centuries in defence of its own interests against the public interest. Having aroused my personal interest in complementary and alternative medicine, I went on to study further the interface between organized medicine and complementary and alternative therapies (see, for instance, Saks 2003) – and from 2002 to 2006 became the Chair of the Research Council for Complementary Medicine, the primary objective of which was to promote evidence-based understanding of the medical alternatives. In the wake of the recommendations of the field-breaking House of Lords Select Committee on Complementary and Alternative Medicine (2000), I became centrally involved in this capacity in setting up a novel Department of Health research committee that, for the first time, was focused on competitively awarding dedicated and extensive funding for post-doctoral fellowships to foster research excellence in complementary therapies – which at this time were on a rising curve of public popularity (Saks 2006).

My work in confronting the professional Minotaur in the UK is also underlined by the research project I led on health support workers around this time. A major Department of Health (2001) consultation document on workforce planning in the National Health Service (NHS) chose only to focus on the professional labour force without mention of the one and a half million health support workers who make up the majority of the health care workforce. However, a report commissioned by the UK Departments of Health and chaired by myself, with a team of colleagues from De Montfort University and Warwick University, highlighted that health support workers were fundamental to the delivery of care and needed to be further regulated to protect public safety (Saks et al. 2000). Following a widespread literature review, focus groups, regional workshops, interviews with influential individuals, and a survey of chief executives in the NHS and Social Service Departments in the UK, the report argued, amongst other things, that a statutory register of health support workers would best advance the general interest given its role in protecting the public. The government, however, did not allow publication of the report for several years largely because of the costs to the state of creating such a register (Saks and Allsop

2007). Nonetheless, the report on the role and functions of health support workers who have a marginalized role in the division of labour (Saks 2008) led to significant debate in government circles, as it served to underline professional dependence on such workers and the case for mandatory health support worker registration that has since frequently been reiterated by health professional bodies – most prominently including by the Royal College of Nursing (2012).

Moreover, I have constructively engaged with mainstream professional bodies in seeking to slay the professional Minotaur in evaluating the regulatory impact in the UK of the case of Harold Shipman, the serial killing general practitioner who is known to have disposed of over two hundred of his patients (Allsop and Saks 2002). Given my track record of research on health professional regulation I was invited independently by the Department of Health and the General Medical Council to assist them in assessing the implications of Shipman for medicine as a self-regulating profession – in the latter case in the context of the report and recommendations on professional regulation in the Inquiry by Dame Janet Smith into the handling of complaints and concerns about general practitioners, General Medical Council procedures and its proposal for the revalidation of doctors (Department of Health 2004). In this process, I was asked to address the General Medical Council and the leaders of all the other health and social care professions to propose ways forward. What followed was a debate about the future of the health professions, in which the government made proposals for wider reform to enhance patient safety in the wake of the Donaldson Review (Department of Health 2007) – resulting in doctors in the UK now having to be revalidated every five years, with regular appraisals (Chamberlain 2015). In medicine in particular, therefore, I contributed to new professional appraisal and re-accreditation arrangement. This has been against a changing political landscape that I have described metaphorically as shifting from a self-regulatory zoo to a circus, with the state as ringmaster, and a safari park with greater emphasis on interprofessional collaboration – as medicine has been restratified with the increasing power of general practitioners against hospital consultants (Saks 2014).

More recently, I delivered a commissioned report to the General Social Care Council about the future of social work education and social work as a profession in England, in the wake of the scandal over the killing of 'Baby Peter', to whom social workers were seen as offering insufficient protection. This report fed into the government's Social Work Task Force that reinforced the value of a social work profession and paved the way to the government establishing new regulatory arrangements for the profession under the Health Professions Council (Saks 2011), which has since been reconfigured into the more multi-professional Health and Care Professions Council (Klein 2013). In this and the other ways described, I have contributed as a sociologist of the professions to the reform of professional groups in health and social care – and thereby to the partial demise of the professional Minotaur in these fields in the public interest in the UK. As such, I have followed in the footsteps of high profile sociologists dedicated to applying their sociological knowledge to the reform of the professions in this country. These include Margaret Stacey, the late Emeritus Professor at Warwick University – who critically appraised to positive effect the role, policies and structure of the General Medical Council as a statutory body responsible for monitoring the standards of medical training and taking disciplinary action, as both a sociologist and a long-standing member of the General Medical Council itself (Stacey 1992).

Slaying the Minotaur: bringing about professional change internationally

Internationally my work in addressing the professional Minotaur is illustrated by my recent presidency and vice-presidency of the International Sociological Association Research Committee on Professional Groups. This has a membership drawn from some thirty different countries who attend the conferences it is regularly involved in organizing worldwide – and has been involved in examining the part played by professions through various theoretical lenses, centrally including neo-Weberianism. This role is linked to my numerous publications in this area in several languages and associated keynote and other presentations in social scientific, professional and government forums in countries in the northern and southern hemisphere. It is highlighted by my involvement with funded projects on the professions in both Europe and North America. In Europe I was most recently engaged as part of the Steering Group for the project 'Rethinking Professions in a World of Transnational Jurisdictions' in the Department of Sociology at the University of Copenhagen – an increasing focus of neo-Weberian work (see, for example, Seabrooke 2014). But my engagement is probably best illustrated by my role in the pioneering project 'Russian Physicians: Their Attitudes and Strategies for Adaptations to Change' from 1998 to 2003, funded by INTAS (the International Association for the Promotion of Cooperation with Scientists from the New Independent States of the Former Soviet Union) and undertaken in collaboration with colleagues from the Russian Academy of Sciences in Moscow. This was distinctive for being one of the earliest neo-Weberian studies in Russia.

This Russian study, based on a survey of over six hundred Russian physicians in three regions of the country, helped to increase our understanding of incipient professional bodies and prepare the ground for professional formation in medicine in a post-Soviet society that had little experience at dealing with professional agendas (see Mansurov et al. 2004). The project was conducted with my long-term collaborator, Professor Judith Allsop, then a colleague at De Montfort University. With my support and especially that of Kathryn Jones in undertaking the study, she went on to play a key part in the Donaldson Review in the UK by providing a commissioned comparative analysis of medical regulation in seven different countries – Australia, Canada, France, Finland, the Netherlands, New Zealand and the USA – which informed government regulatory policy on the medical and other health professions in the UK (Allsop and Jones 2008). In Russia the situation was different, as the medical profession had been disestablished by the Soviet regime in the early part of the twentieth century – when physicians were seen as a class enemy to the socialist state. However, after the demise of the Soviet Union and the founding of the Russian Federation in 1991 there were moves to reprofessionalize medicine (Saks 2015). What the INTAS project uncovered was how little the values of the high number of mostly poorly rewarded physicians had changed since Soviet times, including in their largely positive ongoing attitude to state salaried medical practice. The task here therefore was not so much to slay the Minotaur as to rebuild medicine as a profession based on more human qualities than those of the beast – a task which continues in a political environment where the state remains reluctant to relinquish the reins of power.

In North America I have been involved with a number of ventures in medicine to more proactively slay the professional Minotaur. In the USA this originally took the form in the late 1990s of addressing several hundred physicians on professional ethics in New York State. This was followed by my more recent delivery of the Annual Distinguished Professor Lecture at the State University of Arizona in 2013 highlighting the pitfalls of marginality in American medicine, and a presentation on the changing medical profession at the University of California in 2015. This was in the context of medicine being embroiled in a society which has a far greater individualistic emphasis on the market – with the growing deprofessionalization of once generally very powerful and highly paid physicians through increasing corporatization (Saks 2015). But my strongest neo-Weberian impact on professional policy in North America has been in the more egalitarian and less market-driven country of Canada and its province of Ontario in particular – where I have had a strong long-term association with the University of Toronto, which began with my first academic visit in the mid-1990s and has since developed into a Visiting Professorship in Health Policy in the Institute of Health Policy, Management and Evaluation. This has been associated with a number of keynote addresses to practitioners and policymakers on topics ranging from fostering community hubs to integrating health and social care, in association with the Canadian Research Network for Care in the Community and the Health System Performance Research Network.

One of my higher impact engagements in Canada was as a co-investigator in a large-scale, multi-million dollar project that was led by the University of Toronto and funded by the Canadian Institutes of Health Research from 2006 to 2011 on 'Shifting between Hospitals and the Community: Policy Implications for Care, Clients and Providers', which aimed to enhance professional and other forms of community care in Ontario and beyond (see, amongst others, Williams et al. 2009). Further, in 2014 I was invited by

Health Canada and the Canadian Institutes of Health Research to act as a health policy adviser for both the federal government and the provinces/territories through a Best Brains Exchange Award. This was a very important role in slaying the Minotaur in a system far more dominated by doctors than the contemporary UK – where, under the sway of the medical profession, primary health care is relatively underdeveloped, public engagement is less pronounced and silo-based working has proved more of the norm (Hutchison et al. 2011). This has led to a number of other commitments in collaboration with health policy colleagues at the University of Toronto who are themselves well versed in translating their research into action (see Deber and Mah 2014) – including ongoing projects on the competence of physicians and the role of personal support workers in Ontario. The latter resulted in discussions with the Ontario Health Ministry and invitations to speak in 2015 to large gatherings of practitioners, employers and policymakers in this field at the Ministry-supported annual conferences of both the Personal Support Network of Ontario and the Ontario Community Support Association.

The golden thread: value relevance and applying research in the sociology of professions

As my own work underlines, though, the golden thread leading out of the labyrinth of the sociology of professions is conceptual and is central to the successful slaying of the professional Minotaur. It involves understanding that, in neo-Weberian terms, while value freedom is not possible, the study of the professions is value relevant – and, through this, it can create the possibility of social policy reform for the betterment of society. This is a key message which was set out in the classic article by Gouldner (1964) intriguingly entitled in this context 'Anti-Minotaur: The myth of a value-free sociology'. He argues *in extremis* that the pursuit by social scientists of value freedom is a myth which is liable to create cohorts of sociologists willing to serve in a future Auschwitz. Weber, for Gouldner, was simply striving to separate the expression of political values from academic work – and fully accepted that social science must be value relevant. In this sense, values shape the sociologist's selection of problems, preferences for certain hypotheses or conceptual schemes and the neglect of others – but within such parameters it should be possible for sociologists from any culture or political persuasion to agree. Gouldner, though, identifies an overly simplified interpretation of Weber's position as being akin to a Minotaur – half human, half beast – because, in the pursuit of value freedom, social scientists may be led to reject responsibility for the cultural and moral consequences of their work.

However, despite the merits of Gouldner's stance, the position held by Weber is considerably more subtle. For Weber there is a more positive way of reconciling values and objectivity – not least in relation to the analysis of groups like professions, which, as is argued here, themselves exhibit features of a Minotaur. Most notably, even if values cannot be derived from 'fact', Weber (1949) allows for the analysis of the consistency of values as well as the promotion of research-based understanding of effective means-end relationships in relation to values. This enables sociological inquirers to present various scenarios related to their research in terms of its application to different policy objectives, without directly entering the realm of politics as sociologists by committing themselves to one specific set of political values. As such, sociologists of the professions and other areas could with integrity take greater action in making their research amenable to application in the cause of reform, where this is appropriate. The upshot of this is that the strict search for 'value freedom' in the ivory tower of higher education should be avoided and sociologists need to understand ways in which the application of relevant research in this disciplinary field of the social sciences can be encouraged – for example, through the way that results are communicated, meeting timeframes for political action and making politically visible particular issues highlighted in sociological research (Saks 2012).

This is helpful to research on the sociology of professional groups in modern industrial societies where government is particularly seeking to generate appropriate bodies of applied research to enhance the public welfare. This is well exemplified in Portugal, where a law was established in 2008 requiring professional associations to demonstrate through independent study that they serve a relevant public interest (Veloso et al. 2010). The facilitation of the implementation of sociological research is also prompted more generally in the UK by the Research Excellence Framework (REF) newly introduced by the Higher Education Funding Council. This required universities, with commensurate financial rewards, to provide impact analyses in their submissions, as part of the periodic assessment of research quality for 2014 in competition for extensive recurrent public sector funding. Impact for the REF is seen as "an effect on, change or benefit to the economy, society, public policy or services, health, the environment or quality of life, beyond academia" (HEFCE 2011:26). As such, it is entirely resonant with qualitative, quantitative and mixed methods research – as opposed to the positivistic quantitative research so favoured by American sociologists – in evaluating the operation of professional groups that may lead, in some cases, to recommendations that involve slaying the professional Minotaur (see, for instance, Saks and Allsop 2013).

Conclusion: following the golden thread

When Theseus sailed away from the labyrinth, having slain the Minotaur and made his escape, disaster struck. He had told his father, King Aegeus, that his boat would display a white sail if he had been successful and was alive or a black sail if he had died at the hands of the Minotaur. Theseus, however, forgot to change his sail to white and, seeing the black sail, his father committed suicide by tragically throwing himself from his castle down onto the sharp rocks in the sea (Mills 1997). Our journey could have a similar dispiriting end since, having successfully negotiated the intellectual labyrinth of the sociology of professions, there is no guarantee that sociologists of professions will widely follow the guidance offered in relation to implementing future research on professional groups or indeed adequately publicizing their work in the public domain. To be sure, there have been valuable further developments in more generally understanding the impact of the social sciences and how this may be enhanced, as demonstrated by recent work by Bastow, Dunleavy and Tinkler (2014) at the London School of Economics. However, the way their book is organized still tends to throw too much responsibility for the current level of application of social science research in the external world on the culpabilities of the potential users of such research, and too little on navel inspection by sociologists and others as to how they conduct and present their work. Pleasingly, though, in tune with this chapter, there are references embedded in the text of their book on the need for social scientists to make their research more relevant and accessible to business, government and users in the charitable sector.

Many other related areas of social science have their own Minotaurs to slay to public benefit – from the world of banks and finance which may drag us back into recession to oppressive organizational and management structures that may stifle staff innovation and economic and social regeneration. Indeed, it has been very interesting how the neo-Weberian sociology of professions itself has increasingly addressed this broader environment through a neo-institutionalist approach based on seeing professional groups as one institution striving to occupy the higher ground alongside other institutional forms – from the state to multi-national corporations (Saks 2016 forthcoming). This has been prompted by the growing location of professions in wider private, public and transnational settings, including in large-scale professional service firms themselves, as illustrated by the cases of accountancy and law (Suddaby and Muzio 2015). In looking at this ever wider terrain, I would urge sociologists in their analyses to follow the same golden thread based on the neo-Weberian concept of value relevance, rather than pursuing the chimera of value freedom. As outlined in this chapter, the notion of value relevance has proved extremely helpful in my own career as a sociologist of the professions in enabling the positive application with integrity of research knowledge to policy and practice. In spreading its use to others, it should be stressed that the metaphor of slaying the Minotaur is not a plea to obliterate professions from the landscape, but to further humanize them where they exist and to encourage positive developments in their form and practice in societies where they are emerging.

References

Allsop, J. and Jones, K. (2008) Protecting patients: International trends in medical governance. In: E. Kuhlmann and M. Saks (eds) *Rethinking Professional Governance: International Directions in Healthcare*. Bristol: Policy Press.

Allsop, J. and Saks, M. (eds) (2002) *Regulating the Health Professions*. London: Sage.

Barber, B. (1963) Some problems in the sociology of professions, *Daedalus* 92: 669–88.

Bastow, S., Dunleavy, P. and Tinkler, J. (2014) *The Impact of the Social Sciences: How Academics and Their Research Makes a Difference*. London: Sage.

Beattie, A. (1995) War and peace among the health tribes. In: K. Soothill, L. Mackay and C. Webb (eds) *Interprofessional Relations in Health Care*. London: Edward Arnold.

Becker, H. (1962) The nature of a profession. In: National Society for the Study of Education (eds) *Education for the Professions*. Chicago: University of Chicago Press.

Benoit, C. (1994) Paradigm conflict in the sociology of service professions: Midwifery as a case study, *Canadian Journal of Sociology* 19(3): 303–29.

Carr-Saunders, A. M. and Wilson, P. A. (1933) *The Professions*. Oxford: Clarendon Press.

Chamberlain, M. J. (2015) *Medical Regulation and Fitness to Practice and Revalidation: A Critical Introduction*. Bristol: Policy Press.

Cohen, L., Wilkinson, A., Arnold, J. and Finn, R. (2005) "Remember I'm the bloody architect!": Architects, organizations and discourses of profession, *Work, Employment and Society* 19: 775–96.

Deber, R. B. and Mah, C. L. (eds) (2014) *Case Studies in Canadian Health Policy and Management*, 2nd edition. Toronto: University of Toronto Press.

Department of Health (2001) *A Health Service of All the Talents: Developing the NHS Workforce*. London: The Stationery Office.

Department of Health (2004) *Safeguarding Patients: Lessons from the Past – Proposals for the Future*. London: The Stationery Office.

Department of Health (2007) *Trust, Assurance and Safety: The Regulation of Health Professionals*. London: The Stationery Office.

Ehrenreich, B. and Ehrenreich, J. (1979) The professional-managerial class. In: P. Walker (ed) *Between Capital and Labour*. Brighton: Harvester Press.

Elliott, P. (1972) *The Sociology of Professions*. London: Macmillan.

Esland, G. (1980) Diagnosis and therapy. In: G. Esland and G. Salaman (eds) *The Politics of Work and Occupations*. Milton Keynes: Open University Press.

Foucault, M. (1979) *Discipline and Punish: The Birth of the Prison*. London: Vintage Books.

Fournier, V. (1999) The appeal to 'professionalism' as a disciplinary mechanism, *Social Review* 47(2): 280–307.

Gide, A. (2002) *Theseus*. London: Hesperus Press.

Goode, W. (1960) Encroachment, charlatanism and the emerging profession: Psychology, sociology and medicine, *American Sociological Review* 25: 902–14.

Gouldner, A. (1964) Anti-Minotaur: The myth of a value-free sociology. In: M. Stein and A. Vidich (eds) *Sociology on Trial*. Englewood Cliffs: Prentice-Hall.

Greenwood, E. (1957) Attributes of a profession, *Social Work* 2(3): 45–55.

Halliday, T. C. (1987) *Beyond Monopoly: Lawyers, State Crises and Professional Empowerment*. Chicago: University of Chicago Press.

HEFCE (2011) *REF 2014: Assessment Framework and Guidance on Submissions*. Bristol: HEFCE.

House of Lords Select Committee on Science and Technology (2000) *Report on Complementary and Alternative Medicine*. London: The Stationery Office.

Hughes, E. C. (1963) Professions, *Daedalus* 92: 655–68.

Hutchison, B., Levesque, J., Strumpf, E. and Coyle, N. (2011) Primary health care in Canada: Systems in motion, *The Milbank Quarterly* 89(2): 256–88.

Johnson, T. (1995) Governmentality and the institutionalization of expertise. In: T. Johnson, G. Larkin and M. Saks (eds) *Health Professions and the State in Europe.* London: Routledge.

Klein, R. (2013) *The New Politics of the NHS: From Creation to Reinvention,* 7th edition. London: Radcliffe Publishing.

Mansurov, V., Luksha, O., Allsop, J. and Saks, M. (2004) The Anglo-American and Russian sociology of the professions: Comparisons and perspectives, *Knowledge, Work and Society* 2: 23–48.

Millerson, G. (1964) *The Qualifying Associations.* London: Routledge & Kegan Paul.

Mills, S. (1997) *Tragedy, Theseus and the Athenian Empire.* New York: Oxford University Press.

Navarro, V. (1986) *Crisis, Health and Medicine: A Social Critique.* London: Tavistock.

Nettleton, S. (1992) *Power, Pain and Dentistry.* Milton Keynes: Open University Press.

Parkin, F. (1979) *Marxism and Class Theory: A Bourgeois Critique.* London: Tavistock.

Porter, S. (1996) Contra-Foucault: Soldiers, nurses and power, *Sociology* 30(1): 59–78.

Roth, J. (1974) Professionalism: The sociologist's decoy, *Sociology of Work and Occupations* 1(1): 6–23.

Royal College of Nursing (2012) *Position Statement on the Education and Training of Health Care Assistants.* London: RCN.

Saks, M. (1983) Removing the blinkers? A critique of recent contributions to the sociology of professions, *Sociological Review* 31(1): 1–21.

Saks, M. (1995) *Professions and the Public Interest: Medical Power, Altruism and Alternative Medicine.* London: Routledge.

Saks, M. (2003) *Orthodox and Alternative Medicine: Politics, Professionalization and Health Care.* London: Sage.

Saks, M. (2006) The alternatives to medicine. In: J. Gabe, D. Kelleher and G. Williams (eds) *Challenging Medicine,* 2nd edition. Abingdon: Routledge.

Saks, M. (2008) Policy dynamics: Marginal groups in the healthcare division of labour in the UK. In: E. Kuhlmann and M. Saks (eds) *Rethinking Professional Governance: International Directions in Healthcare.* Bristol: Polity Press.

Saks, M. (2010) Analyzing the professions: The case for the neo-Weberian approach, *Comparative Sociology* 9(6): 887–915.

Saks, M. (2011) Social work in the UK: A changing profession under challenge in turbulent times. Paper presented at the European Sociological Association Conference on Social Relations in Turbulent Times, Geneva.

Saks, M. (2012) The challenge of implementing social science research, *Portuguese Journal of Social Science* 11(1): 71–83.

Saks, M. (2014) The regulation of the English health professions: Zoos, circuses or safari parks? *Journal of Professions and Organization* 1(1): 84–98.

Saks, M. (2015) *The Professions, State and the Market: Medicine in Britain, the United States and Russia.* Abingdon: Routledge.

Saks, M. (2016 forthcoming) A review of theories of professions, organizations and society: Neo-Weberianism, neo-institutionalism and eclecticism, *Journal of Professions and Organization* 3(2).

Saks, M. and Allsop, J. (2007) Social policy, professional regulation and health support work in the United Kingdom, *Social Policy and Society* 6(2): 165–77.

Saks, M. and Allsop, J. (2013) *Researching Health: Qualitative, Quantitative and Mixed Methods*, 2nd edition. London: Sage.

Saks, M., Allsop, J., Chevannes, M., Clark, M., Fagan, R., Genders, N., Johnson, M., Kent, J., Payne, C., Price, D., Szczepura, A. and Unell, J. (2000) *Review of Health Support Workers: A Report to the UK Departments of Health*. Leicester: De Montfort University.

Seabrooke, L. (2014) Epistemic arbitrage: Transnational professional knowledge in action, *Journal of Professions and Organization* 1(1): 49–64.

Stacey, M. (1992) *Regulating British Medicine: The General Medical Council*. Chichester: Wiley.

Suddaby, R. and Muzio, D. (2015) Theoretical perspectives of the professions. In: L. Empson, D. Muzio, J. Broschak and B. Hinings (eds) *The Oxford Handbook of Professional Service Firms*. Oxford: Oxford University Press.

Veloso, L., Freire, J., Lopes, N. and Oliveira, L. (2010) Regulation and the public interest: The Portuguese case of the relationship between the state, science and the professions. Paper presented at the World Congress of the International Sociological Association on Sociology on the Move, Gothenburg.

Weber, M. (1949) *Max Weber on the Methodology of the Social Sciences*. Glencoe: Free Press.

Wilensky, H. (1964) The professionalization of everyone? *American Journal of Sociology* 70: 137–58.

Williams, A. P., Lum, J. M., Deber, R., Montgomery, R., Kuluski, K., Peckham, A., Watkins, J., Williams, A., Ying, A. and Zhu, L. (2009) Aging at home: Integrating community-based care for older persons, *Healthcare Papers* 10(1): 8–21.

5 Social closure

On metaphors, professions and a boa constrictor

Ola Agevall

The tragedy of metaphors

At their best, metaphors and analogies redirect attention, open new lines of inquiry and make us see afresh what has become so quotidian that it escapes our notice. As Richard Swedberg (2014) has argued, they are crucial equipment for theorizing in the social sciences, entering the theorizing process at different junctures and aiding observation as well as explanation. There is therefore good reason to pay attention to the stock of social science metaphors, and to keep construing new ones. This chapter aims to do a little of both.

Metaphors, we may say, are quintessentially novelty items, and as such do not age gracefully. Once productive tensions between vehicle and tenor sooner or later become stale from habituation; all natural languages contain entire petrified forests of once vivid metaphors and analogies which have receded into pseudo-literalness. Indeed, the more striking a metaphor was as a youngster, the more likely it is to be copied, stereotyped and overused, thereby inevitably losing vigour. And once they have been stereotyped, they become clichés – which, ironically, is the case with both 'stereotype' and 'cliché' (Amossy 1991; Amossy and Herschberg Pierrot 1997; Amossy and Rosen 1982) – and cease to be evocative and blend with the other homely linguistic furniture that surrounds us. In other words, the success of a metaphor strips it of those characteristics which occasioned its success. This is the tragedy of metaphors.

The tragedy of metaphors has implications, general and specific, for interpretive work in the social sciences. Long-term exposure to pseudo-literal use may cause us to overlook the genuinely metaphorical quality of an expression in an older work. Conversely, translations may impute metaphorical meaning to what was in fact mere pseudo-literal use. Any interpretation must therefore make assumptions about the vivacity of a metaphor in a particular work. These remarks can translate into a general call for interpretive vigilance, or into empirical inquiries of how actual assumptions are patterned. But they may also serve as a cue to inspect particular concepts and to ask what analytical gains can be achieved from reminiscing about their non-literal youth.

The argument in this chapter is of the latter variety: we revisit the concept of social closure, with the aim of adding new dimensions to the study of social closure in the professions. Our endeavour is part excavation, part exploration. We shall ask what the notion of social closure looked like before it crystallized into the form we now recognize in the sociology of professions. And by thus retracing conceptual evolution, from modern use to classic source, we discern the junctures where the concept was adapted for more specialized and increasingly literal use. This is not to say that the employment of the concept in the classics is somehow archetypal or primal. The wolf is the ancestor of Norfolk terriers and Australian shepherd dogs alike, each being specialized for functions in which wolves would surely perform badly. What the excavation does provide, however, is an overview of the theorizing which has successively shaped the now entrenched concept – and an opportunity to explore alternative ways of refining the original concept.

Metaphor plays a crucial role in this story. Metaphorical work, expanding on the basic spatial analogy of open and closed social relationships, figures prominently in the evolution of the concept. Detecting such metaphorical devices in the works of other scholars is instrumental if we want to understand why the concept was refined in one direction rather than another. Equally important: we too will resort to metaphor in order to suppress the *prêt-à-porter* quality of a long familiar concept and its associated fading imagery. Did you envision social closure as a fortress, jealously guarded for the riches it contains? Fair enough. Now try a different image: that of a small pig consumed by a boa constrictor. We shall encounter the boa constrictor in the last section of the essay, where it will aid us in the task of shaking mental habits. Before we make its acquaintance, we need to examine the concept of social closure up close.

Social closure from Parkin to Weber

While there are several varieties of neo-Weberian profession theories, there is no Weberian one. In Weber's days, the Anglo-Saxon notion of 'profession' as a generic category, describing a distinct class of occupations, had yet to migrate into German (Swedberg and Agevall 2016). What we get from Weber is instead a set of concepts, theoretical props and observations that have been deemed useful in the analysis of the professions. There is a succession of Weberian elements flowing into the study of professions, roughly reflecting the general reception of Weber's work. Definitions of 'profession' have, for instance, alternately been grafted upon and juxtaposed to Weber's concept of bureaucracy, and scholars have resorted to ideal typical concept formation to capture the logic of professionalism.

But while all these uses could well qualify as neo-Weberianism, this term denotes something rather more precise within profession studies. In the apt formulation of Mike Saks (2012:4): "professions are normally defined at root by neo-Weberians in terms of exclusionary social closure in the marketplace sanctioned by the state". Apart from situating social closure at the hub of the neo-Weberian perspective on professions, the quote from Saks also gives us a clue as to how it ended up there. Insofar as the active ingredient here is exclusionary social closure, this is Frank Parkin's hand at work. As Sommer Harrits (2014) argues, the theory of social closure was simply suggested by Weber but gained coherence and elaboration in professional studies primarily through Parkin (see also Murphy 1986, 1988). This is consistent with the history of reception of the concept. It came into vogue in the 1980s; prior to that date, references to the concept are scant and scattered (see amongst others, Dimaggio and Useem 1978a, 1978b; Mulkay 1969; Neuwirth 1969; Parkin 1971, 1974). The main vehicle of diffusion was the innovative and irreverent book by Frank Parkin (1979) *Marxism and Class Theory: A Bourgeois Critique.*

In brief, then, Max Weber provided a point of departure, but it is the work of subsequent scholars that has adapted it specifically to the study of professions, thus refining it in ways that cannot simply be read off from Weber's writings. This is perhaps characteristic of our use of the classics, or indeed what constitutes a sociological classic: by refinement and selective appropriation, an inherited – promising but rough – concept is fitted for more specialized, circumscribed and technical uses. This bears on the previous paragraph, somewhat tempering the tragedy of metaphors. Conceptual refinement and adaptation reconfigures metaphor into literalness, prompting us to pay attention to intention rather than to an amorphous force-field of connotations. And this is generally a good thing. Even so, there is reason to ask what can be gained from retracing the route from modern uses to a classic source. What possible paths were forfeited in the process of refinement? Are there elements of the original that ought to be preserved and brought back into the sociology of professions?

In order to assess this, we need to retrace our steps from Parkin to Weber and compare the neo-Weberian conception of social closure with the Weberian. Max Weber, as we shall see, drew on a very basic spatial analogy, which he used creatively in various parts of his works, and which was built into the architecture of his explanatory apparatus at critical but multiple junctions. Parkin isolated one particular use of the concept, and refined it to suit his theoretical ends – thereby simultaneously sharpening the tool and shedding much of its original variety. In what follows, we shall first discuss the role of social closure in Parkin's project, and how it entered the sociology of professions. Then, in the next section, we examine Weber's broader use. Finally, we draw on the results of this exercise to highlight some features of Weber's analogy and concept-in-use, and illustrate their potential value to profession studies by engaging in novel metaphorical work and applying it to the analysis of the Swedish academic profession.

Parkin's concept

Frank Parkin (1971, 1974) elaborated on closure first in *Class Inequality and Political Order* and then in *The Social Analysis of Class Structure*. As the titles indicate, the immediate context is class analysis and stratification research. The same holds for the work by Parkin (1979) on *Marxism and Class Theory*, but its tone and argument are different. Crafted as a caustic polemic with primarily Althusserian Marxism, it carved out a space for a Weberian analysis, tailored for a joint account of class, ethnic and other communal cleavages. 'Social closure' serves as the framework in which class and communal boundaries are "regarded as aspects of a single problem" (Parkin 1979:42). In all societies, Parkin maintained, the dominant classes engage in what he called exclusionary social closure. "Expressed metaphorically", he suggested, "exclusionary closure represents the use of power in a 'downward' direction because it necessarily entails the creation of a group, class, or stratum of legally defined inferiors" (Parkin 1979:45). But subgroups among those inferiors can themselves erect boundaries against others, in Parkin's parlance, the usurpatory social closure of subordinate classes. In modern capitalism, exclusionary social closure is based on two 'group attributes', property and credentials, and Parkin's main concern was to work out how they shape the characteristics and conditions of reproduction of its dominant classes. Within this framework, professions are centre stage as the prime expedients of credentialism-cum-social closure.

While Parkin's concern was with macro-social features of modern capitalism, within which the professions happen to play a central role, the framework readily translates into a research programme for the study of professions, highlighting the devices through which professional groups secure monopoly, the revenue from professional cartelization, and the relations between profession and state. The sociology of professions had thereby gained several things. Parkin's analysis underscored the overwhelming importance of professions, but from a very different angle than Parsons had done; you could now be sceptical of the harmonic picture of functionalism and still insist that professions were especially important features of modern society. Here was, moreover, a conceptual apparatus and a research programme that could be put to immediate use but which also, and crucially, seemed to summarize important previous work in the field.

Parkin employed the spatial analogy to craft new metaphorical constructions, as in picturing closure from above and from below. He also provided the classic, oft-quoted definition of social closure, familiar in the sociology of professions: "By social closure, Weber means the process by which social collectivities seek to maximize rewards by restricting access to resources and opportunities to a limited circle of eligibles" (Parkin 1979:44). In adopting Parkin's position on social closure, the sociology of professions also inherited features that have been the source of controversy. One of these concerns the imagery evoked by the definition. Professionals would have us believe that they act out of high ideals, but what they are really doing is pursuing naked self-interest, strategically operating to preserve privilege, thereby exploiting the excluded. Was not this an overly cynical way of portraying the professions?

In response to that indictment, it is often claimed that there is no compelling reason to interpret closure along cynical lines. True as this may be, Parkin's account was steeped in voluntaristic, agency-oriented language – no doubt under the sway of anti-Althusserianism – where social entities 'seek' and 'aspire to' exploitative closure and have 'strategies' to attain it. This relates to another feature of Parkin's concept which was passed on to profession research: its exclusive preoccupation with "the closure of economic and social opportunities to outsiders" (Parkin 1979:44). In outline, this is how the concept of social closure is generally understood in profession studies. Proponents and critics may disagree on the merits and scope of the concept of social closure, but there is widespread agreement on the concept itself. In the next section, we shall inquire how this construct relates to Weber's original use.

Weberian social closure

From what materials did Parkin build his refined concept, tailored for modern stratification research? Parkin, it turns out, concentrated on a few specific passages in Weber. His central references go to the same section in *Economy and Society*, that on 'Open and Closed Economic Relationships', supplemented and fleshed out with some forays into other parts of the book. Max Weber's exposition in this section concerns the competition for remunerative opportunities. He stressed that when "the number of competitors increases in relation to the profit span, the participants become interested in curbing competition", thereby prompting participants to seize upon some "externally identifiable characteristic" of outsiders, which in turn serves as "a pretext for attempting their exclusion" (Weber 1978:341–42).

So far, Weber's account appears every bit as conspiratorial as that of Parkin; it quotes material interests as the motive behind closure, and relegates the characteristics themselves to mere pretext. Transposed to the world of professions, this amounts precisely to the cynical theory of professions. What Weber set out to portray in these passages, however, was economic closure – a special case of, rather than coterminous with, social closure. To assess the analytical consequences of this, we turn to how social closure entered Max Weber's thought. In the absence of further specifications, the notion of 'open' and 'closed' social relations is pure spatial analogy. It raises no particular difficulty that 'social relation' is defined abstractly, for even with the most anemically constructed entity, we can conjure up an image of it being closed or open. These properties – an easily intuited yet transferable and abstract analogy – made the metaphor a useful tool for Weber's theorizing, enabling him to subsume a set of particular empirical patterns under a more general concept. To see how the metaphor was brought into play by Weber, we revisit these empirical particulars, focusing, for the sake of brevity, on a single example.

In his essay 'The Protestant sects and the spirit of capitalism', Weber (1970) examined the role of Protestant sect membership in American economic life. He set out to understand why it was important for his American interlocutors to signal their membership in a congregation, and account for the social structure that makes this possible. For this explanatory task, doctrinal specificities are incidental: "What is decisive is that one be admitted to membership by 'ballot', after an *examination* and an ethical *probation* in the sense of the virtues which are at a premium for the inner-worldly asceticism of Protestantism and hence, for the puritan tradition" (Weber 1970:307). The gist of the argument is this: the knowledge that all members of a Protestant sect have passed through ballot, examination, and probation makes membership a sign of certain qualities – in effect serving as a mechanism of trust.

For this to happen, it is crucial that not everyone can be a member. The mandatory membership-by-default in a state church signals nothing; voluntary membership in a sect is ripe with information. Equally important, the signal effect is at work regardless of the reasons for joining. Some may have purposively rational motives for seeking membership in that, observing empirical regularities, actors can calculate that it is good for business to seek membership (hinted at in one of Weber's examples). But the majority of members are presumably in good faith, motivated by sincere religious (value-rational) belief, or perhaps following family tradition. This is not a world of irreligious cynics, but it is a world where cynics are empirically possible and heterogeneity of ends overwhelmingly likely.

Consider next the traces of this argument in *Economy and Society*. The modest abstraction involved – that is, the distinction between voluntary and compulsory association, is preserved there and is used to build other concepts. 'Sect' is defined as voluntary association and is juxtaposed to 'church' as a compulsory association (Weber 1978). What would otherwise be a rather idiosyncratic way of defining 'sect' thus becomes less puzzling when seen against the backdrop of the argument in the essay. It highlights those properties which make a set of behaviours economically relevant, without necessarily being economically motivated. But *Economy and Society* had a much wider scope. Outlined as the third part in *Grundriß der Sozialökonomik*, a gigantesque collective undertaking designed to replace Gustav Schönberg's *Handbuch der Politischen Ökonomie* as the standard handbook of economics, Weber was aiming to provide a toolbox for analyzing all kinds of relations between economy and society, past and present. For that endeavour, he was frequently pushed to further abstractions. This is where the spatial analogy of open and closed relationships came in handy.

Noting that sects are voluntary associations will get you only so far. As soon as you compare social formations across cultures and vast chunks of time, it becomes apparent that there are just as important differences within that set. They differ, for instance, in terms of what it takes to become a member, the procedure to gain admission, the spoils associated with membership, whether or not you can lose membership, and how hermetic the boundary is to outsiders. The metaphor of 'social closure' allowed Weber to introduce a general concept to summarize these various qualities. Weber reserved a place for his new concept in the introductory part of *Economy and Society* in the section where he delineates the basic concepts of sociology (Weber 1978). "A relationship", Weber says here, will "be called 'closed' against outsiders so far as, according to its subjective meaning and its binding rules, participation of certain persons is excluded, limited, or subjected to conditions" (Weber 1978:43).

This highly abstract definition encompasses – but also chimes with – the specification by Weber (1978:45), quoted in the same section of *Economy and Society*, of several manners of social closure:

> Various conditions of participation may be laid down; qualifying tests, a period of probation, requirement of possession of a share which can be purchased under certain conditions, election of new members by ballot, membership or eligibility by birth or by virtue of achievements open to anyone.

Part of this list, obviously, is a verbatim echo of 'The Protestant sects and the spirit of capitalism', suggesting that Weber had this argument in mind when he crafted the concept of social closure. This bears directly on the issue of whether the theory of social closure is inherently cynical.

In his discussion of the Protestant sects, Weber acknowledges that people can mimic religiosity to reap economic benefits. But those benefits will be forthcoming for the truly pious too, whether they want it or not. Just as Mandeville and Adam Smith showed that private vices could turn into public benefits, so Weber shows us how value-rational action may yield private benefits. Weber's point was precisely to undermine the presumption that economically beneficial behaviours must also be economically motivated. That is to say: insofar as this type of argument was the paradigm for Weber's reasoning on social closure, that concept should not, in itself, propel us towards a cynical theory of professions. And indeed, upon introducing the concept of 'social closure' in *Economy and Society*, Weber specifically pointed out that there are different bases for the closure of communal relationships – purposively rational, as well as value-rational, traditional and affectual (Weber 1978).

The section on economic closure, which Frank Parkin drew upon in *Marxism and Class Theory*, is more narrowly concerned with the instrumental, purposively rational type of closure, with would-be monopolists, whose attempts at social closure are motivated by their interest in curbing competition. It is clear that this is a genuine and important subset of social closure, and deserving of scholarly attention. It is also clear, however, that it is merely a subset and that the existence of socially closed relationships in no way warrants the presumption of their purposively rational basis. By thus retracing our steps, from the sociology of professions via Parkin to Weber, we find that Weber's concept of social closure is decidedly more open-ended than the concept which was filtered through stratification theory before it settled in the sociology of professions.

Now there are at least two reasons for resuscitating Weber's original discussion of the concept and putting it to use in the study of professions. First, it provides us with an approach to the analysis of 'social closure in the marketplace sanctioned by the state', which does away with any presumption of purposive rationality but which does not jettison agency. Second, it invites us to consider other forms of social closure than state-backed sanctions of professional jurisdiction, and to inquire how they affect professions and professionalism. To this end, we shall revisit some elements in Max Weber's discussion of closure which were forfeited in the course of subsequent conceptual refinement.

External closure, internal closure and expansion

In his discussion of economic closure in *Economy and Society*, Weber distinguishes between external closure, involving the closing of opportunities to outsiders, and internal closure, concerning the closing of opportunities to insiders. The latter is absent from Frank Parkin's account, and hence from the sociology of professions. His twin concepts of exclusionary and usurpatory closure turn, after all, on the metaphor of power used in a 'downward' versus 'upward' direction and relate to the "closure of economic and social opportunities to outsiders" (Parkin 1979:44).

Internal closure concerns the "appropriation of the social and economic opportunities that have been monopolized by the group" (Weber 1978:343). In this connection, Weber extends the spatial analogy in a different direction to Parkin. He conjures up the image of a container, but goes on to ask in what ways members' access to opportunities can be regulated on its inside. The container is thus fitted with chambers and compartments, barriers and passageways – accessible to all or to some insiders, on a spectrum ranging from a brief period to for life. By reinstating this concept of internal closure, moreover, we gain access to a framework for theorizing the relations between internal and external economic closure.

Here, however, we are moving in uncharted waters. Parkin's refined and by now entrenched concept of social closure is of little help; it was designed solely with external closure and stratification theory in mind. Weber's own account of internal closure, on the other hand, illustrates the bewildering historical variety with regard to internal closure, but he provides no neat typology and little guidance as to how they can be analyzed. If we wish to reintroduce forfeited analytical possibilities, then, we need to do a bit of theorizing of our own and refine the original concept in a new direction. To this end, and to argue the case that such a reintroduction is worthwhile, we too shall draw on the underlying spatial analogy to generate new ideas in the sociology of professions.

The next section is an effort to do just this. It proceeds by way of example – the proof of the pudding is, after all, in the eating – and explores a special case in the sociology of professions – namely, that of Swedish university teachers under university expansion. Sequences of rapid expansion should be of central interest to the sociology of professions. Students of the history of professions are likely to observe in their profession(s) of choice one or more major quantitative leaps when opportunities, clients or the number of practitioners set off in an exponential pattern. Expansion sequences are privileged sites for investigating social closure in the professions, for – as Weber (1978) noted – there is *prima facie* tension between expansion and preserving the revenue accruing from closed economic relationships. They also provide a laboratory for exploring the interplay between external and internal closure, and thus to try out the conceptual equipment we have just recovered.

Meet the boa constrictor: notes on a university reform

At this point, let us introduce the boa constrictor, as we promised at the outset. One of the more peculiar marvels of nature, made possible by cranial kinesis, is the serpent's ability to swallow items significantly wider than its own diameter. Large devoured prey will be visible as a bulge on the boa's body, and will be digested for weeks or even months. The point here, of course, is not to delve into herpetological detail. What our new acquaintance supplies us with is an alternative image which can be juxtaposed to the customary image of social closure – that of the jealously guarded fortress, replete with riches.

Long exposure to the refined concept of social closure does indeed make it difficult to shake the image of a group of insiders set on shutting out aspiring outsiders from gaining access to monopolized opportunities. The presumption of purposively rational action is especially difficult to shed where membership is likely to be, or is perceived to be, associated with social and economic opportunities. But this is precisely what Max Weber refuted in his argument on the puritan sects in America, and conceptualized more abstractly in *Economy and Society* as social closure. People and organizations can enter resource-laden associations without doing so in order to gain access to those resources, or even without aspiring to join at all.

There is a need, then, to bracket the imagery associated with the entrenched concept of social closure. One way of doing so is to juxtapose it to a metaphor with very different properties. This is where the boa constrictor comes in. It offers an image as vivid as that of the fortress: that of an organization or group that is being swallowed and digested by another organization, association, or institution. In many cases, of course, the customary metaphor will still be adequate. But in the presence of a contender, it can no longer be treated as a given. We are invited to be cognizant of the metaphors that guide our thinking. This is the effect we need to achieve if we are to make room for alternative ways of refining the original concept of social closure. With this aim in mind, we turn to the analysis of a specific case – the case, in fact, that got me thinking about boa constrictors in the first place.

Even the most cursory glance at Swedish university statistics makes it abundantly clear that something drastic happened in 1977. From one year to the next, the number of students enrolled in Swedish higher education increased by 50 per cent. Leaps of this magnitude can only be explained by administrative redefinitions: in this case a university reform that incorporated virtually all post-secondary education in the university system. This included nurses, biomedical scientists and occupational therapists in the health sector, and preschool teachers, leisure-time pedagogues and primary to secondary school teachers in the educational sector – all previously situated in special vocational schools. To this should be added the schools of social work, heretofore separate from the university, and a new type of shorter technical education, initiated as a pilot scheme a couple of years before the reform. Among the inclusions were the small but prestigious academies of art, theatre, music, opera, and dance. The most visible change, however, was the creation of a large number of regional university colleges, a new type of higher education unit typically forged by lumping together local teacher training, preschool teacher training, and the newly invented short technical education.

A very considerable expansion of higher education thus came about, not because more people decided to enter the university system but because what they already studied was transferred there. More and new types of students, new types of higher education units and new types of teachers were now contained within a formally unified system of higher education (Agevall and Olofsson 2013, 2014a, 2014b). It is as drastic an expansion as you will get. Now, when a change of this order can be imposed on a profession by *fiat*, it is tempting to view it merely as a sign of defunct external social closure, a breach of the profession's outer barrier that allows outsiders to penetrate its labor market shelter. But something rather more peculiar and interesting is going on here. The teaching staff of the included schools cannot readily be said to be trespassing on professional turf. Rather, the reformed university system had swallowed, in one gulp, a number of discrete educational units, including their students and their staff. It is reminiscent of a boa constrictor that has just devoured some fair-sized prey, the contours of which appear as a large bulge on its body.

The metaphor, admittedly, is not in good taste. Nor can it be pushed very far without becoming far-fetched or misleading. But it does have the benefit of redirecting our attention to other aspects of social closure. Our eyes are drawn to the bulge on the boa: to the sudden inclusion of substantial organizations and their staff in the university system, and how it alters the future character of the new inclusions, the morphology of the profession and the system it inhabits. Having made this point, we can return to Max Weber's discussion of internal economic closure and the imagery it conjures up. With social and economic opportunities closed to insiders, there must be differential access to them and barriers to seal them off. The case of the Swedish university reform of 1977 suggests that external closure interacts precisely with this type of internal closure in non-trivial ways.

Consider first the importance of the notion that some opportunities would remain closed to the new inclusions after their incorporation in the university system. The regional university colleges were founded under the proviso that they be barred from any permanent research appropriations. They were neither to be fitted with professorial chairs, nor with any other arrangement that would divert research funding from the universities and colleges that were already on the inside. The reassurance that internal closure would mimic external closure bolstered the fear that resources would be diluted, thereby making the reform more palatable to the insiders. In want of an established concept for this dynamic, we can refer to it as the mechanism of promised containment.

There are, I believe, numerous other instances where it would be worthwhile to pay attention to the interplay between external and internal closure. Rather than providing a catalogue of diverse suspects, the remainder of this essay will be devoted to detailing a lengthier and somewhat more tangled sequence. External social closure requires some set of criteria which members must meet. Consider, then, the following criteria, laid down in the first two paragraphs of the Higher Education Act of 1977: within the university shall be pursued education, research, and development; all university education shall rest on a scientific basis. How was this delineation of tasks and requirements to be reconciled with the simultaneous inclusion of large educational programmes, in which the overwhelming majority of teaching staff had no experience of scientific research?

There were two ways to ease that tension. The first – to which we shall return – was to act on the university system itself, in the sense of providing a sufficiently encompassing reinterpretation of what it means for an education to be 'based on science'. The second was to change the newly included vocational programmes to meet the criteria. By being pulled into the university system, the vocational schools and programmes came under systemic pressure to become more academic:

> This entailed elevating the scientific competence of program teachers; aligning the program with existing or to-be disciplines that could accommodate bachelor's, master's, and PhD students; and negotiating a new relationship between the imperatives of science and working life. Hence, their instantaneous de jure incorporation was followed by a gradual de facto adaptation to the imperatives of the new institutional environment.
> (Agevall and Olofsson 2013:15)

Thus, while the devoured vocational programmes retained their identity, they were bound to change character as the teaching staff was gradually pulled into the career patterns, hierarchies and disciplinary orientations of the university system. External social closure, in the form of criteria to regulate entrance, worked to alter the incorporated units.

Within these vocational programmes, however, there are still large numbers of teachers who lack scientific qualifications. In several programmes and higher education units they are still in the majority. This brings us back to the question of how the requirement of science-based education was interpreted in such a way that it was consistent with the new inclusions. The roots of this reinterpretation lay in an earlier expansion sequence. Until the late 1950s professors constituted, roughly speaking, the only tenured teacher category at the universities. Each professor was expected to do research as well as teach. After the Second World War, university expansion made it increasingly untenable to retain this compressed career structure. The senior professor (*Lektor*) was introduced in 1958, and the adjunct teacher (*Adjunkt*) in 1965. Rather than insisting on a multiplication of their own ranks, the professoriate accepted the creation and inflation of subordinate, non-professor positions that could take care of undergraduates and trivial tasks, while retaining a monopoly on the most qualified tasks. The cream floated to the top of the new differentiated corps structure.

This is yet another example of how internal closure, the emerging pattern of differentiated access to opportunities on the inside, played an important role for expansion. But it also lowered the entrance requirements to the university and to the profession of university teachers. In contrast to the old professorial chairs, it sufficed to have a PhD to become a tenured associate professor. And as an even starker contrast, 'adjunct teacher' was a catch-all category comprising tenured university teachers who lacked a PhD. This was tantamount to recognizing that teachers need not do, or have done, research themselves. An emerging pattern of internal closure had thereby altered the conditions for external closure.

A new set of slots had thus become available: the main categories of the rapidly transforming university – the associate professor and the adjunct – provided a mould into which new additions could be poured. In this way, the earlier expansion sequence set the stage for the 1977 university reform. Upon entering the university system, the teaching staff of the previously external vocational schools became adjunct teachers. The difference between the old and new incumbents of the university system could then be presented as a matter of degree rather than kind, since adjunct teachers were already allowed as *bona fide* insiders. But whereas the adjunct teachers at the older universities were comparatively few, and inserted in research-intensive environments, the teaching staff of the new inclusions were either predominantly or exclusively adjuncts.

This called for a new reinterpretation of the relation between teaching and research. The phrase 'science-based teaching' was coined, and an avalanche of pamphlets, work groups and instruction manuals provided it with a catechism. Once again, a renegotiation of external closure took place in the wake of changing patterns of internal closure. There is one final twist to this sequence. The massive scale of the 1977 inclusions dramatically inflated the categories of adjunct teachers and associate professor within the university system. They were now in the majority. The morphology of the teacher corps was altered; both the university system and the profession of university teachers received a new structure.

Conclusion

These brief examples will hopefully persuade the reader that there is something to be gained from excavating and reinstating the concept of internal closure, and from exploring and theorizing the interplay between external and internal closure in the professions. There may even be some who are curious to try out the proposed fledgling concepts and figures of thought, in order to see how far they will carry. But even those who remain sceptical of the analytical optic of the illustration have reason to engage with the concept of social closure in the same spirit as we have done here: to look past the received concept, to inquire into its uses prior to latter-day conceptual refinements, and – not least important – to do some metaphorical work of one's own, including in relation to the boa constrictor.

References

Agevall, O. and Olofsson, G. (2013) The emergence of the professional field of higher education in Sweden, *Professions and Professionalism* 3(2): 1–22.

Agevall, O. and Olofsson, G. (2014a) Tensions between academic and vocational demands. In: J. Smeby and M. Sutphen (eds) *From Vocational to Professional Education: Educating for Social Welfare*. London: Routledge.

Agevall, O. and Olofsson, G. (2014b) Social closure and professional expansion. Paper presented at the NORDPRO Conference on the Nordic Welfare Models, Oslo.

Amossy, R. (1991) *Les Idées Reçues: Sémiologie du Stéréotype*. Paris: Nathan.

Amossy, R. and Herschberg Pierrot, A. (1997) *Stéréotypes et Clichés: Langue, Discours, Société*. Paris: Nathan.

Amossy, R. and Rosen, E. (1982) *Les Discours du Cliché*. Paris: CDU et SEDES réunis.

Dimaggio, P. and Useem, M. (1978a) Cultural property and public policy: Emerging tensions in government support for the arts, *Social Research* 45(2): 356–89.

Dimaggio, P. and Useem, M. (1978b) Social class and arts consumption: The origins and consequences of class differences in exposure to the arts in America, *Theory and Society* 5(2): 141–61.

Mulkay, M. (1969) Some aspects of cultural growth in the natural sciences, *Social Research* 36(1): 22–52.

Murphy, R. (1986) Weberian closure theory: A contribution to the ongoing assessment, *British Journal of Sociology* 37(1): 21–24.

Murphy, R. (1988) *Social Closure: The Theory of Monopolization and Exclusion*. Oxford: Clarendon Press.

Neuwirth, G. (1969) A Weberian outline of a theory of community: Its application to the 'dark ghetto', *British Journal of Sociology* 20(2): 148–63.

Parkin, F. (1971) *Class Inequality and Political Order: Social Stratification in Capitalist and Communist Societies*. New York: Praeger.

Parkin, F. (ed) (1974) *The Social Analysis of Class Structure*. London: Tavistock.

Parkin, F. (1979) *Marxism and Class Theory: A Bourgeois Critique*. New York: Columbia University Press.

Saks, M. (2012) Defining a profession: The role of knowledge and expertise, *Professions and Professionalism* 2(1): 1–10.

Sommer Harrits, G. (2014) Professional closure beyond state authorization, *Professions and Professionalism* 4(1): 1–17.

Swedberg, R. (2014) *The Art of Social Theory*. Princeton: Princeton University Press.

Swedberg, R. and Agevall, O. (2016) *The Max Weber Dictionary: Key Words and Central Concepts*, 2nd edition. Stanford: Stanford University Press.

Weber, M. (1970) *From Max Weber: Essays in Sociology*. London: Routledge.

Weber, M. (1978) *Economy and Society: An Outline of Interpretive Sociology*. Berkeley: University of California Press.

6 Regulating the English health professions

Zoos, circuses or safari parks?

Mike Saks

Introduction: the growing challenge of professions

This chapter considers the regulation of professions by innovative use of animal metaphors based on zoos, circuses and safari parks, viewed primarily through the lens of a neo-Weberian perspective. This device – drawing on the strong tradition of employing metaphors in the sociology of organizations – reflects the historical shift from the initially benign thinking by Anglo-American writers on professions about such occupations to more critical notions of professional groups. In this respect, the growing challenge that is felt to be posed by professions has more recently flagged to government and other bodies that these groups require more than just state-sanctioned self-regulation if they are to be kept in check for the benefit of clients and/or the wider public. In this sense, it is argued that the animal metaphors developed mainly from a neo-Weberian framework help the inquirer to understand more clearly the changes in the regulatory framework for professions in the modern world. The application of these metaphors is exemplified by the study outlined in the latter part of this chapter of recent developments in the regulation of healthcare in England. As indicated in the conclusion to this piece, metaphors can be used as an aid to policymaking and to stimulate further theorizing and research in the ever more important field of professional regulation – not least in relation to its consequences for organizations.

The concept of professionalism was once much revered in the Anglo-American sociology of professions. The earlier dominant trait and functionalist schools of thought put professional groups – from physicians to teachers – on a pedestal on both sides of the Atlantic; contributors from these schools argued that professions possess positive, unique characteristics differentiating them from other occupations and generally saw them as beneficial harbingers of progress, in a manner reflecting their own ideologies. Thus, trait writers, who focused on drawing up lists of such perceived attributes of a profession, highlighted such features as their high levels of skills and altruism, and often saw them as paragons of impartiality and objectivity (Millerson 1964). The more theoretical functionalist approach, meanwhile, sought to explain the comparatively strong social and economic position of professions in terms of their implicit agreement to use their talents to engage in the non-exploitative control of esoteric knowledge of great importance to society (Barber 1963; Goode 1960). Such perspectives mirrored popular deferential views of the professions before the emergence of the counter culture in the late 1960s and early 1970s – in which their typically self-policed codes of ethics figured large as protecting the interests of clients and the wider public (Saks 1995).

However, from the 1960s onwards, professionalism was increasingly challenged from a theoretical viewpoint, linked to a more critical social climate with rising rates of public scepticism. Symbolic interactionists were amongst the first to query the earlier self-fulfilling definitions of professions and the consequent reflexive legitimation of professional privileges. They emphasized the parallels rather than distinctions between the work practices of commonly accepted professions and even more lowly and deviant occupations such as janitors and prostitutes (Becker 1962; Hughes 1963). Marxist writers located professions within the class structure of capitalism – typically viewing them as agents of the capitalist class, defending its interests against those of the wider population (Krause 1996; Poulantzas 1975). Thus, lawyers were perceived as sustaining capitalist wage-labour relations (Fine et al. 1979) and welfare professions such as counsellors, educational psychologists and social workers were transformed into upholders of the capitalist social order, to which the well-being of their disadvantaged clients was sacrificed (Esland 1980). Foucauldians, meanwhile, challenged the notion of rational, emancipatory scientific progress inspired by ideologies of professionalism. In so doing, they exposed the disciplinary nature of prisons and psychiatric institutions (Foucault 1979; 1989) – as well as such previously positively regarded areas related to public health like obstetrics (Arney 1982) and dentistry (Nettleton 1992).

In highlighting the disjuncture rather than the unity between professional ideologies and practice, the dominant theoretical critique of the professions that emerged in the wake of the counter culture from the mid-1960s onwards was most strongly based on the neo-Weberian perspective. This was a very powerful strand in a period when traditional deferential approaches to professional authority were debunked, not least for disempowering clients – amplifying the challenge to the classic basis of professionalism in healthcare and other areas (Saks 2000). From a neo-Weberian perspective, professions are seen simply as occupational collectivities that form legally underwritten boundaries against outsiders which serve to protect and enhance their privileges in the marketplace (Freidson 2001; Parkin 1979). This allowed professions to be analyzed without the deferential intellectual baggage embedded in the very definitions of a profession in the earlier trait and functionalist approaches – enabling the involvement of professional interests to be more fully exposed (Saks 1983). In this respect, the self-interested and parochial commitment of professions has been adversely commented on in many areas by neo-Weberian writers, from planning (Cherry 1982) to law (Deflem 2008) – where a key driver of decision making is seen to be the maintenance of, or increase in, the income, status and power of the profession, underwritten by the state.

Within the neo-Weberian perspective, the public interest ideologies of the professions have consequently increasingly been viewed as mechanisms to facilitate their interest-based ascendancy in the politics of work, rather than indicators of the nature of their substantive activity (Saks 2010), as social scientific analysis has focused more on the discourse of professionalism (Evetts 2006). In this light, professions themselves look narrowly focused – particularly when their interest-based actions not only run counter to the public good but also form part of acrimonious boundary disputes with other professional groups (Malin 2000). This impression is further accentuated by neo-Weberian contributors who have highlighted other types of internal divisions within professions centred on group interests, not least in relation to ethnicity and other aspects of the social exclusion agenda (Saks and Kuhlmann 2006). Gender-based relationships of subordination have figured heavily in this equation (Witz 1992); these are well illustrated in professional areas such as medicine and engineering, where males tend to predominate in the most prestigious and well-rewarded posts (Phipps 2008; Riska 2001).

To be sure, some of these critiques are totalistic, do not always align with empirical evidence and, in revealing the limits of professionalism, also succeed in masking the benefits of professionalism captured by earlier trait and functionalist contributors (Saks 1998). However, even the most cynical neo-Weberian writers see professional groups as on occasion subordinating their own interests to the public good, and are aware of situations where the pursuit of professional self-interest coalesces with advancing the interests of clients and/or the wider collective interest – as in the case of professional self-protection against competitors offering services that are dangerous to the public (Saks 1992). Nonetheless, such critiques underline why such parties as governments and corporations in Britain and the USA over the past few decades have striven to manage the professions much more proactively than in the past. This trend has been ever more pronounced in a recessionary climate where there is economic resource constraint alongside the potential for enhancement through technological and other developments related to the professions. Managerialism itself in its many forms is therefore a further challenge to professionalism as cost-effective prioritization, with targets and audit trails, has increasingly become the order of the day (Svensson and Evetts 2010). Although its rationale has sometimes been questioned – not least in critiques of the New Public Management (Dent et al. 2004) – the impact of managerialism from without on professional areas in the contemporary context is clear, not least through a range of forms of governance in the public and private sector.

For the professions, these types of governance are particularly linked to specific configurations of state–profession and profession–citizen relationships in the Anglo-American context (Kuhlmann and Saks 2008). These two areas are interconnected, for actions by the state in relation to the professions have been ever more heavily driven by the desire to enhance the position of its citizens. As such, it can be said that the newly developed culture of consumerism represents a further challenge to the professions in societies that are increasingly risk aware and in which citizens have become a politically protected species (Featherstone 2007). Taking the animal analogy further, this paper analyzes the management of professions from a neo-Weberian perspective using metaphors. Metaphors have already been widely applied within a neo-Weberian account of professions – not least in seeing such bodies as hierarchies and landscapes, such as in relation to 'turf wars' between professions (Liljegren 2012). The analysis here proceeds in an even more novel fashion by first conceiving of professionalism as a zoo containing a range of animals, some of which may be wild and challenging, before moving on to consider professionalism as a circus and then as a safari park.

Animal metaphors have been used in the literature in ways deemed to be offensive (Haslam, Loughnan and Sun 2011), but that is not the intention here. There was also once a view in organizational theory that metaphors were inexact and misleading rhetorical devices, but they have now been increasingly used in this area – as, for example, through the notion of organizations as machines (Cornelissen 2005). The main advantage of metaphors in this context is that they bring new perspectives on the world – aiding theory construction by providing academics with a vocabulary to express, map, and understand phenomena; displaying a plurality and openness of meaning with advantages over more fixed literal language; and having sensory and imaginative qualities that encourage theorists and researchers to see things in a different light. As such, they can help researchers to harness their potential for initiating inquiry and inspire them to explore otherwise obscure links out of their comfort zone. In this sense, there are considered to be two governing rules to help them in their search for novel and creative categorizations and deeper insights through the use of metaphors (Cornelissen, Kafouros and Lock 2005). The first is that it is better to use relational metaphors rather than attributive metaphors, as these highlight interconnected relations between previously unrelated concepts. The second is that the metaphors used should bring together concepts from semantic domains that appear distant from one another and shock academics into seeing a subject in a completely new way. It is held here that conceiving of the regulation of professionalism as a zoo, circus and safari park within a neo-Weberian approach fulfils both of these rules.

Conceptualizing professionalism as a zoo

In the zoo, where living animals are displayed, the professions are taken to represent different types of animal. Traditional modern zoos first developed in the West, initially from private ownership, from the late eighteenth and early nineteenth century onwards (Hardouin-Fugier and Baratay 2004). In most of these, the major attraction is situated in a mainstream compound – generally occupied by dangerous predators like lions and tigers, represented amongst the professions by 'fat cat' doctors and lawyers. A further compound may contain smaller animals with guile, including the wolf and the hyena, which do not carry quite this scale of threat, but nonetheless need to be watched very carefully – particularly when hunting in packs – in a manner akin to accountants and financial auditors. In yet another area, exotic animals like the peacock and the bird of paradise may parade their fine plumage, but lack real bite – much as the architects, who display their resplendent portfolios, while being one of the least financially well rewarded professional groups. In addition, there is typically a more marginalized 'pets corner' in zoos where the guinea pigs, rabbits and other understated forms of domesticated wildlife that are sufficiently docile to touch and feed reside. In the case of professions, these may be represented by dieticians and radiographers, who are relatively subdued, subordinated groups posing a lesser threat to either the public or other professions.

This model of a zoo, however, is not static. The various sections of even a traditional zoo can be, and historically have been, divided into many different spatially and semantically mapped categories based on increasingly sophisticated designs (Croke 1997). Some zoos have prominently located reptile and insect houses, whilst others have aviaries and aquariums as their centrepiece. It can be left to the reader's imagination to discern the types of professions most appropriately represented in such areas – including those professional groups that may be best seen symbolically as crocodiles, venomous spiders, vultures and sharks, or as tortoises, owls and butterflies. In all this, it should be noted that only a selection of animals is contained in any particular zoo, a number of which may be specialized in nature. The selection itself varies over time and is made according to fashion and purpose in both the private and the public sectors in which they operate – in much the same way as the formal accreditation of clusters of occupational groups deemed worthy of state-sanctioned, professional standing (Hardouin-Fugier and Baratay 2004). As such, there are strong parallels with traditional zoos, especially since many countries now have legislation that requires zoos and the specific animals they contain to be formally licensed in a similar manner to the licensure on which professionalism is based (Cooper 2003). Zoos then can be seen to differentiate in the selection process between various types of animals in a parallel way to state regulation differentiating between professions and other occupations in terms of entry and governance.

New species may be added to the collection at any point – as witnessed by the excitement generated a few decades ago by the introduction of the giant panda from China into Western zoos (Norton et al. 1996). Such innovatory moves in the professional sphere are well exemplified by relatively newly professionalized occupations such as chiropractors and osteopaths, who have been at the vanguard of the professionalization of complementary and alternative therapies in the Anglo-American context (Saks 2003b). In sub-sections of this diverse field, practitioners have needed to be herded together to be successful in the professionalization process as a result of the strong prevailing anti-bureaucratic and individualistic ethos which has militated against the development of a common identity. Equally, common species of animal, like the leopard and lynx in the cat family, have some-times been split up in the zoo according to the extant system of categoriza-tion. In an equivalent manner in the professional zoo, criminal lawyers representing individuals would not necessarily at present be placed in the same category as corporate lawyers acting on behalf of large firms given the large differentiation in their rewards (Deflem 2008) – any more than psychiatrists would be placed with top-notch heart surgeons in terms of income, status and power in the pecking order of orthodox medicine (Klein 2010).

Both the conventional and professional zoo is subject to the pressures of managerialism and consumerism. In light of consumer concern about ani-mal rights and the rising public interest in conservation, the more tradi-tional zoo with its tightly regimented space has in late modern times tended to be recast in more open environments by public and private sector man-agers (Young 2003). The professional zoo, however, has moved in a slightly different direction from the classic zoo as a result of managerialism and consumerism as governments and corporations, as well as consumers, have pushed for greater regulation and control of autonomous professions in the public and corporate interest (Kuhlmann 2004). The more liberal past in a comparatively open *laissez-faire* occupational marketplace in much of the eighteenth and nineteenth centuries, followed by an era with greater emphasis on free, self-regulating professions within their own boundaries – in which the leading professions had "virtually complete control over the terms, conditions, and content of their work" (Freidson 2001:184) – has increasingly been left behind. Groups of animals in the professional zoo are therefore to some degree metaphorically penned in behind bars. This has its roots in the imperialistic desire of mid to late Victorians to collect, scientifically categorize and control species and sub-species in the drive for conquest. As such, the creation of zoos – as indeed the professions – may be viewed as embodied in the notion of the panopticon employed by Fou-cault (1979), where human and non-human animals are placed under sur-veillance as part of governmentality in modern societies committed to observing and normalizing behaviour. This has some resonance with the control Weber (1968) anticipated would occur as a result of the rationaliza-tion of modern society through the 'iron cage' of bureaucracy. However, a major distinction from a conventional zoo is that the professional inmates, unlike non-human animals, have in part been instrumental in choosing to be in the zoo and constructing their own form of enclosure in liaison with the state – in particular through exclusionary social closure, the classic neo-Weberian device by which such groups gain a legally enshrined, privileged standing (Saks 2010).

Traditional zoos have been associated not only with entertainment for an audience of visitors but also with public education, research and science (Hardouin-Fugier and Baratay 2004) – providing an obvious link to the knowledge claims and credentialism of contemporary professions (Parkin 1979). They are now increasingly used through in-breeding for the conservation of species that might otherwise become extinct, notwithstanding the debate about how far such animals are bred in zoos simply for public display (Norton et al. 1996). This has parallels with the incestuous reproduction of professional groups, with links between different generations of family members based on educational and social capital, in the ongoing regeneration of the middle class (Freidson 1986). In the professional zoo, moreover, arcane professional practices in classic professions like law and medicine have been preserved within the market shelter of professionalism that are of monopolistic advantage to insiders but little benefit to outsiders – such as excessive restrictions on occupational entry despite high demand for services and an unduly negative approach to innovation (Friedman 1962). In this regard, the limited sized enclosures in traditional zoos are perversely not always helpful to the well-being of non-human animals (Young 2003), but do advantage professional animals in the human zoo in a competitive marketplace. Specialized zoo keepers in this system also have some resemblance to professional bodies, insofar as they care for the particular human animals in their charge – and facilitate the benefits that specific professional groups gain from exclusionary social closure. Such often self-interested professional practices resulting from restricting entry by outsiders are those against which the state has increasingly sought to protect the public and a range of more specific stakeholders through the regulation of professions in recent times, as trust in the traditional mechanisms of professional self-regulation has diminished in government and other circles, if not always amongst members of the public themselves (Svensson 1999).

Conceptualizing professionalism as a circus or a safari park

Conceptualizing professionalism as a zoo has weaknesses, as well as strengths. The issues raised by conceiving of professionalism as a zoo are accentuated as governments in Britain and the USA have striven to achieve an appropriate balance between the use of shackles for the professional animals and allowing them a modicum of autonomy to optimize benefits for, and minimize harm to, both clients and the wider public. Staying with the animal metaphor, this raises the question of whether professionalism might be better conceived of as a circus, rather than as a zoo. This question is prompted by the fact that a circus also contains animals that are subject to various forms of control. A modern circus – which, like a zoo, has late eighteenth-century origins – is typically made up of a company of performers who perform choreographed acts set to music in a circular arena with tiered seating in a large tent (Johnson 1990). For the non-human animals involved, acts range from elephants standing on their hind legs to tigers jumping through rings of fire – extraordinary feats which might be the envy of those trying to encourage interest-oriented professional groups to learn new tricks.

The advantages of conceptualizing professionalism in these terms is that in a traditional circus there is typically a ringmaster with a whip, who keeps the show moving, with animals trained and required to perform to a standard (Daniel 2008). In this sense, the ringmaster plays a key part as a decision maker defining which animals are to be included in, or excluded from, the Big Top – paralleling the state as regards the division between professions and occupations. The role of key players in shaping circus performance, such as the lion tamer, goes beyond that of a zoo keeper who is simply responsible for the care of animals in his/her jurisdiction – and perhaps better reflects the control aspects of professional bodies. Arrangements for controlling performance in a circus therefore may have greater parallels with the desire by government and other stakeholders such as corporations and service users to ensure that professionals operate in a fit-for-purpose manner through education, training and other means. This is not, of course, to say that those endeavouring to use their controlling power always have the appropriate pitch or that animals in zoos and professions do not retaliate or fight back in face of attempts to control their behaviour. Sometimes overly exuberant trainers of non-human animals are mauled to death by their charges in the circus, while professional resistance is illustrated by the adversarial response of lawyers to aspects of the 2007 Legal Services Act that attempted to reconcile consumerism and professionalism in England and Wales (Boon 2010). The concept of a circus may also be favoured in analyzing the professions in countries such as Britain and the USA because historically it has more often involved human beings as performers, from clowns to acrobats (Davis 2002). This creates a greater resonance with the management of professional groups – even if such performers sometimes in the past included 'freaks' and 'oddities' and those conducting daredevil stunts of fire eating and knife throwing (Daniel 2008), who even the most extreme cynics would not associate with the contemporary template of professionalism.

Moreover, the circus has an audience of interested citizens with a stake in ensuring that participants are suitably regulated for their own safety – paralleling the zoo and just like professions themselves. Although animal rights groups have challenged circuses as vehemently for the cruelty involved in training animals as exhibiting captive animals in zoos (Hanson 2002), the integrity of using the circus as a metaphor for professions is accentuated by the recent move towards completely human circuses. These are best illustrated by Cirque du Soleil, a high quality, travelling circus that combines traditional arts and street theatre using performers such as stilt walkers and jugglers, with no non-human animal acts (Babinski 2004). The high standards of this modern Canadian-owned circus, which is now the largest theatrical producer worldwide, reminds us that the wider society, corporations and consumers may do best to continue to keep professional animals in humane, enriched environments, allowing them some autonomy (Young 2003). However, to mitigate risks arising from their unconstrained interests, society may also profit by exerting closer managerial control over them to minimize the limits to, and maximize the advantages of, professionalism. In light of the recent challenges to professions, the arrangements for regulating professionalism in the Anglo-American context do not yet make it 'the greatest show on Earth'.

As the trapeze artist and tightrope walker are aware, though, a safety net is a fundamental requirement in the circus – to protect the performers, as well as the sensitivities of the engaged public as the audience, in case of accidents. The changing nature and form of that safety net and its implications for public policy have captivated neo-Weberian and other recent writers on the professions (see, for instance, Allsop and Saks 2002). However, the final twist in the tale is that the circus metaphor itself has run into difficulty with the recent shift in government policy which has promoted more devolved and de-regulated actions in many spheres in response to the current economic crisis (see, for example, Drolet 2011; Lee and Beech 2011). This poses the question of whether the best current metaphor for understanding the regulation of self-interested professions is the safari park, rather than a zoo or a circus – as now increasingly *laissez-faire* policies provide greater opportunities to promote collaboration between groups of professionals than are apparent in a traditional zoo or circus. This is especially so given the growing political emphasis on fostering effective and efficient joined-up working in public and private corporations to achieve key outcomes in difficult economic times (see, for example, Kuhlmann and Saks 2008). This policy shift – which has paradoxically not yet led to the de-regulation of professions themselves despite the emphasis given to free market ideology – takes us more towards safari parks at a time when they are becoming more popular for containing and displaying non-human animals, while zoos and circuses are becoming either more open or extinct (Young 2003).

The currency of the safari park metaphor is increased by the fact that such arrangements have typically been based on segregation, with the onus on putting more social animals together to intermingle and roam free – in order to replicate their natural habitat within a broader, more loosely policed estate (Young 2003). This has parallels in the way in which professional jurisdictions have been shaped in the interactions between different occupational groups in the system of professions in controlled environments – with socially constructed boundaries, ranging from the rigid and robust to flexible and permeable (Abbott 1988). To add to the value of this metaphor, safari parks have public audiences, who typically are in vehicles rather than being ambulant or seated as in zoos or circuses respectively. In a similar fashion to professional groups too, the protection of the clientele in an arguably more exposed environment also remains paramount given the potential hazards posed by the wild animals involved. In this sense, Britain and the USA seem to have come full circle from the Victorian notion of the African 'big game' safari (in which hunters typically picked off the weaker of the species to bring back trophies from jungles) to that of predators and prey otherwise existing in a natural symbiotic balance. This milieu mirrored the open and competitive marketplace experienced by occupational groups before professionalism based on exclusionary closure emerged in the mid to late nineteenth century in the Anglo-American setting (Brint 1996; Perkin 1989). Today the overseas safari has primarily become a tourist event (Pickford and Pickford 2011), complementing the controlled in-house safari park experience that parallels the more carefully managed environment of professional regulatory regimes.

We shall now turn to illustrate the application of the relational animal metaphors employed here from a very different domain within a neo-Weberian perspective by analyzing their applicability to the case of the regulation of the English healthcare professions, in the organizational environment of the National Health Service. In this context, Table 6.1 sets out the nature of the landscape in terms of the types of animal metaphors, the main defining regulatory feature of these and the associated policies for healthcare professions in England.

Table 6.1 Animal metaphors and government policies for healthcare professions in England

Animal Metaphor	Main Defining Regulatory Feature	Associated Government Policies for Healthcare Professions in England
Zoo	Segregated cages of animals with keepers characterized by exclusionary closure	Conservatives (1979–97): Professional self-regulation with restriction on medical powers
Circus	Ringmaster with centralized control of the animals in terms of performance	Labour (1997–2010): Modernization of state regulation of health and care professions to protect public
Safari Park	Devolution and de-regulation – with greater collaboration between the animals	Coalition (2010–15): The Big Society and interprofessional collaboration in health and social care

Applying animal metaphors to the regulation of healthcare professions in England

This case study focuses on recent attempts by the Conservative, Labour and Coalition governments in England to reform the professional regulation of healthcare, in light of growing evidence of the frailties of the existing system of professional self-regulation, which threatened to prejudice the health of the wider public. It has the virtue of highlighting some of the key issues involved in managing professions, as well as accentuating their changing nature and form, in terms of the metaphors of zoos, circuses and safari parks. In this respect, there was disquiet in government circles over the environment from the late 1970s and early 1980s, which was then based heavily on the autonomous self-regulation of healthcare professions. The environment at this time seemed most akin to a zoo in which the professions concerned had played a large part in constructing their own caged enclaves. Government concern was centred on the drive to improve quality and standards in the face of, amongst other things, advances in medical knowledge, changes in the patterns of illness and growing user demand (Allsop and Saks 2008). Most immediately, it was driven by the increasing publicity given to practitioners who behaved like 'rogue elephants' and caused harm to patients, while not being quickly picked up by professional self-regulatory processes. This was illustrated in medicine by the doctors involved in generating unacceptably high mortality rates for heart surgery on children at Bristol Royal Infirmary and in removing deceased children's organs without consent at Alder Hey Hospital in Liverpool (Allsop and Saks 2002). Such concern was also raised about other species of health professions, including in nursing with Beverly Allitt, who killed a number of small children in her area of practice (Davies 1993). It was underlined by the case of Dr Harold Shipman, the mass serial killing general practitioner who murdered over 200 patients without discovery over several decades (Allsop and Saks 2002). As a result, reviews recently took place of a wide range of professional groups penned in the healthcare enclosure. What happened subsequently in terms of the regulatory response of the government, though, may for various reasons be most suitably depicted in terms of the metaphors of first a circus and then a safari park – as opposed to a zoo, which seems to fit most appropriately the earlier phase of the regulation of healthcare professions.

Professions as a zoo

Starting with this earlier phase, from the mid-nineteenth to the mid-twentieth century, groups of human animals enjoyed considerable professional self-regulatory freedom in their compounds – depending on their place in the pecking order. As such, the variegated professionalizing environment was probably best depicted as a zoo up to the second half of the twentieth century. The zoo metaphor was particularly applicable to the 'top dog' role of medicine in this period, as doctors have been the dominant players in asserting their interests since their *de facto* monopoly was established with the 1858 Medical Registration Act that created the exclusionary social closure leading to the collective social mobility of medical practitioners in terms of income, status and power (Parry and Parry 1976). This elevated the medical professions from a position in which there was a relatively open field where the various groups involved in healthcare – from herbalists and homoeopaths to apothecaries, surgeons and physicians – competed with each other in a largely unregulated habitat (Saks 1992). The pre-eminent, interest-based, position of doctors in the health professional zoo was reinforced by the 1911 National Insurance Act and the 1946 National Health Service Act, which gave them a monopoly over the delivery of state-funded healthcare services, facilitated by the close relationship between the state and the profession centred on the medical–Ministry alliance (Saks 2003a).

The boundaries of the health professional zoo also expanded during this period, with the growth of the range of limited and subordinated professions with their own regulatory enclosures. These new professions did not effectively challenge the position of medicine. The allied groups of professions such as dentists, opticians and pharmacists characterized by 'limitation' were restricted to a specific part of the body or therapeutic method. By the same token, health professionals like nurses, midwives, occupational therapists and physiotherapists, marked by 'subordination', took on delegated tasks from doctors (Turner 1995). This paralleled the increasing expansion and differentiation of zoos in the last half of the nineteenth and first half of the twentieth century, as more and more species became available for display in the market (Hardouin-Fugier and Baratay 2004). It also paralleled the dramatic expansion of the professional division of labour over this period, whereby it seemed that all occupational groups were becoming professionalized (Wilensky 1964). Just as in the professional zoo more broadly, though, the profusion of healthcare professions underlined the standing of the dominant profession – in this case medicine – which continued to hold sway over other health professions.

Nonetheless, in the wake of the counter culture in England in the 1960s and 1970s, the incoming Conservative government from 1979 onwards went on the offensive in terms of increasing control of professions both generally and in the specific realm of healthcare, as their monopolistic position was seen to hinder market forces (Alaszewski 1995). What followed were largely unsuccessful attempts to bring to heel the creatures in the health professional zoo, especially those seen to be dangerous predators like medicine, through a variety of measures. The attempt to create an 'internal market' based on the split between purchasers and providers did not fundamentally alter the balance of power as far as the health professions were concerned, even if it did mean that opticians were stripped of some powers, such as the ability to exclusively sell spectacles. The reforms in the early 1980s instigated by businessman Sir Roy Griffiths of Sainsbury's, which were intended to extend the principles of the private sector into the National Health Service, placed health professions under the managerial control of general managers. However, these were also subverted in this case by the fact that doctors themselves largely became such managers (Saks 2003a). Meanwhile, the Patients' Charter that was introduced to advance consumer rights at the beginning of the 1990s was too formalistic and limited to make a real impact in light of the distinctly disempowering ethos of biomedicine, based on objective scientific indicators that did not engage the experience of the patient (Saks 2002). As such, the zoo metaphor – in which professions were prime movers in constructing their mainly self-regulating cages in face of citizen and government oversight – continued to reign supreme.

Professions as a circus

This set the scene for the Labour government, which – in its period of office from 1997 to 2010 – took a stronger line in modernizing the health service, in view of rising concerns about the powers of self-interested professional groups in healthcare and their impact on public safety (Allsop and Saks 2002). This weakened the applicability of the zoo metaphor with its emphasis in neo-Weberian terms on self-regulation. Following several commissioned reviews, there was major reform of the regulation of health professions, including in medicine, with various improvements related to revalidation procedures, registration and quality assurance protocols for medical education; fitness-to-practise procedures; lay representation on the General Medical Council; the replacement of the United Kingdom Council for Nursing, Midwifery and Health Visiting and the English Nursing Board for Nursing, Midwifery and Health Visiting by the more accountable Nursing and Midwifery Council; and the development of the less explicitly subordinated Health Professions Council in place of the Council for the Professions Supplementary to Medicine (Saks 2003a). These reforms were paralleled in social care by the formation of the General Social Care Council with balanced lay, professional and employer representation (Davies 1999). In addition, the Council for the Regulation of Healthcare Professionals – which later became the Council for Healthcare Regulatory Excellence under the Labour government – was formed to promote the interests of the public as an oversight body (Allsop and Saks 2002).

These reforms centrally involving an engaged public audience had a greater overt impact than those of the Conservative government that preceded it – thus encouraging the metaphor of professionalism as a circus rather than a zoo with the enhanced role of the state as an effective ringmaster, quelling at least some of the resistance of dominant animals in the circus tent. All the reforms were influenced too by the desire to raise standards in the health professions, in much the same way as there has been recent pressure to increase the standards in zoos and circuses (Young 2003). However, there was still scope for further regulatory reform led by the state as circus ringmaster. This was highlighted by the Shipman Inquiry, the fifth report of which focused on the systems for monitoring the work of doctors (Shipman Inquiry 2004). The previous Shipman Inquiry reports from 2002 onwards on death disguised, the police investigation, death certification and controlled drugs had suggested that the delays in detecting the Shipman case were not only related to flaws in the regulatory mechanism of the medical profession, but also factors such as the monitoring role of Primary Care Trusts. Nonetheless, a number of the recommendations made in the fifth report of the Inquiry – such as for independent adjudicators in investigations and greater clarity over the purpose of general practitioner appraisal – pointed to the need to further reform the General Medical Council to enhance the protection of user interests. Further actions to improve conditions in the health professional circus were therefore explored by the government-commissioned Donaldson and Foster reviews (Saks and Allsop 2007).

The main aim of the Donaldson review was to strengthen procedures for assuring the safety of patients in situations where a doctor's performance or conduct posed a risk to patient safety or the effective functioning of services; to ensure the operation of an effective system of revalidation; and to positively modify the role, structure and functions of the General Medical Council (Department of Health 2006a). The parallel Foster review aimed to reinforce the procedures for ensuring that the performance or conduct of non-medical healthcare professionals and other health service staff did not pose a threat to patient safety or the effective functioning of services; to ensure the operation of effective systems of continuing professional development and appraisal for non-medical healthcare personnel and make progress towards revalidation where appropriate; and to ensure the effective regulation of healthcare staff working in new roles within the healthcare sector and of other staff in regular contact with patients (Department of Health 2006b). These reviews therefore recommended a range of measures upholding safety parameters – to which zoos and circuses also had to adhere in relation to both non-human animals and their clients (Johnson 1990) – from defining a good doctor to ensuring greater regulatory coordination and consistency between medical and other forms of healthcare (Saks and Allsop 2007).

A White Paper entitled *Trust Assurance and Safety – The Regulation of Health Professionals in the 21st Century* emerged thereafter in government's role as ringmaster with a number of key proposed reforms, including assuring the independence of regulatory bodies; ensuring continuous fitness to practise; clarifying the role of regulatory bodies in education; providing more information about health professionals; reviewing the regulation of new roles and emerging professions; regulating certain unregulated professions through existing statutory regulatory bodies; and harmonizing regulatory practice and legislative provision (Department of Health 2007). These presaged a more transparent system of regulation, paralleling the behind-the-scenes insight for consumers increasingly being introduced into zoos and circuses to encourage understanding of animal habitats (Hanson 2002). Another aspect of the White Paper was its concern with implementation (Department of Health 2007). In this regard, for example, a working group was set up to consider the practicalities of regulating Traditional Chinese Medicine, herbalism and acupuncture – given the long-standing desire to develop a system of statutory rather than voluntary regulation for forms of complementary and alternative medicine posing the greatest potential threat to public health (Saks 2005). Later the government brought out an expert report setting out the principles and next steps for implementing the proposed new revalidation system (Department of Health 2008). This case study shows the determination of the government to ensure that even the most powerful and self-interested of the animals are sensitively secured in their compounds as part of the changing framework of regulation of the health professional circus.

Professions as a safari park

The foregoing case study of healthcare professions highlights the different ways in which the Conservative and Labour governments up to 2010 sought to tighten control of professions for public benefit – ultimately strengthening the security of the individual enclosures in the circus so that the animals did not escape. The notion of more broadly flung professional groups running wild in the current Anglo-American context in a relatively uncontrolled manner and causing damage to the public, clients or indeed corporate interests was not appealing, given the societal benefits of appropriately regulated professional groups (Freidson 2001). However, at this point the safari park metaphor came more into focus with the rise to power of the Liberal Democrat and Conservative Coalition government from 2010 onwards with a more devolved and de-regulatory ideology. As part of this, it is now looking to create more de-regulation in relation to professions and other services under the rubric of the Big Society (Ishkanian and Szreter 2012), which does not sit so easily with the metaphorical concept of a tightly controlled a Big Top with the ringmaster at the centre. This philosophy is set out in the present government's better regulation agenda, in which self-regulation is encouraged as an alternative to traditional command and control to increase efficiency and economic growth – together with greater integration of the health and social care professions.

In this process, a new White Paper, *Equality and Excellence: Liberating the NHS* (Department of Health 2010), was introduced. Subsequently the 2012 Health and Social Care Act was passed providing for devolution of power to the public and the professions; enhancing patient choice of healthcare professionals; and giving responsibility for commissioning care to accountable groups of general practitioners. Related to this, following the regulatory furore over 'Baby P' – who died at the hands of his mother and her boyfriend as a result of services not being properly joined up (Shane 2009) – the government determined that social work would be regulated by a new integrated Health and Care Professions Council rather than the General Social Care Council, bringing the health and social care professions together. Health and well-being boards have also been introduced, which are seen as key forums for professions in the health and care system to work together to improve the health of local populations, all of which have shades of the safari park. This convergence was underlined by the establishment of the renamed and more inclusive Professional Standards Authority for Health and Social Care – which was formerly called the Council for Healthcare Regulatory Excellence. In complementary fashion, the Law Commission is also in the process of reviewing the health and social care professions to establish a more streamlined, transparent and responsive system of regulation.

This expanded regulatory focus is highlighted by the growing recognition of the importance of joined-up working between professions and professionals in health and social care (Pollard, Thomas and Niers 2009), underpinned by more eclectic qualitative, quantitative and mixed methods of health research from a multi-disciplinary base (Saks and Allsop 2013). Although there are potential downsides to collaborative interprofessional working, such as the time it can take to bring to fruition and the complexity of communication channels, there are many benefits in terms of a patient/client centred approach to health and social care – even if this has all too rarely been translated into practice by the professions (Malin 2000). This underlines that the safari park, in which selected animals mix together for the good of the public, is now perhaps a better metaphor for understanding the regulation of health and social care professions in England, rather than a zoo or a circus. This is because there is a greater and more positive interface between groups of self-interested professional animals than in a traditional zoo or a circus, given increased government emphasis on de-regulation and collaborative working.

However, if we are moving into a more open mode of regulation, do we need such segregation – or by extension professional regulation – in health and social care or elsewhere? Or should the government take the ultimate step of going back to the law of the jungle in de-regulating the professions and let the market totally determine the public interest? The government is still clearly concerned that in the metaphorical safari park the health and social care professional animals do not escape from their compounds and harm both clients and the wider public. However, it is possible to conceive of a de-regulated world without professional zoos, circuses or safari parks. There are, though, upsides and downsides to this world without professions and indeed professional regulation. On the positive side, it could cheapen the cost of services by exposing existing professional groups to more competition, lead to less central state intervention and result in more direct consumer control (Friedman 1962). On the other hand, there may be enhanced

risks if consumers contract for services in medicine and other currently professionalized areas in a position of *caveat emptor* ('let the buyer beware'),
rather than being part of a system supported by formal ethically controlled
expertise. The loss of a self-supporting professional mechanism of expert
peer control based on members' subscriptions could also carry heavy financial replacement costs for government, further increase bureaucracy and
eliminate a useful buffer between individuals and the state (Stacey 1992) –
thereby underlining the preferred use of the zoo, circus and safari park metaphors in depicting and organizing the English healthcare environment, even
if there may be other helpful metaphors such as those based on wildlife
conservation and management within the jungle, which stop short of the law
of the jungle itself.

Conclusion

Metaphors, such as those drawn from the animal kingdom within a
neo-Weberian perspective in this context, therefore, can increase our
understanding of the different modes of regulating professions. In this
regard, it has been suggested that the ability of a metaphor to advance
and clarify theoretical understandings of organizations is based on the
extent to which that metaphor is seen to capture multiple relevant features of such entities and the ease with which it is understood (Cornelissen and Kafouros 2008). As has been seen in the case of healthcare,
the metaphors of zoos, circuses and safari parks certainly seem to fulfil
these criteria. As such, they will surely stimulate the further development
of theory and research in the field of professional regulation in future –
whether from a neo-Weberian standpoint in relation to thinking about
the texture of the relationship between professions and the state or from
the way in which interest-based professional groups interrelate with each
other. Thus, in terms of the metaphors and the case study of healthcare
in England – and the increasingly interlinked area of social care – current
government policy appears to have moved beyond the zoo and the circus
towards the safari park.

  However, it is important to note that at any one time, the applicability
of these metaphors overlap and interpenetrate – giving rise to a shifting
mixed economy within the reforming agenda with no inexorably fixed
point of destination. The precise conjuncture in other modern Western
health systems – including in Europe and North America – may or may not
differ. The move towards the law of the jungle, though, perhaps remains a
step too far in terms of the real risks that the interests of professions pose
to clients and the general public in liberal democratic societies. In understanding the regulatory relationship between such key parties as the professions, the state and citizens in future at a time when professional groups
have come under serious challenge, it is hoped that conceptualizing professional groups as clusters of animals in a menagerie – whether it be a zoo,

circus or safari park – can be extended to a wider range of professions in the Anglo-American context and other countries where professional exclusionary social closure prevails. These metaphors inspire greater flexibility in our thinking about professional groups more generally and their regulation by government and other bodies, including in organizational frames of reference themselves. In this latter case, such metaphors may also be capable of application in creative ways, especially given recent international developments in fields such as accountancy and law, where the regulating emphasis for individual practitioners has been based more on organizations as entities than professional bodies (Tricker 2012). As such, the applicability of animal metaphors in the field of professional regulation can stretch as far as the imagination of both regulating bodies and the inquirer will sustain.

References

Abbott, A. (1988) *The System of Professions: An Essay on the Division of Expert Labour*. Chicago: University of Chicago Press.

Alaszewski, A. (1995) Restructuring health and welfare professions in the United Kingdom: The impact of internal markets on the medical, nursing and social work professions. In: T. Johnson, G. Larkin and M. Saks (eds) *Health Professions and the State in Europe*. London: Routledge.

Allsop, J. and Saks, M. (eds) (2002) *Regulating the Health Professions*. London: Sage.

Allsop, J. and Saks, M. (2008) Professional regulation in primary care: The long road to quality improvement, *Quality in Primary Care* 16: 225–28.

Arney, W. (1982) *Power and the Profession of Obstetrics*. Chicago: University of Chicago Press.

Babinski, T. (2004) *Cirque du Soleil: 20 Years Under the Sun, An Authorised History*. New York: Harry N. Abrams.

Barber, B. (1963) Some problems in the sociology of professions, *Daedalus* 92: 669–88.

Becker, H. (1962) The nature of a profession. In: National Society for the Study of Education (eds) *Education for the Professions*. Chicago: University of Chicago Press.

Boon, A. (2010) Professionalism under the Legal Services Act 2007, *International Journal of the Legal Profession* 17: 195–232.

Brint, S. (1996) *In an Age of Experts: The Changing Roles of Professionals in Politics and Public Life*. Princeton: Princeton University Press.

Cherry, N. (1982) *The Politics of Town Planning*. Harlow: Longman.

Cooper, M. E. (2003) Zoo legislation, *International Zoo Yearbook* 38(1): 81–93.

Cornelissen, J. P. (2005) Beyond compare: Metaphors in organizational theory, *Academy of Management Review* 30(4): 751–64.

Cornelissen, J. P. and Kafouros, M. (2008) Metaphors and theory building in organization theory: What determines the impact of a metaphor on theory? *British Journal of Management* 19: 365–79.

Cornelissen, J. P., Kafouros, M. and Lock A. R. (2005) Metaphorical images of organization: How organizational researchers develop and select organizational metaphors, *Human Relations* 58: 1545–78.

Croke, V. (1997) *The Story of Zoos: Past, Present and Future*. New York: Scribner.

Daniel, N. (ed) (2008) *The Circus 1870–1950.* London: Taschen.

Davies, C. (1999) Rethinking regulation in the health professions in the UK: Institutions, ideals and identities. In: I. Hellberg, M. Saks and C. Benoit (eds) *Professional Identities in Transition: Cross-cultural Dimensions.* Södertälje, Sweden: Almqvist & Wiksell International.

Davies, N. (1993) *Murder on Ward Four: The Story of Bev Allitt.* London: Chatto and Windus.

Davis, J. M. (2002) *The Circus Age: Culture and Society Under the American Big Top.* Chapel Hill: University of North Carolina Press.

Deflem, M. (2008) *Sociology of Law: Visions of a Scholarly Tradition.* Cambridge: Cambridge University Press.

Dent, M., Chandler, J. and Barry, J. (eds) (2004) *Questioning the New Public Management.* Aldershot: Ashgate.

Department of Health (2006a) *Good Doctors, Safer Patients: Proposals to Strengthen the System to Assure and Improve the Performance of Doctors and to Protect the Safety of Patients.* London: The Stationery Office.

Department of Health (2006b) *The Regulation of the Non-medical Healthcare Professions: A Review by the Department of Health.* London: The Stationery Office.

Department of Health (2007) *Trust, Assurance and Safety – The Regulation of Health Professionals in the 21st Century.* London: The Stationery Office.

Department of Health (2008) *Medical Revalidation – Principles and Next Steps: The Report of the Chief Medical Officer for England's Working Group.* London: The Stationery Office.

Department of Health (2010) *Equality and Excellence: Liberating the NHS.* London: The Stationery Office.

Drolet, J. (2011) *American Neoconservatism: The Politics and Culture of a Reactionary Idealism.* London: C. Hurst & Co.

Esland, G. (1980) Diagnosis and therapy. In: G. Esland and G. Salaman (eds) *The Politics of Work and Occupations.* Milton Keynes: Open University Press.

Evetts, J. (2006) Short note: The sociology of professional groups – new directions, *Current Sociology* 54(1): 133–43.

Featherstone, M. (2007) *Consumer Culture and Postmodernism,* 2nd edition. London: Sage.

Fine, B., Kinsey, R., Lea, J., Picciotto, S. and Young, J. (eds) (1979) *Capitalism and the Rule of Law: From Deviancy Theory to Marxism.* London: Hutchinson.

Foucault, M. (1979) *Discipline and Punish: The Birth of the Prison.* Harmondsworth: Penguin.

Foucault, M. (1989) *Madness and Civilization: A History of Insanity in an Age of Reason.* London: Routledge.

Freidson, E. (1986) *Professional Powers: A Study of the Institutionalization of Formal Knowledge.* Chicago: University of Chicago Press.

Freidson, E. (2001) *Professionalism: The Third Logic.* Cambridge: Polity Press.

Friedman, M. (1962) *Capitalism and Freedom.* Chicago: University of Chicago Press.

Goode, W. (1960) Encroachment, charlatanism and the emerging profession: Psychology, sociology and medicine, *American Sociological Review* 25: 902–14.

Hanson, E. (2002) *Animal Attractions: Nature on Display in American Zoos.* Princeton: Princeton University Press.

Hardouin-Fugier, E. and Baratay, E. (2004) *Zoo: A History of Zoological Gardens in the West.* London: Reaktion Books.

Haslam, N., Loughnan, S. and Sun, P. (2011) Beastly: What makes animal metaphors offensive? *Journal of Language and Social Psychology* 30(3): 311–25.

Hughes, E. C. (1963) Professions, *Daedalus* 92: 655–68.

Ishkanian, A. and Szreter, S. (2012) *The Big Society Debate: A New Agenda for Social Policy?* Cheltenham: Edward Elgar.

Johnson, W. (1990) *The Rose-tinted Menagerie*. London: Heretic Books.

Klein, R. (2010) *The New Politics of the NHS: From Creation to Invention*, 6th edition. Oxford: Radcliffe Publishing.

Krause, E. (1996) *Death of the Guilds: Professions, States, and the Advance of Capitalism, 1930 to the Present*. New Haven: Yale University Press.

Kuhlmann, E. (2004) Post modern times for professions: The fall of the 'ideal professional' and its challenge to theory, *Knowledge, Work and Society* 2: 69–89.

Kuhlmann, E. and Saks, M. (eds) (2008) *Rethinking Professional Governance: International Directions in Healthcare*. Bristol: Policy Press.

Lee, S. and Beech, M. (eds) (2011) *The Clegg-Cameron Government: Coalition Policies in an Age of Austerity*. Houndmills: Palgrave Macmillan.

Liljegren, A. (2012) Key metaphors in the sociology of professions: Occupations as hierarchies and landscapes, *Comparative Sociology* 11(1): 88–112.

Malin, N. (ed) (2000) *Professionalism, Boundaries and the Workplace*. London: Routledge.

Millerson, G. (1964) *The Qualifying Associations*. London: Routledge & Kegan Paul.

Nettleton, S. (1992) *Power, Pain and Dentistry*. Buckingham: Open University Press.

Norton, B. G., Hutchins, M., Maple, T. L. and Stevens, E. F. (eds) (1996) *Ethics on the Ark: Zoos, Animal Welfare, and Wildlife Conservation*. Washington DC: Smithsonian Books.

Parkin, F. (1979) *Marxism and Class Theory: A Bourgeois Critique*. London: Tavistock.

Parry, J. and Parry, N. (1976) *The Rise of the Medical Profession*. London: Croom Helm.

Perkin, H. (1989) *The Rise of Professional Society: England Since 1880*. London: Routledge.

Phipps, A. (2008) *Women in Science, Engineering and Technology: Three Decades of UK Initiatives*. Stoke-on-Trent: Trentham Books.

Pickford, P. and Pickford, B. (2011) *African Safari: Into the Great Game Reserves*. Oxford: Beaufoy Publishing.

Pollard, K., Thomas, J. and Niers, M. (eds) (2009) *Understanding Interprofessional Working in Health and Social Care: Theory and Practice*. Basingstoke: Palgrave Macmillan.

Poulantzas, N. (1975) *Classes in Contemporary Capitalism*. London: New Left Books.

Riska, E. (2001) *Medical Careers and Feminist Agendas: American, Scandinavian and Russian Women Physicians*. New York: Aldine de Gruyter.

Saks, M. (1983) Removing the blinkers? A critique of recent contributions to the sociology of professions, *Sociological Review* 31(1): 1–21.

Saks, M. (ed) (1992) *Alternative Medicine in Britain*. Oxford: Clarendon Press.

Saks, M. (1995) *Professions and the Public Interest: Professional Power, Altruism and Alternative Medicine*. London: Routledge.

Saks, M. (1998) Deconstructing or reconstructing professions? Interpreting the role of professional groups in society. In: V. Olgiati, L. Orzack and M. Saks (eds)

Professions, Identity and Order in Comparative Perspective. Onati, Spain: Onati International Institute for the Sociology of Law.

Saks, M. (2000) Medicine and the counter culture. In: R. Cooter and J. Pickstone (eds) *Medicine in the Twentieth Century.* Amsterdam: Harwood Academic Publishers.

Saks, M. (2002) Empowerment, participation and the rise of orthodox biomedicine. In: R. Byrt and J. Dooher (eds) *Empowerment, and Participation: Power, Influence and Control in Contemporary Health Care.* Dinton: Quay Books.

Saks, M. (2003a) *Orthodox and Alternative Medicine: Politics, Professionalization and Health Care.* London: Sage.

Saks, M. (2003b) Professionalization, politics and complementary and alternative medicine. In: M. Kelner, B. Pescosolido, M. Saks and B. Wellman (eds) *Complementary and Alternative Medicine: Challenge and Change.* London: Routledge.

Saks, M. (2005) Regulating complementary and alternative medicine: The case of acupuncture. In: G. Lee-Treweek, T. Heller, S. Spurr, H. MacQueen and J. Katz (eds) *Perspectives on Complementary and Alternative Medicine: A Reader.* Abingdon: Routledge/Open University.

Saks, M. (2010) Analyzing the professions: The case for the neo-Weberian approach, *Comparative Sociology* 9(6): 887–915.

Saks, M. and Allsop, J. (2007) Social policy, professional regulation and health support work in the United Kingdom, *Social Policy and Society* 6: 165–77.

Saks, M. and Allsop, J. (eds) (2013) *Researching Health: Qualitative, Quantitative and Mixed Methods,* 2nd edition. London: Sage.

Saks, M. and Kuhlmann, E. (2006) Introduction, special issue on the Professions: Social inclusion and citizenship: Challenge and change in European health systems, *Knowledge, Work and Society* 4: 9–33.

Shane, J. (2009) *It Must Never Happen Again: The Lessons Learnt from the Short Life and Terrible Death of Baby P.* London: John Blake Publishing.

Shipman Inquiry (2004) *Safeguarding Patients: Lessons from the Past – Proposals for the Future.* London: The Stationery Office.

Stacey, M. (1992) *Regulating British Medicine: The General Medical Council.* Chichester: Wiley and Sons.

Svensson, L. G. (1999) Professionals as a new middle class: The Swedish case. In: I. Hellberg, M. Saks and C. Benoit (eds) *Professional Identities in Transition: Crosscultural Dimensions.* Södertälje, Sweden: Almqvist & Wiksell International.

Svensson, L. G. and Evetts, J. (2010) Introduction. In: L. G. Svensson and J. Evetts (eds) *Sociology of Professions: Continental and Anglo-Saxon Traditions.* Gothenburg: Daidalos.

Tricker, B. (2012) *Corporate Governance: Principles, Policies and Practices,* 2nd edition. Oxford: Oxford University Press.

Turner, B. (1995) *Medical Power and Social Knowledge,* 2nd edition. London: Sage.

Weber, M. (1968) *Economy and Society: An Outline of Interpretive Sociology.* New York: Bedminster Press.

Wilensky, H. (1964) The professionalization of everyone? *American Journal of Sociology* 70: 137–58.

Witz, A. (1992) *Professions and Patriarchy.* London: Routledge.

Young, R. J. (2003) *Environment Enrichment for Captive Animals.* Iowa City: University of Iowa Press.

7 Boundaries of social work or social work of boundaries?

Andrew Abbott

I would like to pose a basic problem in the history of social work, or, rather, the basic problem that the history of social work has posed to theorists of occupations and professions. I can perhaps best illustrate that problem by listing some of the people present at the National Conference of Charities and Correction (NCCC) in 1884 in Louisville, Kentucky. As is well known, the NCCC was a lineal ancestor of social work, and indeed the conference would later be known as the National Conference of Social Work.

There was Mrs J. S. Sperry of the Ladies Benevolent Union Hospital of Pueblo, Colorado; Mr J. G. Knapp, statistical agent for the US Agricultural Department for Florida; Dr Theophilus Powell, Medical Superintendent of the giant Georgia Lunatic Asylum at Milledgeville. There was Dr H. Z. Gill of the Illinois Southern Penitentiary at Chester, and Frederick Wines, the great Illinois charities reformer. There was Mrs L. D. Lewelling, Matron at the Girls' Reform School in Mitchellville, Iowa; Amasa Pratt of the Ohio Deaf and Dumb Institute; and the Reverend L. F. Cain, Chaplain at the Indiana State Prison in Jeffersonville.

If we were to look ten years later, we would find not only these old familiar faces, but also some new groups. We would find Charles Henderson and Edward Bemis, Professors in the University of Chicago's Departments of Sociology and Political Economy. We would find Mrs. Anna Lowell Woodbury, President of the Washington DC First Mission School of Cookery and Housework, and Ursula L. Harrison, Superintendent of the Illinois School of Agriculture and Manual Training for Boys. We would find the Reverend George Hoover of Iowa's Educational Aid Association, Miss Maud M. Virgin of the Charity Organization Society of Burlington, Iowa, and Miss C. C. Barnwell of a Baltimore institution called the Dispensary for Plaster of Paris Jackets. We would find probation officers, overseers of the poor, trustees of mental hospitals and other state institutions, superintendents of institutions for orphans and the deaf, and heads of banks for the poor. Everything conceivably related to social reform – from alcohol to education to lunacy to vocational training to probation work is contained in this meeting somewhere.

If we look at this same list in 1912, we find a major change. For one thing, the list is much longer. Many of the institutional authorities who came to earlier meetings are still there, but there is now an immense silent membership, which does not necessarily come to the annual conference. Most of these are women, and many are called agents or visitors or, in some cases, social workers. Many list no title at all. These are the foundation of the new occupation that will eventually take the name social work. It is, in fact, already in existence by this point, already possessing training schools and journals, soon to get an association and a labour exchange.

What is important, however, and would become more so if we were to follow these lists later into the new century, is that many aspects of welfare-related work present in the earlier lists are going or gone. Probation is present but will gradually disappear. The connection with education is tenuous and will grow steadily weaker. Areas like manual training, home economics and kindergartens are no longer evident. By contrast, the connection with psychiatry is strong and getting stronger.

This set of connections is the great problem of social work history. Why was it that certain task areas became part of social work and other parts did not? I will take three approaches to this question. The first draws on that literature in the sociology of professions that has emphasized professional functions. The second draws on the 'contested jurisdictions' view of the development of professions that I set forth in *The System of Professions* (Abbott 1988). The third sets forth a new version of the theory origin of social groups, using social work as an example of what I think is the most general process by which new social groups are created.

Let me start out, as I did myself, with the functional view of professions, which dominated studies of professions from the Second World War to the early 1970s. To the functionalists, as their name implies, understanding a social entity's function was crucial to understanding its nature. Despite their name, however, the functionalists spent more time on the structures than on the functions of professions. For it was they who came up with the notion that professions should be identified by certain 'traits' that marked them as a particular and special kind of occupation.

Indeed, one of the most celebrated articles of this school of analysis was written about social work by Ernest Greenwood (1957), an article entitled 'The attributes of a profession'. For Greenwood, the crucial list of attributes of a profession included five things: skill based on theoretical knowledge, a period of formal training and education, an occupational organization, a code of ethics or conduct and some form of community-sanctioned licence. Other writers proposed additions and replacements to this list. These included competency testing, altruistic service, public service, application to the needs of others, fiduciary relations with clients, loyalty to colleagues and fee-based remuneration. These new traits, combined with the old list of skill, training, organization, ethics and licensing, make up the usual functionalist conception of a profession.

Note that, as I said, the basic idea of the functional view of professions was actually about structure, not function. Something was a profession if it had a certain structure. But it turns out that a more purely functionalist account could be found to explain the tasks of social work, and indeed, it was that theory with which I undertook my first studies of the profession.

When I began to study social workers in the field, on the outpatient psychiatric floor of the University of Chicago Hospital in 1972, I noticed that while the social workers spent some of their time in one-to-one therapy, they also seemed to spend an enormous amount of time on the phone. At the time, I was mainly interested in the uses of psychiatric knowledge. I had gone to the field trying to figure out how psychiatric knowledge was actually used in practice, largely with an eye to demonstrating that practical knowledge and academic knowledge were quite far apart. Because of this interest, I treated the phone work of the clinic social workers as a minor diversion. Such is the danger of having one's theoretical questions too formalized.

My whole notion of social work changed radically when, a year later, I began what would turn out to be five years of fieldwork and other research at Manteno State Hospital in Manteno, Illinois. I was still interested in psychiatric knowledge, even though I had been told there was no psychiatric knowledge to speak of at the hospital, but I now began to find social work knowledge and psychological knowledge to be just as interesting as psychiatric knowledge. For they, too, were radically different in the state hospital setting. In particular, there was at Manteno a serious disjunction between social work as a turf of work and social work as an identified credential. People with social work credentials were doing quite a few different things; some were administering psychological tests, some were running wards and programmes, some were doing particular kinds of therapy, and some were doing what I would later learn was called casework. On the other hand, the state civil service classification of social worker was largely occupied by people without credentials, certainly without master's-level credentials. And these people were emphatically doing casework: spending whole days on the phone, taking patients to appointments and hearings, and generally managing the then-flourishing process of deinstitutionalization.

It was in response to this empirical reality that I developed what would be my first theoretical analysis of social work, an analysis in the high functionalist vein. Like most other young sociologists, I had been influenced by the writing of Talcott Parsons. Parsons always analyzed things into fours – not threes, like Freud, but fours. This was because there were four 'functions', by which Parsons meant there were four basic tasks any collectivity had to accomplish in order to survive. It had to adapt the external environment to its own needs, it had to set goals for itself, it had to hold itself together, and it had to maintain its concept of itself. These four functions were memorized by a generation of sociologists under the names adaptation, goal attainment, integration, and latent pattern maintenance, and the schema took the name of the initial letters of these concepts, AGIL.

To those who know my later work, it may seem surprising that I ever took Parsons seriously. But I have an abstract streak, and I found the system fun, a kind of game. Yet although I would now regard a Parsonian analysis of the turf of professions as completely wrong-headed, it managed to produce a surprisingly apt result in the case of social work.

The game in Parsonian functionalism was to set forth a list of functions, then to go looking in the social world to see the institutions carrying out those functions. One always began with a set of AGIL boxes and then tried to fill them in with the likely suspects. Wherever you started, you could have four main items. Then any lesser items (like lesser professions, or less social institutions, or lesser anythings) would have to be treated as somehow brokering between the main divisions, dealing with what Parsons called 'flows across boundaries'. These brokers themselves occupied subboxes in the big boxes; every box in the AGIL schema was itself broken into four AGIL boxes, which in their turn were divided, and so on.

Parsons was nothing if not grandiose. He himself had decided that the four functions of the entire human world were carried out by what he called the four 'levels' of action: the body, the personality, the social system, and the cultural system. It seemed to me that this meant there should be four principal professions. I at once decided these were medicine for the body, psychiatry for the personality, law for the social system, and religion for the cultural system. Of course, if I had known anything about the history of European universities, I might have wondered why arts, rather than psychiatry, was not the fourth profession. For it is from the four-faculty university of the Middle Ages that the three 'ancient professions' of law, medicine, and divinity in fact descend, and arts, not psychiatry, was the true fourth to those three.

My pretty theory had a major problem. Social work was clearly a major force in my area of empirical work, yet it seemed a fifth wheel in the four-functional world. The solution seemed obvious and very much in the Parsons tradition. Social work must be the profession of interstitiality, the profession whose job was to mediate between all the others. In any empirical sense, that was what the social workers of Manteno did. Many of them had pretensions to some sort of therapeutic expertise. Many of them actively did groups, one on ones, token economies, and other such things. But the heart of what they did was to broker between doctors, lawyers, and psychiatrists on the one hand, and patients, institution, and, sometimes, family on the other. The social function of social work was intersystem translation.

Thus, my own empirical sense came together with my theoretical scheme, absurd as it was, and they made a good marriage. This brought me my first notion about the relation between social work and boundaries. Social work was about boundaries: boundaries between institutions, boundaries between professions. In this general sense, social work was 'social work of boundaries', just as we might speak of social work of the aged or of the mentally ill. In the most general sense, I felt, social work was about bringing all professional forces together in order to articulate and concentrate their resources as best might be for the particular client. Thus, it was that I came very early to one part of my title, the notion of 'social work of boundaries'.

Like all functionalist notions, my idea of social work as boundary occupation rested on a profoundly idealistic concept of the occupation. It worked best when construed as a kind of idealization of what was there in actuality, an Aristotelian goal (in Greek, an *entelechy*) toward which the profession pointed. Indeed, there were in the social work tradition works that fit my case exactly, not least among them Mary Richmond's great *Social Diagnosis*, with its careful characterization of the many dozens of agencies and professions dealt with by social workers on a regular basis (Richmond 1917).

In practice, however, there was an obvious disjuncture between my theory and reality. As I said, the certified social workers at Manteno worked all over the map. A surprising number were administrators of one sort or another. Others were scattered around in a variety of alternatives to traditional casework. There was also my nagging memory of the social workers at the University of Chicago Hospital, who, deep down, had clearly preferred doing therapy to being on the phone. If doing boundaries was the functional heart of social work, why weren't some social workers more excited about doing it?

At this point I got distracted from social work in particular, for I suddenly noticed that most professions were not doing what the functionalists – and indeed the general public – thought they were doing. How many doctors were spending all day with patients on the wards? How many lawyers spent time trying cases in court? How many clergy spent time on the street saving sinners? I gathered these empirical findings under the concept of 'professional regression'.

Professional regression referred to a process by which a profession 'regressed' into itself. High status in the professions, I argued, went with being able to talk purely professional talk, being able to rule out the confusions and difficulties that clients often present to professional knowledge schemes. Curiously, it was the very complexity and interwoven character of clients' problems that presented the most glaring challenge to professional knowledge, even though the whole point of professional knowledge was to deal with client problems. Hence it was that doctors wanted to deal only with patients' medical problems, not with the psychiatric and social ones. Professionals would have high status before their peers only if they could remain separate from such defiling complications. This would be easiest if they dealt with pure professional knowledge in itself. Ergo, high-status professionals would spend more of their time talking to other professionals than to clients, or, even better, would consult with other professionals in such a way as to never speak to clients at all. Only the English barristers had managed this perfectly; for them it was more or less unethical to speak to a client directly, rather than through a solicitor. But American surgeons were close. This theory also explained why academics – who speak generally to nobody but other academics – enjoyed high status despite their low pay. Their professional purity gave them the status that their salaries did not.

This argument worked for social work, as for the others. Indeed, it seemed to work best there. For if the profession's concept of itself was as the profession of interstitiality, then the profession's concept of itself was inherently impure. *Ex ante*, social workers would flee such a definition of self; they would try to slide out of it into something that could be made and kept pure. Psychiatric knowledge, on which personal therapeutic practice in social work is based, was an obvious good alternative. Thus my theory nicely explained why psychotherapeutic practice was of higher status than casework, why the University of Chicago social workers giggled with horror at the days I spent talking to social workers at Manteno.

More deeply, the idea of professional regression implied that, eventually, whole professions might move away from their original areas of work. If enough professionals pursued high status, there would be no one left in the original professional heartland. Indeed, here was an idea that helped me in my original problem of explaining how psychiatric knowledge could be used in mental hospitals without the necessity of any psychiatrists working there. The Manteno hospital had only one board-certified psychiatrist on full-time staff for a hospital of 3,500 patients, even though the American Psychiatric Association had once been called the Association of Medical Superintendents of American Institutions for the Insane. Here was a nearly complete desertion, and one undoubtedly explained by professional regression.

At the same time, it was clear at Manteno that social workers, along with psychologists, were invading the turf the psychiatrists had left behind for their offices in Chicago's Loop. At Manteno, the certified members of these lower status professions outnumbered the one psychiatrist and clearly overshadowed the unlicensed foreign physicians who made up the rest of the medical staff. They were younger, more energetic, more enthusiastic. It was clear that the vacuum was being occupied by new groups.

All this may seem a simple inference today, but it took me a long time. I had, by this time, left Manteno and moved East to teach at Rutgers University. Having at last returned to sociology full-time, I could now make the theoretical leap that my experiences at Manteno had implied. If all professions were in motion most of the time, then the world of professions was simply one large, conflicted turf. There were conflicts over clients, over status, over resources, over licensing, above all over something that I would come to call jurisdiction, the more or less exclusive right to dominate a particular area of work. Two years of listening to others' studies of the histories of professions at Princeton's Davis Center seminar persuaded me that only such a theory could account for the incredible diversity of histories in the professions.

Curiously, I looked far outside the professions to find theory that could help me comprehend this turf-based theory of professions. In my original paper on this subject (in 1982), I took most of my theory about competing professions from the theory of race relations. Race relations had been an old standby of my department at Chicago, and I had dutifully read the area for my doctoral preliminary examination. Now I borrowed and applied Park's theory of the race relations cycle, Lieberson's comparison of external and internal colonization, and van den Berghe's attribution of race relations to the division of labour. Above all, I remembered the community studies of race relations in Chicago – Franklin Frazier's analyses of bounded black communities, Gerry Suttles' books about racial boundaries, and so forth.

In this new theory of mine, the history of professions became a history of turf wars. I theorized the professions as living in an ecology. There were professions and turfs, and a social and cultural mapping – the mapping of jurisdiction – between those professions and turfs. Change in this mapping was the proper focus of studies of professions and happened most often at the edges of professional jurisdictions. These edges could be studied in the three arenas of workplace, public and state and admitted different kinds and levels of settlements, ranging from full and monopolistic jurisdiction to much looser forms of purely intellectual jurisdiction or clientele differentiation.

In short, this was a theory of boundaries, for social work as for all other professions. But in this case, it was not a question of social work of boundaries but, rather, of boundaries of social work. In this new theory, set forth eventually in *The System of Professions*, the content of social work's jurisdiction was not a fixed thing set from the beginning, elaborated by some process of functional differentiation. Rather, it was a contested, turf-driven matter (Abbott 1988).

From my new theory, a number of implications immediately followed for my understanding of social work. First, one could not understand social work within the static framework of the functionalists. There was no transcendent 'function' of interstitiality that social work came into being to serve. Even though interstitiality would exist no matter what the arrangement of the system of professions, the shifting relations among other professions were continually changing the meaning of that interstitiality. Where in one decade, the chief brokering needs might lie between educational institutions and jails, in another, more might lie between hospitals and families.

Nor was social work best understood, as Parsons undoubtedly would have understood it, as something that differentiated out of religion as the society became more complex and demanded a more functionally specific set of professions. Rather, the functions of social work, like those of the other professions, emerged from a continuous process of conflict and change. The larger social and cultural structure produced from time to time new problems that were potentially professionalizable. The various professions and would-be professions then attempted to shape these problems into coherent jurisdictions by creating intellectual processes of diagnosis, inference, and treatment. At the same time, the competing professions would be forwarding their claims in the workplace, before the public, and within the apparatus of the state and settling them, as I noted before, in a variety of ways.

Thus, social work must stem, originally, from some set of underlying changes in the society and the surrounding professions. It was, in fact, clear just which social and cultural changes those were. The island communities of America had been destroyed in the late nineteenth century. The cities filled with the restless young. Millions of immigrants flooded the country. Industrial employers became larger and less interested in their workers. The workplace became more bureaucratic and more demanding. Moreover, these changes were accompanied by a cultural shift toward social Darwinism, a vision of society as a winner-take-all competition in which the losers would be thrown aside, bent and broken, because of their inability to meet the demands of modern civilization.

Confronted with these changes, the local institutions that had previously provided some vague measure of social security to a relatively stable local population could do little. At the same time, a profound impulse had urged a wide variety of groups to enter the new area, which we might loosely call 'problems of social order and welfare'. It was conceived in philanthropic terms, but also in hierarchical terms. It was an area calling for science, but also for altruism. It was an area that involved people in crime, in illness, in education, even in industry. The area's very complexity bespeaks its inchoate, undefined character. This was, indeed, the world I described in listing the occupations of members of the National Conference of Charities and Correction in its early years.

Social work had clearly condensed out of this vast and complicated turf. But my theory of turf competition did not really say how that condensation happened. Where did entities like social work come from?

My original solution to this problem was rather *ad hoc*. In thinking about social work and similar cases, I developed the notion of enclosure, a concept I remembered from my undergraduate years as an English historian. The agricultural revolution of England in the seventeenth and eighteenth centuries was driven by a process of enclosing common land, a process in which the wealthy took over the commons at bargain prices and used them to raise sheep for the new woolen trade. Typically, professions emerged from enormous and complex areas like social welfare by a somewhat similar process. It seemed that a coalition involving both new people and people from prior professions would separate itself and claim a particular, defined turf within the complex area. Social work was by no means the only example, for psychiatry emerged in much the same way. For a contemporary example outside social welfare, consider the complex occupational terrain in the area of information provision. It was ironic that the rise of social work was indeed a matter of 'enclosing the commons', for the metaphor of the commons was taken over by the emerging social welfare movement and used, as in other places, as the name of one of the original Chicago settlement houses.

With the notion of enclosure, I had moved fully from a theory about social work of boundaries to a theory about boundaries of social work. Instead of seeing the field as shaped by an inner function or purpose of transcending interprofessional boundaries, I saw it as shaped by conflicts on boundaries. Social work attracted and lost various subfields: probation, kindergartens, manual training, and so on – not because they were closer to or further from the inner nature of a social work of boundaries, but because other occupations had come and taken some of them away, while other subfields remained securely protected within the bosom of social work.

There were, however, obvious problems with this theory. On the one hand, psychiatric social work was clearly one of the foundation fields of social work, yet it had been contested with the psychiatrists and psychologists in the child guidance clinics from their first beginnings. It was hardly a calm, enclosed heartland. On the other hand, while probation work appeared central to social work throughout the early years of the National Conference of Charities and Correction, which, indeed, enshrined the connection of social work and probation in its very title, it eventually disappeared so completely from the thing we call social work that, today, we have a hard time wondering what the two might ever have had in common.

The problems were not only with social work. My turf-based view of professions depended on some embarrassingly strong assumptions. About the contested boundaries between professions, I was presuming that they could be specified, that they did, in fact, separate professions, and that they were the zones of interprofessional action (because they were the zones of interprofessional conflict). Indeed, I presumed a kind of spatial structure to these contested boundaries, implicit in the phrase 'at the core of a profession'. Here was a deep assumption of professions as more or less convex bodies, with secure heartlands deep behind their boundary territories. Yet psychiatric social work was an example of a subfield that was at once central and contested.

Beyond these implicit presuppositions about boundaries, I presumed something much more profound, as I noted in the closing chapter of *The System of Professions*. In arguing mainly about interprofessional conflict, I tended to take for granted the existence of the professions doing the conflicting. This had been necessary, of course. One has to take some things as given, and if I was to make conflict the focus of attention, the bodies in conflict were the obvious thing to presuppose. But when I argued about the emergence of professions in border territories, or about the gradual dissolution of professions without jurisdictions, or about the transformation of professions via amalgamation and division, I was taking for granted the notion of acting bodies called professions, capable of being split or joined, capable of coming into or losing some kind of permanent existence. Yet I had no clear way of imagining how such bodies came into existence. The metaphor of enclosure did not account for why professions coalesced under some circumstances and remained inchoate in others.

This issue of coalescence was intimately related to the issue of which tasks ended up within a new profession like social work. Perhaps coalescence was possible only because certain tasks ended up within the new jurisdiction and certain tasks did not. That meant thinking of boundaries as crucial to the very formation of a professional entity like social work.

Curiously enough, then, my attempt to figure out where social entities like social work come from takes me back to the second of my two title phrases: 'social work of boundaries'. My first (functional) theory held that the Aristotelian aim of social work was to be a social work of boundaries, to work systematically across interprofessional boundaries and, by doing so, to link the other professions in the service of a single client. I replaced that with the system-of-professions argument, the argument that what mattered was not 'social work of boundaries', but rather the 'boundaries of social work'. The field took its shape from interprofessional competition at its margins.

But there is another sense for the original phrase 'social work of boundaries', a sense applicable to this problem of coalescence. It is the sense of social work as a social entity actually created by pulling certain boundaries together, the idea that it is 'social work [made out] of boundaries'. In short, I am proposing that social entities come into existence when social agents tie social boundaries together in certain ways. The first things are the boundaries. The second are the entities.

In social work, there are a number of historical facts that seem to suggest that we think of boundaries first. For one thing, the subspecialties emerged as firm entities well before the general profession did. The medical school and psychiatric social workers emerged as coherent groups before the American Association of Social Workers. This suggests that boundaries between groups handling interprofessional relations (the incipient social workers) and other professions first appeared separately, within sub-areas, within single organizations. These local boundaries preceded more general ones between social work as a whole and other occupations.

Even more important, it is clear that the task shakeout – the disappearance of probation, kindergartens, home economics, and the like – long antedated all the professional organizations, which appeared only in the late 1910s and 1920s. Kindergartens were clearly bound for the school system by the turn of the century, as were industrial education and home economics (thus, for example, leading to the eclipse of the Boston Cooking School, whose Fannie M. Farmer wrote the bible of early-twentieth-century cooking). The break with probation came a little later but followed the same trajectory. But if such task realignments came first, before the amalgamation of the various groups into 'social work' as a whole, local boundaries and differences were clearly determining the shape of that whole.

I am, therefore, arguing that the crucial formative years of social work came well before the period at the centre of the standard account, which is 1900 to 1920. The standard account of the formation of social work views the profession as arising out of a turf competition between the charity organization societies with their 'scientific' ethos of casework and the settlements with their chaotically comprehensive services and their broad social agendas. The usual view is that the settlements more or less lost out to the new scientism of Mary Richmond and others. The settlements' broad interests in reform and preventive services were replaced by the narrow, vocational, casework-centered approach of the social work schools.

However, there is crucial evidence of structure in the task areas of social work well before this whole conflict. John Mohr's work on the thousands of charities listed in the New York Charity Organization Society directories between 1888 and 1917 shows that implicit lines of demarcation emerged between different kinds of potential clients by the turn of the century. Moreover, one can see those lines emerging as well in occupational data describing the graduates of the first School of Social Work, the School of the New York Charity Organization Society, begun in 1898. In 1904, there was a retrospective on the School's first 207 graduates. Of these, 167 had identifiable volunteer or paid employment; many of the remainder were women who had married and left any kind of work behind. Of these 167, over one-third (58) were involved in charity aid societies as visitors, agents, supervisors, editors, or general secretaries. Another 22 were involved in specific charities. However, 16 were teachers, running all the way from professors of sociology to instructors in kindergartens. Fourteen were settlement workers, running clubs, music schools, and various other activities. Thirteen worked for governments, mostly for New York City as tenement house inspectors. A mere four entered probation and medical work. These career tracks were already making the divisions of social work clear, even before the public battle of the charity organization movement and the settlement movement had reached the boiling point. The structuration, as we might call it, of careers and tasks was already evident. Local boundaries, although not firm, were falling into coherent shapes (Mohr 1992).

That the structuration of the task field became clear even before there was much centralized institutional structure may well explain the success of the later structures on which the organized entity called social work is based. In particular, I shall argue that in these various sub-areas like probation and family work, boundaries began to emerge between different kinds of people doing the same kinds of work, or between different styles of work with roughly similar clients, or between one kind of workplace and another. It didn't really matter what these boundaries were, at first. They began as simple inchoate differences. They were not boundaries of anything but, rather, simple locations of difference. They were not associated from one workplace to another; they were not consistent from one client type to another; they were not necessarily stable over time.

For example, kindergartens began in the 1880s to be conducted by people with a wider variety of backgrounds than before: some from education, some from volunteering, some from churches. These people also differed in some cases by gender, by class, by level of education. Rapid expansion of the earlier movement drove this difference. In the probation field, the dimensions of difference were different. In probation, the profound dimension of difference was clients (who differed given the differing aims of state laws), and, hence, structure. Adult probation demanded largely legal professionals, while child probation was dominated by the newer aims of the child welfare movement. Both kindergartens and probation thus became sites of difference, and, hence, boundaries in my sense. However, the differences were not necessarily similar across areas, or even across given instantiations of a type of institution in a single area.

Social work came into existence when various social agents like the leaders of the settlement and charity organization movements, the heads of state boards, and the superintendents of institutions began to hook up these sites of difference into larger proto-boundaries, and then into larger units. (And, of course, recalling the 'system of professions argument', one must remember that leaders of other professions and proto-professions did so as well, the most important of these being the newly powerful occupation of school superintendents.) Thus, in one part of social welfare, a gender proto-boundary may have emerged. That is, gender differences may have come to be the organizing differences in a set of institutions or work sites that are somehow adjacent in social space. In these, men were fighting with women about how some particular set of tasks was to be done, and both were aware that similar fights existed in adjacent units. The best example of such a boundary was psychiatric social work, an area in which men (psychiatrists) and women (psychiatric social workers) did largely the same thing under different professional banners. In another part of the social welfare area, differences of training have taken a similar, decisive shape; there were two kinds of training in sharp opposition, even though men and women may have been on both sides. (A good example of this was in kindergartens, where the older, specially trained Froebelians were overwhelmed in the 1880s by less trained workers coming into kindergartens via the settlement houses.) In yet another, what mattered was a similar opposition between people who had connections to churches and those who did not. (Friendly visiting itself was such an area.) Social work emerged when actors began to hook up the women from the first area with the scientifically trained workers from the second with the non-church group in the third. All those people are placed 'within' social work, and the others ruled outside it. An image is then developed to rationalize this emerging reality as a single thing. Unfortunately, in the process of making such a hookup, certain areas (like probation) may have proven too distant, in some sense, to have one of their parties included in the emerging thing called social work.

Along another dimension, a single boundary may have been crucial. An important boundary in home economics, industrial education and kindergartens was that between services that were school based and those that were settlement-house based. By linking the school 'sides' of these boundaries together, school administrators achieved a more secure expansion into the non-traditional curriculum than they otherwise might have.

Thus, I come to the notion that social entities actually emerge from boundaries and that the phrase I initially intended in a functional sense – social work of boundaries – in fact describes, in quite another sense, the realities of entity creation. Once the entity is created, of course, there arise intergroup competition and 'boundaries of social work'. But while the phrase 'boundaries of social work' describes the central determining factors around the profession at any given time, the phrase 'social work of boundaries' captures the idea that local sites of difference always exist – even within various inchoate areas of welfare-related tasks today – from which new professions or sub-professions could emerge.

All this is very well for me the theorist of occupations and social structures. I have essentially told a story of how the history and current reality of social work have shaped my own thinking about occupations more generally. But what does all this mean for those who wonder about the future of the profession as it moves through its centennial?

To answer, I shall raise some issues that my own theories suggest are likely to be crucial for social work in the near future. Remember that I am not, at present, an expert on this particular occupation. But I am someone who has thought a lot about how and why occupations change and who can, perhaps, foresee some change in social work.

First, I think social workers should not be disturbed about the structure of the occupation, which may at times seem amorphous, uncontrolled and uncontrollable. Most of the 'ideal-typical' professions like law and medicine are moving rapidly away from the relatively rigid structures characteristic of professions earlier in the century. Now more doctors and lawyers are salaried than self-employed. More of them work in large organizations with other imperatives than health or justice. There is more and more explicit internal diversity in terms of careers. Most of the professions are starting to look like engineering: a large multifarious field, with several subfields, with serious internal hierarchies and status differences, with different levels of certification and with short career structures that often lead directly into administration. It is clear that this amorphous kind of occupation is replacing the tightly organized, small professions of the earlier part of this century. Social work's experience is not unique.

Second, in terms of competing professions, the situation is quite unclear. Social work has often taken my first notion of its function – social work as a discipline of connections across boundaries – as its heart. Probably the vast majority of what people with the title 'social worker' actually do in the USA is indeed connecting together services provided largely by other professions and other institutions. In many cases, this work of connection takes place within organizations completely controlled by other visions of professional function – hospitals, psychiatric clinics, schools and courts. In all these institutions, social workers have often conceded control to other professions, a cession that, for example, was quite explicitly made in psychiatric social work in the 1920s. Thus, in one main part of its work, social work is perpetually at the mercy of changes in other professions.

Ironically, these changes are sometimes positive. The new economics of hospitals has meant an emphasis on discharge planning, with a consequent rapid upswing of social worker employment. Thus, the very decline in 'helping' within the hospitals has benefited social workers who plan for the less expensive 'helping' outside.

Outside this institutional sector, in the free-standing practice jurisdiction, is the clinical social work that consists of talking with upper- and middle-class people about personal problems. Here, the competition social work faces is severe. The doctors control the medications crucial to a large segment of this clientele, and the psychotherapeutic and psychological knowledge used most often comes from elsewhere, although some techniques (for example, brief psychotherapy) have come from social work. Social work's chief advantage here is its price, which is on average less than that of psychiatrists and psychologists. But with third-party payers picking up substantial portions of the bills, this advantage may be less important than it seems. This 'personal problems' area of social work will never become central to the field but will always remain a kind of suburb to which elites can flee from the central problems with which social work is concerned. But its implications for the future of social work are great. We have only to think of the relations of suburbs to cities to imagine how great those tensions can become.

If psychotherapy is the suburbs, then public assistance is the city. This third major jurisdictional area remains to the social workers alone. It comprises those on public assistance, a clientele that claims the attention of over one-third of social workers generally, but of only one in twenty professionally certified social workers. The good news is that no other profession wants this group, which makes it a fertile ground for professional work, as psychiatrists found in the last century. The bad news is that central parameters defining what can be done with the group are set by other agents, chiefly the state with its school attendance laws, its means tests and its sudden reallocations of resources. It is noteworthy that although psychiatrists and librarians, for example, both built their occupations on institutions funded by the state, both branched out rapidly as that funding became precarious. Indeed, psychiatrists left government institutions almost altogether.

I think even more profound challenges to social work have to do with larger social changes and forces. First, I think it not unlikely that social workers may face substantial changes from new developments in information science. The caseworker's stock-in-trade has always been a complex knowledge of routines and practices within a wide variety of welfare institutions and policies. This knowledge may soon sit in computers in easily retrievable form, a development that might, as in library science, enable social work staffs to be cut even as they provide more services. This would probably already be happening if social workers were not paid so little that governments cannot save much by replacing them. However, the possibility is there, and I would not rule out a technological transformation of this area rather like the one in health.

The second larger change has to do with the profession's means of support. Social work's major funder, although not necessarily its major client, is government. And democratic government, as Aristotle tells us and as recent history makes clear, is given to sudden and violent change. Our government is clearly planning to cut funding for those social welfare programs that employ many social workers, like family assistance, while maintaining funding for those social welfare programs that do not, like social security and unemployment. It is true that these cuts will affect the 'official' certified profession less than the unofficial, uncertified one. But the cuts will be drastic nonetheless and will affect those areas of social work most clearly identified with the heartland concept of casework. The main conclusion is that since one main jurisdiction of social work is heavily dependent on the state and since that area of social work that is not heavily dependent on the state is closely contested by other professions, the profession is perpetually in a precarious position.

A final issue concerns the profession's sources of legitimacy. This issue comes close, I think, to involving the heart of the field.

Like so many other occupations, social work has emphasized rationalization and 'scientific' knowledge as its foundation. This language was central to the original formation of social work out of the various boundary disputes of the 1880s and 1890s. It was crucial to the consolidation of the profession after the Second World War. However, it works only within the profession. The larger public's image of social work is quite simple and well captured in the first sentence of the section on social work in the Bureau of Labor Statistics publication that thousands of vocational counsellors use to guide teenagers toward employment. Social workers, says the *Occupational Outlook Handbook*, 'help people'. The central public image and the central public legitimacy of social work come not from science, but from altruism.

Social work is unusual in having retained a public image based on a character trait. Most other professions have given up justifying themselves on the basis of character, which was the foundation of most professional authority in the nineteenth century. The military profession has turned 'from warriors to managers', the doctors from trusted health advisers to technological sorcerers. Social work has claimed to be scientific, but the public, which has changed its opinion of soldiers and now, at last, of doctors, seems unwilling to believe it. The altruist image is reinforced by social work's public connection with populations despised and feared by the general population – the poor, the criminal, the mentally ill. It is also reinforced by the field's pathetic salaries – on average, two-thirds of those of nurses with equivalent training – which the public imagines could attract only those whose true goal is to realize other values. I think that the public is not totally mistaken in this view. Social work does, both in my experience and in the historical record, have more altruists in it than most other professions. And social work schools do not stamp out idealism in quite the same way as do medical schools.

But altruism has a price. Along with the dispossession characteristic of many social work clients – the dispossession that calls for altruism in those who would help – goes another quality. Many of social work's clients are not so much dispossessed as politically controversial; not only the criminals, the poor and the mentally ill, but also the problem schoolchildren, the drunk drivers and the child abusers. Just as corporate lawyers benefit directly from the power, status and income of their wealthy clients, so also social workers suffer in the public eye from their client associations, even while the public expects social workers to keep these difficult people out of sight and mind and even though the public reserves the right to criticize. (One has only to read the self-righteous columnists of one's local papers to see social workers portrayed as villains in child abuse case after child abuse case.)

In its early years, social work had some protection in these attempts to specialize in the despised classes. There was the belief in science, of course, but there was also a powerful consortium of philanthropists, university professors, clergy and other social notables who supported the initial efforts of the profession. Those allies, it seems to me, have largely fallen away. Philanthropy itself has professionalized, and programme officers want to make their own reputations with creative new programmes rather than frankly facing the enormous problems confronting the old ones.

The environment, in fact, looks in many ways as it did one hundred years ago. Again, we have a welter of social services so confused that no one can figure it out. Again, the populations to be served are often both difficult and despised. Again, there is a diffuse sense that those institutions that ought to be caring for individual welfare in this society are failing in that task. It was from such a complex conjuncture that the old profession of social work emerged. It emerged through the drawing together of groups that represented particular sides of various debates over welfare. It was a coalition of diverse and diversely different groups, a 'social work of boundaries'. I think we are at a juncture where such a new coalition could easily emerge.

It is not clear to me what that coalition is, but I have a sense that it could be pulled together by linking those who are willing to think about new technologies for doing what we once called social work with those who want to take a life-course or long-range perspective on group and individual clients and with those who are not afraid to face squarely the political controversies that could lie ahead. It will be a surprising coalition; the new entity is not to be found by simply extending old debates. Social workers must look around at all the various controversies and envision a new way to pull various parts of them together. It will be, again, a social work of boundaries.

References

Abbott, A. (1988) *The System of Profession.* Chicago: University of Chicago Press.
Greenwood, E. (1957) Attributes of a profession, *Social Work* 2(3): 45–55.
Mohr, J. (1992) *Community, Bureaucracy and Social Relief.* PhD dissertation, Yale University.
Richmond, M. (1917) *Social Diagnosis: Russell Foundation.* New York: Sage.

8 Gender in law and the metaphor of Justice-as-a-Woman

An evolutionary socio-legal perspective

Vittorio Olgiati

Introduction

The aim of this chapter is to offer a general overview of historically determined socio-legal contexts, basic patterns and recurrent appraisals of a thousand-years-old metaphor: Justice-as-a-Woman. Starting from ancient civilizations, up to contemporary society, an unusual analytical approach will be provided to enlighten the case in point: the coupling of evolutionary dynamics of law-in-action, as a political-institutional device, and the idea of Justice as its basic frame of reference. Accordingly, pivotal epochal stages are outlined which, in the course of centuries, marked the recurrent 're-stylings' that – in different countries and for different reasons – characterized the updating of the metaphorical representation of Justice-as-a-Woman not only as a pivotal ideological *leitmotif*, but also as a veritable communicative mirror of the many facets that law-and-society entailed, and still entails, as regards pivotal socio-institutional human relationships.

For this purpose a variety of theoretical and empirical insights drawn from the sociology of law and the sociology of the legal profession will be outlined to offer an understanding of the relevance that the metaphorical image of Justice-as-a-Woman has had in the course of human civilizations, and relate it to what might be defined as the 'state-of-the-art' position that it has at present, in an age when growing numbers of women are officially provided with higher legal education and professional credentials that enable them to act in Law Courts. This makes for a veritable process of 'femininization' of legal practices and performances whose 'body of knowledge' is now available under the label of socio-legal 'gender studies'. To a large extent such studies have been oriented towards empirical surveys to provide data about the number, status and role of women involved in legal practice (Schultz and Shaw 2003): an enquiry whose interest was and still is indeed 'on demand' to monitor the dimensions and potential socio-legal consequences of such access on the broader dynamic of law-and-society at large. Yet, empirical surveys do not provide the valuable insights that are at the core of Law as an historically determined cultural domain and Law Courts as complex communicative systems. In this respect, it was not by chance that a socio-legal scholar such as Niklas Luhmann, in the Introduction of his work *Rechtssoziologie* (1972), explicitly defined the early empirical sociology of the legal profession as a 'sociology without law'. However, in spite of this, it is fair to add that the rise of 'Gender Studies' opened the way to a critical concern about official Law practices, Court decision making and even parliamentary legislation. This was epitomized by, for example, the study by Hanne Petersen (1996), who wrote from an explicit gender-oriented perspective in the significantly entitled *Home Knitted Law*, to fill the gap between the formal-official detachment of the idea of Justice in the practice of Law Courts and emphasize the need to reset the broader normative realm (Olgiati 2011).

Given the above, a basic question is still outstanding: if Gender Studies on the current feminization of the legal profession mark a significant epochal turn, can 'gender-oriented' legal performances and attitudes be conceived of as a signal for the rise of a new socio-legal age concerned with a great transformation, especially as regards the idea and the image of Justice? This question is not new and has been debated since ancient times. Indeed, even though the idea of Justice has often been related to the question of what sort of Law, it never hinged on the assessment of legal technique alone, but rather provided cognitive guidelines about specific human interactions, those of women included, up to the point where the self-same ideal of Justice was transformed into the metaphor of Justice-as-a-Woman. In this light, this study will explicitly use this ancient metaphorical model as an analytical frame of reference to enlighten its uninterrupted re-appraisal in the course of most relevant historical stages of Western civilizations. More precisely, an attempt will be made to outline the image of Justice-as-Woman not only as recurrent *leitmotif* in the long history of legal theory and practice, but also as a still pertinent conceptual tool to critically understand the contemporary interplay between law and society.

The early narrative on gender and law: the metaphor of the 'tree of life' in Eden's Garden

To understand the evolutionary social, political and institutional conditions that, over the course of centuries, allowed women to officially gain more or less generalized legal access to the legal profession, and consequently the power to act in Court, we need to look back thousands of years. Here we should note the extraordinary cultural impact of the *ratio juris* of a metaphor that can be found in the Bible, Genesis 2.9: the metaphor of the Tree of Life and the Trees of Knowledge of Good and Evil. As is well known, this original metaphor represents the unconstrained happiness of human conditions of Adam and Eve in Eden's Garden: a happiness, however, that was lost as soon as Eve, seduced by a snake, disregarded the warning made by God about the forbidden apple, offered it to Adam and both ate it. What then occurred to our ancestors – and it is occurring today – is equally well known: instead of living in peace and harmony forever, human beings were, and still are, routinely facing a variety of interpersonal conflicts, quarrels, fears and threats, each and all sooner or later requiring the authoritative enforcement of the power of Law as a quest for Justice.

The extraordinary historical importance of such a biblical metaphor for the history of human civilization, as well as the deep-rooted influential impact that it had on the evolutionary assessment of theories and practices about Law and Justice in the course of thousands of years is a matter of fact that cannot be ignored or undervalued. Since then, the symbolic value of the Tree of Life as well as the image of the Trees of Knowledge have been represented in different ways according to specific cultural traditions, as it is documented by a number of ancient books and paintings made in the course of different historical civilizational periods in areas such as the Middle East (Mesopotamia, Egypt), Europe (Greece, Italy), South America (pre-Columbian countries), Asia (India, China, Japan). So much so that the same metaphorical reference can be found in another ancient religious book: the *Rigveda*, a book in which the Tree of Life symbolically recalls the 'path of human life' between vices and virtues. In this respect, what is relevant for the historical evolution of basic peaceful human interactions and, consequently, for the practice of Law and the idea of Justice, is not only the bio-psychological difference between men and women, but also and, above all, the increasing structural/functional logic of the broader social dynamic based on the artificial construction of different binding social ladders: an enterprise that, in the course of centuries, has been theorized and performed as a pivotal political-institutional rule.

Bachofen's Mutterrecht: the first sociological theory about 'material' natural law

As is well known, rituals and the contents of ancient religions have been, and still are, precious sources of knowledge as regards the historical evolution of Law in different ages of civilization in different countries, as they provide a direct representation of the dialectical coupling between Law-as-fact and Justice-as-ideal. Having said this, however, it is impossible to ignore an additional side of the same coupling – that is, the cognitive insights provided by its original source: the law enforced since proto-historic times as a veritable 'material' natural law for explicit purposes of human survival. The very first study about the existence of such a material law in the early stages of human civilization is the book by Johannes Bachofen (1943) explicitly titled *Mutterrecht* (or 'Mother's Law'). Significantly, due to its singular theoretical framework, as well as its uncertain analytical sources, this study constitutes a unique masterpiece of the early rise of what has been, and is now, called the sociology of law.

The core issue of Bachofen's *Mutterrecht* is explicitly epitomized by the title – highlighting that women, in ancient times, assessed and ran a proper feminine legal system. Unfortunately, lacking full documentary evidence,

Bachofen could take advantage only of his selective perception of the inner meaning and value of the scanty variety of historical records that he had at hand. For this reason, his scientific research could be merely based on the remains of ancient symbolic representations of human interactions and social performances, or remains of ancient religious doctrines, ceremonies and rituals, as sources oriented towards the regulation of human life. However, altogether Bachofen was able to outline three main stages of socio-legal civilization as they developed in archaic societies of the Mediterranean area.

The first stage of civilization – defined as 'etherism' – was a stage of pure natural law: a law allowing the expression of human instincts, including free, spontaneous, occasional sexual interactions between men and women. This kind of law emphasized biological imperatives – survival and procreation – performed without any sort of limitations. The second stage of civilization occurred as soon as women were able to mix sexual intercourse and socio-psychological attitudes with direct reference to their 'norm-oriented' fertility, and therefore with the material value of 'natural' maternal law as a pivotal source of social life. In turn, and besides, women were able to relate such maternal law to the material rule-of-justice stemming from social interactions based on recurrent human reciprocation and revenge. To the extent that Nature, Law and Justice were evolutionary pillars of social dynamics, women gained the highest social, religious, political and legal status roles. Bachofen defined this historical period as the 'ginecocratic' stage of natural material law, otherwise called the actual law of material life and later defined it as 'equity' and 'justice' given the primacy of maternity. The third stage of civilization occurred at the time when men gained power, established a soldierly-driven political system and enforced new, harsh rules to radically deconstruct female-oriented natural law; in brief, all sort of public acts, including religious ceremonies in particular, turned entirely into male-ruled socio-legal performances. Such a new order was not based on customary rules, but on the new idea of *imperium* as a state form, defined according to the new notion of *public potestas* as the superior legal device of a veritable spiritual and paternal natural law called *jus positum*.

Unfortunately – as already outlined above – a number of theoretical insights and historical references provided by Bachofen's work were not supported by empirical evidence due to the lack of original documentary sources. For this reason, since its first edition, Bachofen's study has been disregarded as a proper 'scientific' work, to the point where it was disputed whether a 'female law' ever existed (Cantarella 1995). In spite of such criticisms, however, it is possible to argue the opposite – that in some historical circumstances women were able to create and enforce rules stemming from living imperatives of social life. At any rate, whether or not a *Mutterrecht* really existed, the whole study can be conceived of as a metaphorical socio-legal narrative, as Bachofen explicitly aimed to challenge the exclusive scientific validity of male-centred academic legal theories of his time.

Justice-as-a-Woman metaphors in early socio-legal systems

Having quoted Bachofen's work and outlined the different stages of civilization in which – according to his theoretical approach – a maternal law arose, developed and declined, it is now worth focusing on cultural legacies and institutional consequences of the law-in-action in subsequent periods of civilization. In this respect, what paradoxically becomes really significant is not so much the kind of production and enforcement of official rules and/or binding decisions, but the socio-political attempt to enforce highly refined communicative strategies of political governmentality, based on the coupling between Law and Justice by means of an explicit (and appealing) substantiation of the idea of Justice-as-a-Woman as a basic iconic communicative model.

According to Western literature specifically devoted to the topic (for example, Jacob 1994; Prosperi 2008; Sanza 2013; Sbriccoli 2003) the most ancient representation of the Justice-as-a-Woman metaphor dates back to ancient Egyptian civilization: it is a portrait of the Goddess Ma'At in the act of weighing the merits and faults of a dead human being. The portrait represents the Goddess holding in her hair, fixed by lace, an ostrich's feather, symbolic of equality of treatment. Metaphors of Justice-as-a-Woman were also recurrent communicative devices in the Middle East: for example, in ancient Mesopotamia the ideological-political meaning was the assessment of durable peaceful living conditions. As far as European countries were concerned, historical records show that in ancient Greece the Justice-as-a-Woman metaphor was epitomized by two different divine female figures: the Goddess Themis (Justice) provided with the power to address and assess her decisions, and the Goddess Hestia (Essence) – mentioned by Plato – enacting law-making according to what had resulted in a just and truthful manner in the course of cross-examination in Court. In early narratives Hestia (renamed Vesta in ancient Rome) was also represented as the only Goddess who, being the essence of anything that is becoming, was placed at the centre of the Universe and conceived of as immovable.

In ancient Rome recurrent metaphorical images were those of the Goddess Vesta and Dike (otherwise called Astrea) who, under the label of Ore lived in the sky – both held in their hands a scale and a sword while keeping their eyes wide open. Mention should also be made to a marble *bas-relief* at the *Ara Pacis Augustae* in Rome, dated from the thirteenth century before Christ. It shows different ways in which women wore the toga, at that time called *toga virilis*, as a rule borne by high-ranking men with high civil and religious status roles. Among symbolic devices that for ages provided specific communicative meanings to either printed or carved metaphorical images of Justice-as-a-Woman in ancient Rome, the following tools had the highest normative value and the most meaningful socio-political implications: the *Scale,* held with the right hand, as a symbol of equity based on circumspection and mature deliberation; the open or blinded *Eyes* (later on: the

Bandage), symbol of neutrality, impartiality and equality; the *Sword,* symbol
of power and severity, held, by rule, by the left hand, as a male icon of the
sun; the *Seat,* symbol of clemency and repair, which allows the right *Leg* with
an uncovered *Knee* to be held out, ideally to allow concerned human beings
to embrace it as a significant juncture of the body.

The above metaphorical mix of material and symbolic items concerned
with the image of Justice-as-a-Woman in ancient Rome never implied a confu-
sion or overlap about its basic meaning, as for centuries the theoretical and
empirical contents of official law and legal culture were based on the unquestioned narrative of Roman mythological Law-and-Justice's interplay, explicitly based on a *politeist* religious system centred on feminine features – epitomized
by the Goddess Themis (Justice), daughter of Sky and Land, surrounded by
three other Goddesses provided with specific high qualities: Minerva (Wisdom),
Venus (Beauty), Cerere (Fertility), They were accompanied by the virgin Ves-
tals to keep apart male Gods epitomized by Mercury (God of Thieves), Mars
(God of War) and Bacchus (God of Intemperateness) whose tasks were concerned with robberies, misconduct and harsh conflicts. Such a mythological
narrative began to be put into question and lose its own original socio-legal
meaning as soon as women were allowed to practice law, as their interpretations of legal doctrine and their attitudes in and out of Court proceedings
were a matter of scrutiny at official levels. Critical evaluations became increasingly generalized in the course of time, as they matched the broader
socio-institutional crisis that later led to the fall of the Roman Empire – when
the number of women acting as legal practitioners was growing and, as a
reaction, anti-feminist speeches and works such as those made by renowned
jurists such as Papinian, Ulpian and Gaius began to have a large resonance.
According to Papinian, for example, women's condition and performance had
to be conceived of as inferior to that of men, while, according to Ulpian,
women could not be judges or hold a magistracy or bring a lawsuit or act as
procurators because 'they are like children'.

Needless to say, such critical statements deeply undermined the traditional
ideal of the feminine as a valuable representative agent of both Justice and
Law. In turn, due to ongoing arguments about women's *infirmitas sexus,*
only a relatively small number of women – thanks to their high social status,
brilliant personalities and individual intellectual gifts – were able to react and
continue to act in Court on behalf of their own or other people's interests.
This was, for instance, the case with women such as Lelia, mentioned by
Quintilian; Lauronia and Manilia, who become targets in a *satira* by Giove-
nale; Amnesia and Ortensia, both quoted for their different attitudes in
Court; and Afrania, recorded by Ulpian as *improbissima foemina.* Some
other women, whose names are not known, were able to act as Arbitrators
up to the time of the Emperor Justinianus, when their right to act was officially abolished. In any case, what actually caused a significant change as
regards women as legal practitioners was the rise and spread of two radically
different, but intertwined, epochal developments: the diffusion of the

Christian religion and the fall of the Roman Empire. In this respect, it is worth noting that women were actually among the most reactive agents able to cope with such new cultural, legal and political patterns.

At the same time, however, basic traits of the Justice-as-a-Woman metaphor were still pivotal reference frames for socio-legal systems in other countries. In this regard, the case of a Far Eastern country such as Japan is quite interesting. Indeed, given the slow and difficult communicative linkages across the world, it is still possible to hypothesize that there was a flow of such metaphorical traits. Under the legal domain of the Samurai – twelfth century AD – Justice was represented as a well-dressed young Virgin with long black hair; provided with a mirror, symbol of truth; and holding the sword-of-paradise, these being the items established according to the Confucian principles of the first rule of the perfect Samurai (Mazzoleni 2015).

Law, policy and justice as a gender issue in the Middle Ages: the case of English Common Law

The epochal changes that occurred in Europe as a consequence of the fall of the Roman Empire and the spreading of Christian religion cannot be fully understood without reference to the so-called barbarian invasions and the long duration of their original socio-legal, political-institutional and religious imprint. In this respect, the most significant turn *vis-à-vis* the previous Roman Empire was not so much due to different normative patterns enforced in different European regions, but the enforcement of a new, unexpected, constitutional model by a woman called Teodolinda, daughter of the Duke of Bavaria and an active supporter of anti-Arian factions. In 589 Teodolinda married Autari, the King of the Longobards in Milan. On Autari's death, she married the Duke of Turin, who in 616 also died. After the death of her second husband, she officially proclaimed in 625 her takeover of the Longobards' kingdom as Queen in order to ensure the lineage of the ruling family to her young son Adaloaldo. Such an extraordinary constitutional takeover – gained without bloodshed – not only opened the way to new concerns about women's social, institutional and political commitment at a time of harsh, conflictual institutional conditions in which women's rights were not equal to those of men, but also established what is still a basic general principle of the royal Common Law system, as epitomized by the monarchical models currently in force in England and Holland.

Yet all that shines is not necessarily gold. What has been said above occurred at nearly the same time as the enforcement of the well-known Salic Law, which was updated three times between 511 and 597 and revised twice, in 763–64 and 768–79, to regulate women's entitlement to royal succession to the Crown (Hotman 1686). The issue was debated with reference to the most renowned Roman Law doctrines, among which – not by chance – those professed by Ulpian and Papinian, whose legal statements, according to the Law of Quotations published in 426 by Theodosius II and Valentinianus III, could not be put under discussion by any judge. Significantly, however, the anti-feminist content of such a Law raised a strong reaction in England, as the attempt to restrain female rights was clearly contrary to the inner *ratio juris* of the customary principles and practices of English Law.

The harsh debate about women's socio-legal standing raised by the interpretation of Salic Law left a deep mark in the course of the following centuries throughout all Europe, as it revolved around the evolutionary characters of the theory and practice of political-constitutional systems. Yet, in spite of this mark, ancient iconographic traits of Justice-as-a-Woman neither changed nor withered away, as documented by a statement written as early as 1320 by a French theologian, Jean de Hesdin, to any potential portrait-painter: "What will we make clear about this? Firstly to be depicted as a virgin, because justice must be certain and is immaculate and uncorrupted" (quoted by Ripa 2011). The above debate, however, reached a veritable turning point in the fourteenth century, when a French woman of Italian origin, Cristine de Pizan, published a book entitled *Le Livre de la Citè des Dames* [The Book of the City of Ladies] (de Pizan 1999). This book explicitly advocated, among other things, women's authority as a mirror of their own skills and knowledge in contrast to recurrent criticism about legal incompetence and emotional ineptitude in public affairs, and promoted the right, as learned women, to hold a special position at political and constitutional levels as in early medieval law. This claim involved not only replacing the traditional male head of the political body with a female one, but also raising attention to the popular calls for a female-oriented administration of Justice (Gianlongo 2005).

The extraordinary resonance that de Pizan's book had throughout Europe was further emphasized by its translation into English in 1521, historically epitomized by advancement of the debate on rights already going on in England. Indeed, as has been shown by Peter Goodrich (1993) in an essay significantly titled 'Gynaetopia: Feminine genealogies of Common Law', since the Middle Ages the attempt to undermine the customary rationale of women's socio-legal standing in ancient English Law was repeatedly contradicted by English jurists by not only asserting a variety of evidence about local living experiences and jurisprudential guidelines, but also by recalling the symbolic and material value of the notion of Justice. In this light, it is by no means surprising that the same debate deepened throughout subsequent centuries. Proof of such a reactive move is provided by a number of written sources, among which – according to Goodrich – special relevance needs to be accorded to works written by English scholars such as John Fortescue in 1466 and John Selden in 1610. Such works benefit from the ongoing continental debate on the advocacy of feminine causes to challenge the *ratio* of the rules of civil Roman Law, still included in English Common Law, concerning the limited legal status role of women. In brief, they provided clear documentary evidence that such a space-time technical/logical contradiction not only was merely extemporary, but also emphasized the normative value of the 'two faces of Justice', that is, the 'truth of justice' revealed by reason and the 'truth of justice' as a proper feminine character. They were therefore two sides of the same coin which, on the one hand, were an explicit sign of both the grace and providence of the laws of nature, and, on the other, proved the historically determined mismatch of the dual normative facets – civil and common – of the self-same English Law at both legal and constitutional levels.

In Fortescue's work, in particular, such a Janus-headed duality was also a mirror of the intertwining of a number of socio-legal experiences due to the variety of historically determined cultural and institutional changes. A plurality and variety of issues that the metaphor of what Fortescue called the *prosographia* of the 'feminine face of Justice' reflects the inner value of the concurrent logic of what Selden, in his turn, called the *prosopopeia*. This metaphor allows us to ascribe different meanings – such as nature, culture and habits – to law. Some scholars at the time considered all the basic Common Law sources concerning women – statutes, cases, opinions, sayings, arguments and judgements – related to women's interests, duties and advantages. Accordingly, almost all recurrent socio-legal relationships in which women were concerned or involved were discussed with specific regard to the impact upon their sexual difference, so as to outline either good and valuable patterns or questionable character and bad effects.

The Renaissance ideals: towards new visions of Justice-as-a-Woman

From the thirteenth to the seventeenth century in England the main focus as regards legal and constitutional issues was oriented towards solving the mismatch between the original male and female, civil and common, normative technicalities of Common Law. Meanwhile in continental Europe the same focus was theoretically and empirically oriented towards the assessment of new legal systems in which the idea of Justice had to be culturally and politically secularized to officially match it with the new ideological imperatives of 'good government' as well as 'fair law making and fair sentences' proclaimed by newly established ducal and royal powers. In this respect, a major effort to assess the legitimacy of such new constitutional systems was devoted to politically exploiting once again the communicative potential of ancient metaphorical narratives by substantially reframing and updating their original rationale in line with two new opposite epochal developments: on the one hand, the standing of learned women in society and, on the other, the reaction against rising schismatic religious movements such as the Lutheran Reform. Evidence of such mainstream movements can be summarized here with reference to Italy.

As regards women's legal learning, the newly created educational system – the University – somehow allowed selective access of women into Law Faculties. In turn, the lack of explicit rules about legal practice made it possible for some women to act in Court. This was so in the case of Galeana Salvioli from Bologna, Domitilla Trivulzi from Milan and Isotta Nogarola from Verona. Other women, such as Accursia, Bettisia Gozzadini, Milanzia dall'Ospedale and Bettina Calderini, having obtained a Law degree, were entitled to teach law in Law Faculties. In their turn, Giovanna Bianchetti and Maddalena Buonsignori became renowned jurists, while Eleonora d'Arborea gained a high reputation as a judge and legislator. In fact, Eleonora d'Arborea, acting as Queen of the land of Arborea in Sardinia, in 1395 promulgated a revolutionary Statute – the *Carta de Logu* – stating the equal standing of all citizens before the law, including the principle of equality of treatment between brothers and sisters in the matter of the law of succession. The cultural wave fostered by the Renaissance also allowed a further leap ahead as regards higher education in general, and legal education in particular, conceived of as a professional source. This was shown by the case of Giustina de Rocca, who acted as lawyer and judge and followed a diplomatic career, Prospera Porzia Malvezzi from Bologna, Emilia Brembati from Bergamo, Vittoria Galeota from Napoli and Maria Vittoria Delfini-Dosi. A special mention is also deserved by Maria Pellegrina Amoretti, who, having achieved a law degree at the University of Pavia, published in Latin a study to support the legal principle of equal rights between men and women (Olgiati 2003).

Given the above, the metaphor of Justice-as-a-Woman was instrumentally valued at both political and communicative levels – at a political level in order to emphasize the legacy of late outcomes of the 'Fights-for-Investitures' (ended in 1122) as epitomized by the icon of Justice as a *Roman Eagle* and as a symbol of *Remission of Sins* in the Universal Judgment, and at a communicative level in order to assess the new ruling elite's institutional cultural policy about law-and-order, as epitomized by the number of artistic works specifically devoted to represent Justice as a communicative metaphor by the most renowned painters of the time (Jacob 1994).

In 1302/1305 Giotto painted Justice-as-a-Woman with the *Scale*, to represent the Court's decisions as assessments of a balanced status in civil life preventing corrupt judges from acting according to their own will; the *Sword*, complemented by body armour; and the *Seat*, as mercy and generosity. Giotto also painted a Universal Judgement in the Scrovegni's Chapel in which he distinguished Virtues from Vices. In this painting, he represented *Justice* as a woman and *Injustice* as a man: one in Paradise, holding neither a balance – as she uses her hands to weigh the issue at stake – nor a bandage, to evaluate the same issue; and the other in Hell, acting as a judge, wearing royal clothes and holding a staff. In 1311 the sculptor Giovanni Pisano did not represent Justice-as-a-Women as sovereign power, but as an agent able to dispense grace, as a sign of temperance. In 1337 Ambrogio Lorenzetti painted Justice either as a virtue stemming from God or as a real woman providing peace, order and remissions of sins. From 1359 onwards a number of other artists painted, printed or sculptured Justice holding both swords and scales as still suggested by ancient Roman tradition. Andrea Mantegna in 1489 painted Justice with ears and sight. Sebastian Brant in 1494 made the very first portrait of Justice-as-a-Woman with a bandage, as a sign of judges' impartiality and incorruptibility. Albrecht Dürer in 1499 painted Justice as either a godly or human woman to emphasize the value of Law. From 1508 to 1511 Raffaello Sanzio also painted Justice holding both sword and scale, according to the classic model.

Yet, in 1558 at the rising apex of the Inquisition, Peter Brueghel painted a bandaged Justice, in a city square where hay-forks, gallows, stakes and torture covered the whole space. About a century later, in 1649, Theodor van Thulden painted the kiss of Justice and Peace to epitomize the Westphalian Peace Treaty. In turn, as late as 1712, Hugo Grotius put on the title-page of his masterpiece *De Jure Belli ac Pacis Libri Tres* a traditional Justice-as-a-Woman provided with a bandage, sword and scale. As can be seen, in about two centuries only, the thousand-year-old metaphorical meaning of Justice-as-a-Woman endured the most radical overlapping meanings that have ever occurred!

The Enlightenment's turn: law as a mirror of metaphorical constitutional principles

The above-mentioned painting by Brueghel as early as 1558 against the horrors of the Inquisition's legal policy cannot be undervalued, as, since then onwards, the image of Justice-as-a-Woman could not be heralded anymore as a univocal model provided by a univocal meaning. So much it was and it is so that in 1737, Johann Preysler painted a quite surprising paradoxical blind Justice, in a world enlightened by Law. By contrast, the title-page of a Court sentence concerning a woman, pronounced in Rome in 1770, showed the female image of Justice without a bandage, but provided – as occurred in ancient Roman Empire – with a scale and a Roman axe, typical icons of the self-same Inquisition.

Yet this is not all. As an explicit reaction against the socio-institutional impact of the Inquisition's bloody proceedings, as early as 1622, Lorenzo Priori radically overturned both the whole meaning and nature of the metaphor: he did not print in the title-page of a volume entitled *Pratica Criminale* a Justice-as-a-Woman image at all, but the city of Venice without a bandage, with a *Scale* (the feminine symbol of the moon) and a *Sword* (the masculine symbol of the sun) to show an actual example of fair and ordered living conditions. At the same time, an equally renowned artist such as Veronese painted in his turn a similar metaphor: Venice sustained by Peace and Justice. In the course of this, he made two marble statues representing Venice-as-Justice – one provided with a *Sword* and *Scale*, the other evoking the image of a fair socio-political life in Venice's Ducal Palace.

As we can clearly understand, the fact that the self-same Republic of Venice, as such, turned out as a model of Justice was remarkable: for the first time the ancient Justice-as-a-Woman icon was dropped abruptly, and a 'State-model' was heralded as a living metaphor of what has been – and is now – called the

'Rule-of-Law'. Accordingly, since then the ideal of a fair social, legal and political life was not related to the age-old image of Justice anymore as it was before, but rather grounded directly on the qualitative nature of governments as provided by the use of Law-as-Reason, supported, in turn, by two new metaphors: the *Light of Knowledge* and the *Reflexivity of Mirrors*. As regards the *Light of Knowledge*, there is no need to recall here its ancient content including moral ideals. Equally, as regards the *Reflexivity of Mirrors*, there is no need to emphasize – as Jeremy Bentham outlined in his Panopticon – its potential to improve the *Light of Knowledge*, as mirrors merely replicate the variety of visual perceptions of what is defined as 'scientific' reality.

Yet, what has been just said is not all. The fact is that the 'Enlightenment's turn' implied a radical cultural, political and institutional reframing of the self-same idea of Justice as a reflexive hypostatization of any particular State's model: a matter that could not but raise a reaction on the part of other States run according to different socio-legal orders. So much so that visitors to the Royal Palace of Caserta, built by the Bourbons near Naples from the second half of the eighteenth century onwards, enter a large hall and see a painting on the ceiling representing the ancient Roman Goddess Astrea – Justice – surrounded, on the one hand, by Hercules (symbol of mighty force) and, on the other, by *Truth* and *Innocence* (symbols of the human quest for salvation), both compelling *Prepotence*, *Ignorance* and *Error* – typical patterns that go against *Reason* – to go away. The metaphorical message that such a painting still provides at a structural/functional level is clear: the new image of Justice not only cannot be let alone, but also can successfully be enacted only by virtue of the subsidiary efforts of other agents provided by singular skills, techniques and expertise supported by their specialized legal Knowledge, Power-to-Act, and Truth searching devices. In other words, the new theoretical and practical conception of Justice turned out as a part of the new 'Doctrine of State's Interests', otherwise called its *Raison d'Etat*, whose performances necessarily implied new systemic couplings and new socio-legal intertwining supported by utilitarian and managerial use of both Law, as a technique, and Justice, as a goal. Given all the above, it is not surprising that – due to such a radical ideological turn – a number of enlightened legal scholars, such as Cesare Beccaria, became strong promoters of the Universal Rights' Declaration, enforced in 1789: a legal act that Francisco Goya epitomized with two metaphorical paintings on 'The Divine Reason' (1804–26): one in which Justice does not hold the sword, and the other in which Justice holds a Law book.

The age of law as a system: claims for rights, the impact of mass media and the idea of justice

Among the most relevant outcomes of the Enlightenment concerning law-in-action and law-in-theory was the assessment of two new conceptions of *Reason* as a primary guideline of/for social order, although Justice played a basic role: the first one was epitomized by Montesquieu's new metaphor of a social dynamic governed by the rational logic of the *esprit des lois*, and the other was outlined by Rousseau, representing the metaphor of 'human life' as a primary condition of/for socio-legal progress and a basic ethical value. Within this ideological and political frame of reference the 1789 Declaration of Universal Rights was heralded as a major stepping point. Paradoxically, however, it was not at all of use to actually allow women to gain full citizenship rights equal to men, even in spite of the record of women's legal expertise from the thirteenth to the seventeenth centuries. Within this general context a utilitarian and managerial use of both Law and Justice and Law as Justice was increasingly undertaken based on the criteria outlined by Bentham's Panopticon. In turn, a significant role was also played by new epochal developments such as nationalism as a civil and political ideology, social movements as instrumental political procedures, and economic conflicts as outcomes of the ongoing mode of production.

Given the above, the rise of women's movements claiming to be officially entitled to practice law in Court deserve a special mention here. Of particular interest is the case raised in the last decades of the nineteenth century by Lidia Poet from Turin, as she was the very first woman in Europe whose application to the local Bar to be enrolled as lawyer was officially accepted. This enrolment, however, was immediately revoked by the Court of Appeal in Turin in 1883 and a year later the same judgement was confirmed by the Court of Cassation. Meanwhile, though, Poet's case gained a wider, long lasting, international resonance (Olgiati 2003) – so much so that this early attempt opened the way to the first official entry of a woman to the contemporary legal professional system in Sweden in 1897. Since then, up to 1930, almost all European States allowed qualified women to act as lawyers in Court. The entry of women in Courts as judges occurred much later, around the 1950s. Since then, the feminization of legal professionalism – as is well known – shows a rising exponential curve, while, by contrast, the idea of Justice has been subsumed *de facto* into the jurisprudential rationale of written nation-states' constitutions, thereby raising a question that cannot be avoided: what kind of idea of Justice acted, and still acts today, as a complement to and/or fulfilment of Court decision making and Law-in-action?

Paradoxically, an answer to the above question can be found beyond and outside the province of official Law and traditional theories of Justice, as it implies a direct reference to socio-legal expectations outside the State and within society. It also implies innovative theoretical and normative devices able to shape social dynamics, among which, in particular, are those fostered by what we now call extra-State high-tech governmentality and mass media communication. In this respect, a significant development as regards the common understanding of the form and substance of the interplay between Law and Justice was made, first, by the scientific assessment of biological metaphors related to human life and social environment grounded on Darwin's concepts of 'evolution' and 'organism' and, second, by the use of such biological metaphors as sociological concepts within the new disciplinary area of the Sociology of Law (Rottleutner 1986). In turn, since its early assessment, the formal/official enforcement of positive law as a State-run legal system led not only to the once sacral value of law's production and enforcement to wither away, but also to a search for empirical evidence to assess 'judicial truths' increasingly based on cultural premises, political issues and ideological aims that reject sacred and moral evaluations and directly call for factual cognition and actual experience.

In this respect, a remarkable critical example is provided by the number of paintings made, from the last decades of the nineteenth century and the first decades of the twentieth century, by Gustav Klimt, all of which are explicitly reactive against the Justice system in force at his time. In fact, Klimt's paintings represent the traditional metaphor of Justice-as-a-Woman, which are not in line with the traditional historical model at all. Indeed, all his paintings show the image of beautiful women, dressed according to the *belle époque* fashion, but Klimt variously titled them in a harshly critical vein as, amongst other labels, 'disgraceful jurisprudence', 'naked truth', 'golden tarot' and 'dark machine'.

What actually paved the way to such an explicit deconstruction of the age-old meaning of the image of Justice cannot be understated: the rise of the epochal crisis of State-run positive law as univocal *ratio juris* (Romano 1910) and, after the First World War, the rise of a new type of social communication: that of the mass media – including, in particular, the daily news, film movies and, later, TV series. Such new tools not only enabled the dissemination of a mix of real and/or fictional pictures about the dynamics of Law and society, but also emphasized emotional events such as social disasters and criminal actions as sources of social attraction able to enlarge their share of the audience (Brint 1994). In this respect, written and visual transmission of socio-legal events in which the Law is at stake do not actually raise today any stable ideal of Justice, but rather opportunities for entertainment, debate and show business. Indeed, the kind of communication provided by mass media and high-tech devices do not offer a univocal meaning or reference model, and even less enhance a shared narrative of the socio-legal value concerning what both Law and Justice could and/or should be able to achieve – so much so, that, paradoxically enough, in an age of feminization of the legal profession and legal pluralism, the metaphor of Justice-as-a-Woman does not anymore have an unquestioned and meaningful appeal.

Conclusion

Having outlined basic historical records on the topic of this essay, the inner meaning of the above mentioned metaphors of Justice-as-a-Woman constructed by Gustav Klimt cannot be underestimated: they were, and still are, an explicit sign of cultural complaint (and socio-legal reaction) against the whole domain of what is now called 'governmentality' – a domain that, at present, is characterized by a widespread institutional fragmentation leading, in its turn, to a veritable technical and political destabilization of all basic areas of the jurisdiction of Justice (Commaille 1999). Such a destabilization is connected to the rise of new goals and performance of national systems of Justice at the territorial level that undermine intimate human feelings and expectations at the broader social level. As a consequence of this trend, it is not by chance that – lacking strong ethical constraints – current outcomes, such as the so-called miscarriage of Justice might foster what has been, and continues to be, labelled from an evolutionary socio-legal perspective 'vindictive Justice' (Terradas Saborit 2008).

References

Bachofen, J. J. (1943) Das Mutterrecht. In: J. J. Bachofen (ed) *Gesammelte Werke.* Basel: K. Meuli.

Brint, S. (1994) *In an Age of Experts. The Changing Role of Professionals in Politics and Public Life.* Princeton: Princeton University Press.

Cantarella, E. (1995) *L'Ambiguo Malanno: La Donna nell'Antichità Greca e Romana.* Milano: Einaudi.

Commaille, J. (1999) La déstabilisation des territories de justice, *Droit et Société* 42(43): 239–64.

de Pizan, C. (1999) *The Book of the City of Ladies.* London: Penguin.

Gianlongo, A. (2005) *Donne di Palazzo Nelle Corti Europee, Tracce e Forme di Potere dall'Età Moderna.* Milano: Unicopli.

Goodrich, P. (1993) Gyneatopia: Feminine genealogies of Common Law, *Journal of Law and Society* 20: 276–308.

Hotman, A. (1686) *Traitè de la Loi Salique in Opuscules Francoises des Hotmans.* Paris: M. Gullieme.

Jacob, R. (1994) *Images de la Justice: Essay sur l'Iconographie Judiciaire du Moyen Age à l'Age Classique.* Paris: Le Leopard d'Or.

Luhmann, N. (1972) *Rechtssoziologie.* Hamburg: Rowohlt Taschenbuch Verlag.

Mazzoleni, E. (2015) Iconologia Giapponese della giustizia: Tre ikonemi, *Heliopolis: Culture, Civiltà, Politca* 13(1): 85–92.

Olgiati, V. (2003) Professional body and gender difference in court: The case of the first (failed) woman lawyer in modern Italy. In: U. Schultz and G. Shaw (eds) *Women in the World's Legal Professions.* Oxford: Hart.

Olgiati, V. (2011) On women lawyers' voice in Europe: Scenarios for a legal education agenda. In: J. Langer (ed) *Analysis and Visions for Europe: Theories and General Issues.* Frankfurt-am-Main: Peter Lang.

Petersen, H. (1996) *Home Knitted Law: Norms and Values in Gendered Rule-Making.* London: Dartmouth Publishing.

Prosperi, A. (2008) *Giustizia Bendata: Percorsi Storici di una Immagine.* Torino: Einaudi.

Ripa, C. (2011) *Iconologia dall'Antichità e da Altri Luoghi.* Charleston: Nabu Press.

Romano, S. (1910) Lo stato moderno e la sua crisi. In: G. Zanobini (ed) *Scritti Minori*, Volume I. Milano: Giuffré.

Rottleutner, H. (1986) Les metaphors biologiques dans le pensée juridique, *Archives de Philosophie du Droit* 31: 215–44.

Sanza, M. T. (2013) *Le Narrazioni della Legge*. Napoli: ESI.

Sbriccoli, M. (2003) *La Benda della Giustizia*. Ordo Juris. Milano: Giuffré.

Schultz, U. and Shaw, G. (eds) (2003) *Women in the World's Legal Professions*. Oxford: Hart.

Terradas Saborit, I. (2008) *Justicia Vindicatoria: Consejo Superior de Investigaciones Científicas*. Madrid: Fareso.

9   Engineering the soul
Construction and sacrifice in the teaching profession

Lixian Jin and Martin Cortazzi

Introduction: metaphors and teachers

This chapter focuses on the profession of teaching seen through an analysis of metaphors in China and Iran. We first examine public discourse metaphors for teachers which are circulated by Chinese policymakers and the media: some are significant elements in ancient Confucian traditions. Mainly we investigate the metaphors for teachers held by current teachers themselves (the professionals) and by students (their clients) to show far more complex relations. Through metaphor analysis we demonstrate networks between technical-cognitive dimensions of the profession (where the teacher is 'an engineer' who constructs knowledge and skills in society) and aspects often overlooked by those working outside education: affective, aesthetic, moral and spiritual dimensions ('the soul') in which teachers in China and Iran are presented as providers of warmth, care, cultivation and beauty and as moral and spiritual exemplars (symbolized as teachers who 'sacrifice'). Such Chinese and Iranian metaphors have social implications for the teaching profession elsewhere and applications in internationalizing contexts.

Scholars have long since considered that metaphors are important for learning and, therefore, to teaching and to considerations of teaching as a profession. Thus in ancient China, well before the second century BC, judging by the Confucian classic the *Li Ji* [Book of Rites]: "The scholars of ancient times learned the truth about things from analogies" (cited in Lin 1938:250). Current cognitive approaches to metaphors see this kind of analogical leap as essential to thought (for instance, Gibbs 2008; Holyoak and Thagard 1996; Lakoff and Johnson 1980; Ortony 1993) and therefore to reflective thinking and learning about, with or from professions. Essentially, in this context, a metaphor is a comparison through the transfer of meaning. In the cognitive linguistic terms used here, for the metaphor: 'A teacher is the sun', the 'target' (i.e. the topic) is the teacher and the 'source' for the comparison is the sun. The source (usually a more familiar or better understood element) is used to generate inferences ('entailments') about the target in order to make essential or perhaps overlooked points or to present ideas framed through different angles of vision.

For 'a teacher is the sun' metaphor, users participate interactively by seeking systematic correspondences ('mappings') about the relevant elements, perhaps as part of an overall pattern or schema involving more linked metaphors ('a metaphor network'). Using students' words, the sun has 'energy' and 'warmth' and is 'essential for life and growth' – in this view, teachers show such qualities. The target-source relations involve uncertainty about which features of the source are relevant in teaching contexts. They involve ambiguity: metaphor users often see different possible interpretations, especially from personal, traditional, institutional or socio-cultural variations in framing. Metaphors involve creativity: entailments can surprise us through extension beyond an obvious range by using prior knowledge relationships about or within the source. So here, the sun as 'a source of light' uses the common metaphor of 'knowledge is light' to represent how teachers give knowledge, illumine the mind, and aid enlightenment. However, our research shows an extension to the metaphor in China: to give us light and warmth, the sun burns itself up, suggesting a theme of teacher 'sacrifice' for the benefit of learners and society. In Iran, our investigations show sacrifice in the same metaphor is elaborated by combining entailments: the sun can be used for spatial orientation, direction and guidance, so a teacher gives guidance through devotion and the sacrifice of burning up. This gives extra nuances to Western notions of 'teacher burn-out'.

This example may suggest some social implications for the teaching profession. The study of such metaphors broadens the range of public perceptions of teachers and brings different insights. This is significant because teaching as a profession has the distinctive element that everyone as a learner has experienced the work of teachers practically daily and continually over years of schooling. Such personal images derived from schooling are necessarily limited and are often memories dated by at least one generation. Within education, researchers have investigated metaphors with a number of purposes, including: first, to refine, elaborate and extend their metaphors – especially for trainee teachers – because they are considered influential for classroom practice; second, to examine teachers' ideas about their profession; third, to examine students' conceptions of teachers, which is vital to develop learner-centred approaches; fourth, to ascertain the roles of metaphors in the classroom and within educational discourse; fifth, in multicultural and international contexts of education, to compare metaphors cross-culturally and interculturally and hence explore different cultural orientations to teaching and learning (Cameron 2003; Cortazzi and Jin 1999, 2012, 2013, 2014; Jin and Cortazzi 2011b, 2013; Wan and Low 2015).

The metaphor 'a teacher is the sun' might be considered teacher centred (in a heliocentric classroom or education system); however, these entailments show it to be quite learner centred (giving students knowledge and developing student growth). For parents and policymakers, the cognitive aspects are in general publicly acknowledged, but perhaps the affective dimensions (giving warmth) are overlooked, while the professional dedication and dimension of sacrifice seem virtually ignored in public debate about teaching in Europe or North America. Greater recognition of these dimensions might aid appreciation of the profession and enhance its public status. This is important not just to benefit teachers but also to support education and therefore to benefit learners. Thus the Chinese and Iranian metaphor meanings studied here may bring humane insights for Western discussions of professions. They may have application in contexts of teaching international students from locations where such metaphors prevail. If, for instance, students expect warmth and sacrifice from Western teachers and for some reason fail to see these dimensions evident in classrooms, they may feel disappointed or disillusioned, with potential consequences for their participation and learning (Cortazzi and Jin 2013).

The main emphasis of this chapter, though, is to present analyses of metaphors concerning the profession of teachers in China and Iran. Our datasets are elicited from participants within education who are both teachers and students. With reference to China, we give significant examples of metaphors used frequently in public discourse: these construct the teaching profession from outside. This provides a broad and significant perspective, since teachers in China work in the largest education system and represent the largest number of teachers in any country (around 13 million). Within professional contexts we then examine widespread examples of metaphors from our research data concerning teachers in China and in Iran, as a potentially contrasting case. We analyze metaphors as 'metaphor networks' and 'landscapes' or patterns of metaphors and entailments to give a picture of teachers from inside Chinese and Iranian cultures. This shows some of the richness and complexity of professions and metaphors.

Teachers as engineers and cultivators

The phrase 'engineer of human souls' was apparently coined by Yury Olesha, a Russian writer who used it humorously while meeting Stalin in the house of Maxim Gorky; Stalin later cited 'writers are engineers of human souls' at a 1932 writers' conference giving impetus to the notion that professional writers and intellectuals are essentially in the service of the state. This became most visible in a literary movement known as 'Soviet Realism' (Westerman 2011). The connection of the phrase specifically with teachers emerges in the long novel by Skvorecky (1984), *The Engineer of Human Souls*, in which a Czech professor of literature (like the author), having left his country with the entry of Soviet troops in 1968, works with students in Canada to teach them about seven writers, interspersing this with flashbacks and reminiscences of his life in the Nazi and Soviet eras.

In China, Deng Xiaoping reintroduced the phrase in 1979 after the Cultural Revolution to emphasize the role of writers, artists and intellectuals in 'ideological education of the masses' (Pantsov and Levine 2015). The metaphor had already made its way into official Chinese descriptions of teachers in the 1950s as part of a stream of metaphors designed to construct the profession in public campaigns (Jin and Cortazzi 2011a), then under the Soviet Union's influence. Teachers in China as 'engineers of the soul' were seen mechanistically in the positive socialist terms of the 1950s and 1960s as 'brain power labourers', 'advanced producers', 'machine tool makers', and 'people's heroes'. In some periods, notably during the Great Leap Forward (1958–1959) and the Cultural Revolution (1966–1976), most teachers were officially seen as obstacles who represented 'bourgeois' or 'feudal' groups who were said to be holding back progress. Many teachers were openly reviled as 'freaks' and 'monsters' or 'stinking number nines' – a category which put teachers in ninth place in a publicized list of 'enemies of the people'. With others they were publicly shamed and often exiled to remote rural areas for 're-education'. A few teachers perceived as having an acceptable political alignment were 'weapons in the class struggle', 'warriors' and 'red thinkers'. In the 1980s and 1990s, technical-mechanistic metaphors for the profession were popular: 'technicians', 'machinists', and again 'engineers of the soul'. As engineers, teachers are seen as technical professionals using tools and machines to provide knowledge and skills for students: they 'construct the nation'.

However, some popular images for teachers of the 1960s and 1980s have humane and moral associations that go beyond the merely technical. Teachers were often described as 'red and expert': 'expert' encapsulates the technical skills or cognitive expertise, while 'red' has more than the obvious socialist colouring overtones because it is held to signify moral worth. Similarly, in the commonplace 1980s Chinese term for 'education', *jiao yu* ('teaching and cultivating') or *jiao shu yu ren* ('teaching books and cultivating people'), the scholarly knowledge base or book-centred approach is complemented with a humane approach of moral 'cultivation' which echoes centuries of Confucian tradition. The orientation to the education of teachers in China has been described ideologically as 'to cultivate cultured persons as teachers with lofty ideals, high morality, strong discipline and a sense of mission as educators, 'the engineers of the human soul' and 'the gardeners of the nation' (Lin and Yang 1989, cited in Leung and Hui 2000).

Further metaphors of the 1990s and 2000s reinforce this sense of mission with moral virtues: teachers are 'golden key-holders' because they are held to open doors to the future of China's youth and they have roles of guidance as moral models, seen in terms of light as 'candles' and 'lamps'. In the 1990s we photographed a large official sign near the main gate of a Normal University which predominantly trains teachers: it said in both English and Chinese, "Keep in mind that as a teacher of classes you are also an educator of students, an instructor of their lives and a leader of their moral virtues." Increasingly in official metaphors in the 2000s and 2010s teachers are seen as 'performers', 'conductors' and 'directors' in classrooms because they are considered to orchestrate processes of guidance for students in more participatory and applied learning processes, rather than merely being transmitters of knowledge. Teachers in the 2010s are 'cultivators of students' ability', 'nurturers of creativity and future professionals': they have the knowledge and pedagogic skills to enable students to be successful in an increasingly competitive society, if students themselves make efforts.

It might be thought that the historical metaphors for teachers have mostly passed from public awareness. However, they resonate in leaders' statements; for example, from Li Lanqing, a previous vice-premier who was responsible for education in China, who approvingly links Confucius, 'cultivation' and the teaching profession:

> China has a long tradition of respecting teachers and valuing education. Confucius, the great educator, lived . . . over 2,500 years ago, and was later given the title 'Great Sage and Teacher'. . . . The ancients pointed out, "For a country to become strong, it must honour teachers . . . the goal is to make teaching an enviable profession . . . the ancients pointed out . . . the goals of this reform [of education]. First, to cultivate high-calibre professionals . . . cultivating more talents . . . cultivate as many professionals as possible".
>
> (Li 2004:3/25/69/118)

Many of the above metaphors are current among students and teachers, too. Some images are reflected in teacher's titles, with professional role differentiation: *shifu* as used by apprentices to address their 'master' is transferred to address a teacher as 'a craftsperson'; *laoshi* means an 'old master' and is commonly used in direct address by students to teachers to show respect; *xuezhe* ('a learned person') connotes a respected scholar and may be used in scholar-to-scholar address; *xiansheng* ('born earlier') is little used now, except to address the most senior and well-known scholars.

Some metaphors and titles are commonly circulated via the Internet, as seen in this humorous example sent on Teacher's Day in 2015; in mainland China this is 10 September (Confucius' birthday) – other professions do not have such a national day:

> In Chinese, a teacher is *laoshi* ('old master') or *shifu* ('master craftsman'); in English 'a teacher'; the fake name is *'the engineer of the soul'*; the name beside is 'educational worker'; the pet name is 'a gardener'; the nickname is 'a candle'; the economic definition is 'low income class'; the sociological definition is 'member of a survival group'; the political definition is 'old number nines'; the habitual way of calling them is 'intellectuals'; the government name is 'civil servants'; the social welfare definition is 'an income adequate social group'; and the true name is 'poor people'.
>
> (anon, WeChat Internet site on 9 September 2015, trans. Jin)

Teachers as tradition: guides and treasures

This historical continuity of metaphors for teachers becomes more evident when we examine the Confucian tradition. Confucius characterized himself as a tireless teacher and learner. He is regarded as a symbol of education and social ethics. This is internationally visible in the naming of the Confucian Institutes established by China in many countries to teach the Chinese language and culture. Arguably, the first professional teachers on any scale were those in China in the ancient Confucian academies whose main purpose was to nurture scholars. These academies of classical learning were mostly private institutions; some were specifically recognized by the emperors. First established around the year 725 in the Tang dynasty (618–907), they quickly spread all over China; in the Yuan dynasty (1271–1368) most became schools for the elaborate Imperial examination system which gave successful students access to official positions at the local, regional or national level as the normal employment for scholars. Such academies endured for a thousand years and only ceased in 1898.

Within academies, teachers were generally respected and often treated with reverence. Importantly, though, some well-known texts critically evaluate the practices of some teachers, who apparently encouraged repetition, rote-learning and reading aloud with little understanding. Such criticisms demonstrate the gap between the ideal and the practices of some professionals. Thus the poet Han Yu at the Imperial University in 802 criticized teachers who simply tested students' ability to memorize and recite texts because: "This is not what I would call passing on the tradition or resolving doubts. . . . I do not see the wisdom of this". He repeats the metaphor that the teacher is the tradition, centrally concerned with transmission, yet teachers can learn creatively from anyone, since the tradition is egalitarian: "Confucius said, 'When three people walk together, there will certainly be one who will be my teacher'". So for Han Yu neither teacher nor student is better as such than the other: "One has simply learned the tradition earlier than the other. . . . My teacher is the tradition . . . neither rich nor poor, old nor young; where the tradition is, there the teacher is" (Hartman 1986:163–64). As the tradition, a teacher transmits, but also innovates, since Confucius proposed both of these as criteria to be a teacher: "Be thoroughly versed in the old, and understand the new – then you can be a teacher" (Confucius 2007:21).

The Confucian classic the *Li Ji* (second century BC or earlier) elaborates the metaphor of the teacher as a 'guide', with the further criterion of a good teacher as one who develops students to think for themselves:

> In his teaching the superior man guides his students but does not pull them along; he urges them to go forward and does not suppress them; he opens the way but does not take them to the place. Guiding without pulling makes the process of learning gentle; urging without suppressing makes the process of learning easy; and opening the way without

leading the students to the place makes them think for themselves. Now if the process of learning is made gentle and easy and the students are encouraged to think for themselves, we may call the man a good teacher.
(Lin 1938:246–47)

Another Confucian classic, the *Book of Xunzi* (third century BC), emphasizes metaphors for the teacher as *a* 'cultivator', a 'nurturer' and a 'treasure': "Of all the methods of controlling the body and nurturing the mind . . . none are more important than getting a teacher"; "therefore the possession of a teacher and of precepts is the greatest treasure a man can have"; "if a man has a teacher, he will exalt self-cultivation" (Xunzi 1961:32/60/162). The *Xunzi* stresses how the critical element cited above is a possible quality of teachers: "He who criticizes me and does so correctly is my teacher" (Xunzi 1961:24).

Evidently, and contrary to one popular impression, the central texts of the Confucians do not support teaching or learning as mere transmission of book knowledge via rote-learning. The influential thinker Wang Yangming (1471–1529) famously emphasized: "The sages said that knowledge is the guiding idea for action and that action is the practical work of knowledge. Knowledge is the beginning of action and action is the consummation of knowledge" (Cleary 1991:44). Ming dynasty scholars (1368–1644) repeatedly see teachers as 'cultivators', for example: "We lecture on learning so that we can cultivate virtue" (Cleary 1991:67).

Interpreting teacher metaphors through patterns

In the research reported here, we collected metaphors for teachers from participants through elicitation and analyzed them looking for underlying patterns and socio-cultural conceptions. These contemporary patterns echo, elaborate and extend the Confucian and more recent traditions of China. This approach draws on cognitive linguistics research by Lakoff and others (for instance, Lakoff 1993, 2008; Lakoff and Johnson 1980), but we follow a cultural interpretation of this (Kövecses 2005, 2006) in order to investigate perceptions of teachers in their social contexts of education (Cortazzi and Jin 1999; Jin and Cortazzi 2011b).

To complement the metaphors found in public discourse, we elicit metaphors from students and teachers in universities. We ask each participant to complete a form by writing up to three metaphors for a 'teacher' and explaining the reasons for choosing each one (the entailments). Broadly, the elicited metaphors complement our other research with questionnaires, interviews, classroom observation and photos, alongside text analysis for Confucian metaphors (Jin and Cortazzi 2008). As this is an open-ended elicitation task, participants between them usually write a wide range of metaphors: after all, with imagination they can write practically any metaphor. Many metaphors are creative and reveal reflective thinking, others are commonplace within their cultural contexts; some participants wrote very little, others wrote more than we asked. In this way, we collected 1,175 metaphors written in English from 596 students in China in three universities in central and eastern China, together with 413 metaphors from teachers in China and a further 785 metaphors from 393 students in Iran in two universities in northern and southern Iran. Student data were gathered in classrooms. The metaphors from teachers in China were elicited at extended teacher development sessions attended by university teachers from over one hundred universities, with two or three teachers from each; ten teachers were from universities where student data were obtained and these were their particular teachers; overall, the teachers represent a wide range of universities all over the country.

In our analysis, as researchers and teachers ourselves, we do not always know what particular metaphors for teachers imply. We may guess or impose our own interpretation; however, to know the meaning intended by participants we need to examine not only the metaphors but also their entailments. Thus when students in China say a teacher is a 'piece of chalk' or 'ice', from a British perspective both are considered negative: the 'chalk' is dry and white, and 'chalk and talk' is considered an over-long explanation likely to bore learners, while 'ice' is cold and an icy person shows dislike or unfriendliness. However, for these Chinese students, teachers as 'chalk' "teach their knowledge to us but lose their youth gradually", "they leave marks of knowledge, sacrificing themselves as they melt away", "they write down the most beautiful texts, even down to the last bits of chalk". As 'ice', teachers in hot summers "are melting, running themselves out to wet students' dry hearts". Thus these metaphors are positive for students. They represent an underlying concept of teacher devotion and sacrifice. Cross-culturally, the meaning of metaphors can often be a surprise.

The teacher as an 'engineer of the soul' (given by 62 students in China) has entailments that both echo and elaborate the understanding of previous generations. As 'engineers', teachers are "constantly designing and modifying students", "with superb skills, making us in different shapes from ordinary and dull materials". "We are the materials, the teacher makes tall buildings of students' souls"; "they build the road of knowledge for us"; they "design a blueprint for the future of the motherland", "cultivate talents for future generations to continue the civilization", "make young hearts beautiful by using their ingenious skills", "guide us to sow the seeds of civilization", "clean out rubbish and waste and let us be healthy." "Every student has been cultivated by teachers since kindergarten, this is a vacant land, a building is gradually and steadily constructed with the command of the engineer, digging the foundation, adding decoration, until a magnificent building stands up". "They bring wisdom to our souls"; "they are selfless to offer themselves, enriching others"; "they have a great moral quality to educate us".

Teachers and sacrifice

Interestingly, Chinese students' metaphors for teachers often make comparisons with other professions or occupations. Some highlight an entertainment function (for example, a 'musician' or a 'magician'), roles relating to knowledge (for instance, a 'miner' digging for knowledge or a 'merchant' selling knowledge), or giving of guidance, advice or direction (such as a 'counsellor', a 'traffic policeman' or a 'tourist guide'). A salient case is the teacher as a 'gardener' (a Confucian 'cultivator'). This seems to contrast with 'engineer of the soul'; it is apparently less mechanistic or technical and more oriented to growth and development. Current students see a teacher as a 'gardener': "cultivating people; making students grow", "hardworking, producing beautiful flowers for the motherland", "making our shortcomings disappear by trimming the flowers", "silently sowing with sweat and care", so with sacrifice "a teacher's sweat pours onto the flowers of the motherland" and "his sweat pours onto the plants, making himself suffer".

Further consideration leads to the idea of metaphor networks. A series of metaphors on the same topic may each have distinct entailments which do not immediately relate to each other. However, in our datasets the meanings of given metaphors for 'teacher' often clearly overlap and combine, as shown above, with the teacher as an 'engineer of the soul' (we term this 'a spread of entailments'). Conversely, several different metaphors for 'teacher' may share a very similar entailment; this indicates cognitive salience (which we call a 'key entailment'). When there are multiple reciprocal mappings across metaphors, this shows the richness of a wider metaphor pattern: we call the resultant mapping 'a metaphor network' and a wider, even more complex network is 'a metaphor landscape'.

Underlying concepts for 'a teacher' can thus be revealed for even just a few metaphors by mapping metaphors and their entailments. In our Chinese data, a teacher as an 'engineer of the soul' and a 'gardener' (166 examples) are compared with a 'parent' (56 examples) and a 'friend' (76 examples). In our analyses we require at least two mappings before a candidate metaphor or entailment is accepted into a network. Although in these particular data, the teacher as a 'parent' does not 'show self-sacrifice' in the way that an 'engineer' and a 'gardener' are said to do, clearly students will recognize how parents do sacrifice for children – they just do not mention this in these data. Such gaps might be filled by further research: the network patterns show us where to look. In this network, using participants' own words, the teacher metaphors as an 'engineer of the soul', a 'gardener', a 'parent' and a 'friend' mean that a teacher 'cultivates talents', 'nurtures growth', 'develops knowledge' and 'moral qualities', 'cares for learners', 'shows self-sacrifice' and 'patience', 'talks heart to heart' and 'beautifies lives' and 'works for the motherland's future'. We comment below on the multiple professional dimensions involved here.

The above metaphors compare teachers with other people, but teacher sacrifice can be seen metaphorically in the activities of animals and insects. A 'teacher' can be an 'old cow', a 'bee', or a silkworm and with others these comprise a further metaphor network. In the UK, to call a teacher 'an old cow' is a gender-based insult because it carries the meaning that the teacher is unpleasant, stupid or ugly. In contrast, in China the 'cow' metaphor (45 examples) shows admiration and praise: the teacher is 'hard-working', 'tireless' and 'productive', 'silently suffering', 'only serving society', destroying itself gradually and 'leaving its spirit forever'. One student elaborated this devotion and sacrifice: "We are the plough; she drags the plough ahead with every difficulty; she won't stop working until she gives out all her strength." As a 'bee' (43 examples), a teacher in China is "selflessly working hard for others, spreading the pollen of knowledge", "transporting knowledge, most diligently, adding sweetness and scented taste to our spiritual life". In a more culturally specific metaphor, the teacher as a 'silkworm' (20 examples) is "devoting their whole life to others", "producing selflessly until the last minute of its life", "it sacrifices itself but gives silk to create the most beautiful clothes for people."

This metaphor network of sacrifice in Chinese metaphors includes major characteristics of 'having devotion', 'being hard-working' and 'suffering' to 'give guidance' and 'enrich knowledge', but also to 'create beauty', 'help others' and 'serve society'. Each attributed professional characteristic relates to others in a network. A major sacrifice metaphor in this network is that the teacher is a 'candle' (114 examples): teachers "burn themselves out to give life to others", "sacrifice themselves to light the road to others", "give knowledge to light up our future", "give out all their energy to make us understand", and as a 'red candle', they "sacrifice themselves to bless us with brightness and warmth at the cost of their life".

Teachers as burning candles, prophets and light

In many obvious ways, Iran is quite a different context from that of China; however, regarding metaphors for the profession of teachers it turns out that China and Iran have much in common, though with different emphases. Culturally, metaphors resonate throughout the literary and scholarly history of Iranian civilization. The Persian language (*Farsi*) is noted for its wide use of rich metaphors. These are particularly evident in the expression of poetry: Persian mystical and spiritual poetry constitutes one of the world's great literary traditions (for example, the works of Rumi and Hafiz), often translated into European languages. Many poems, however, need detailed commentary referring to metaphors (for instance. Arberry and Schimmel). This suggests that comparison with metaphors from China may be valuable.

In Iran, too, the teacher as a 'candle' is significant (82 examples) (Cortazzi et al. 2015), although, as might be expected, it is not 'red'. A teacher "burns and gives light to students", "as a burning candle, they brighten our lives, give us brightness and heart", "they enlighten our minds", "students learn with the guidance, encouragement, help and sacrifice of teachers", "they show warmth, affection, devotions and love, they sacrifice themselves", "they devote their life to teach us", and "teachers burn so students learn". In some Iranian metaphors there is a clear religious element which is rarely explicit in our Chinese data. Thus in Iran a teacher is a 'prophet' (24 examples): "they guide us through darkness, they teach everything that we need", "show us the correct way of living in order to reach salvation", "rescue humans from the chains of ignorance", "they deliver a message – it's up to you to apply it". A teacher as an 'angel' (14 examples) includes: "they devote themselves to us", "they guide us and have purity", "a rescuing angel – always bestows the best inspiration on my soul", "they are always with us and the effects of their teaching remain with us forever".

Metaphors of the teacher as 'light' are prolific in both sets of data (153 Chinese examples; 37 Iranian); more specifically, as the 'sun' (125 in China; 21 in Iran), as the 'moon' (28 in China; 12 in Iran), as a 'star' (56 in China; 11 in Iran), as a 'candle' (237 in China; 81 in Iran) and as 'fire' (24 in China; 7 in Iran). Both sets of metaphors form networks to indicate how teacher knowledge, enlightenment and sacrifice seem salient, as does guidance, though this is emphasized more in Iran (which matches the roles of 'prophets' and 'angels'). Teacher guidance is seen in Iran with strong Islamic associations in a predominantly Muslim population. Such comments as "teachers guide us on the straight path" or "show us the right path" cannot be said there without thinking of the opening verses of the Holy Book, the Qur'an, "guide us to the straight path", also translated as "guide us on the right way" or "show us the straight way". These words are recited in daily prayer and the teacher metaphor gives evidence of a spiritual perspective. Of course there is a Muslim minority in China, so the same point would apply to this relatively small group, but it is not evident in our data. 'Light' in both contexts has associations of knowledge and, in participants' words, 'enlightenment', which may well have strong Buddhist associations for some in China but for others it is often clearly in contrast with 'darkness'. In China, 'darkness' means a lack of knowledge, while in Iran it connotes spiritual ignorance and lack of moral guidance, but the Chinese emphasis is that the teacher is expected to give help to students in difficulty and support those with problems.

Dimensions of teacher landscapes

To summarize the 1,589 Chinese metaphors for teachers, we give an overview of dimensions of metaphor landscapes through networks. Some of the features for a teacher as 'sacrifice' and teacher as 'light' have been shown as metaphor networks (see also Cortazzi and Jin 2012; Cortazzi, Jin and Wang 2009; Jin and Cortazzi 2008). The teacher as a 'source of knowledge' network meshes with the teacher as 'light' network to include many metaphors centred on helping students progress through deep teacher knowledge, the teacher as being tireless, giving guidance and direction, with nurturing and protective functions, and being a source of energy, love, hope and warmth. In turn, another network in this landscape is associated with 'giving care' and 'direction', with strong elements of how teachers have 'an enduring effect', show 'friendship and closeness', and 'cleanse and purify' learners from errors and undesirable qualities.

The general professional characteristics of a teacher are represented in a huge variety of complex metaphors in these landscapes: without analyzing the entailments and considering metaphor networks, the overall patterns might well be overlooked in a reduced understanding of the insider view. For Chinese metaphors of teachers, three meta-characteristics or dimensions of professionalism emerge from these networks which echo the Confucian traditions: the deep importance of 'cultivation', 'knowledge' and 'morality'. 'Cultivation' is traditionally understood at three levels – a teacher should be cultivated; a teacher should cultivate learners; and teachers should enable learners to develop their own self-cultivation. Similarly, 'knowledge' has three levels related to the teacher's deep knowledge, the teacher developing the students' knowledge and the teacher inspiring the student's desire for continued learning for further knowledge. 'Morality' also has three levels applied to the teacher's professional self as a moral model, the pedagogic interaction in which implicitly morality is developed by the learners and how teachers foster learners' own inner morality.

An overview of the 785 metaphors for teachers in Iran has been analyzed to show five dimensions of metaphor landscapes (Cortazzi et al. 2015) to give this insider view of the profession:

- Aesthetic: Teachers show beauty and give knowledge of beauty.
- Affective: Teachers show students their care, patience and love.
- Cognitive: Teachers develop learners' knowledge, inspire them, give guidance, solve problems and promote intellectual growth.
- Moral: Teachers show learners moral truth and through their example show how to be a moral person.
- Spiritual: Teachers show sacrifice, devotion, guidance on 'the straight path' and they inspire the soul.

These dimensions should not be seen as a list for this profession in Iran but holistically, as a cycle of mutually influencing elaborate schemas. They are all interrelated networks. While there are no 'engineers' in our Iranian data (as it happens) three or four dimensions of this landscape relate directly or indirectly to the 'soul'. These 'soul' dimensions seem crucial for the metaphor landscapes in Iran; evidently from the Chinese analyses they are highly significant in China, with the reservation that the spiritual dimension might rather be seen as a moral dimension, without the overtly religious associations of scripture.

Positives outweigh negatives

These metaphor landscapes are overwhelmingly positive, perhaps surprisingly so as inside views where some disappointment, disillusion or disasters with teachers might be anticipated. Students have, after all, spent years in classrooms with some less-than-ideal teachers. There are certainly a few negative metaphors for teachers. These include attempts at humour and mixed positive-negative metaphors. Examples in Iran are: a teacher is a 'killer' – "they kill motivation and murder enthusiasm"; an 'extra-terrestrial' – "the things they say are alien to students"; a 'transient despot' – "they make you listen and obey them but you understand the reasons later"; and a 'jellyfish in the knowledge sea' – "they look amazing but if you get too close you may end up being paralyzed". Some from China are: a 'durian' – "it smells terrible but when you try to eat it, it is delicious"; a 'two-edged sword' – "transmitting knowledge to us but at the same time killing our ability to analyze"; and a 'surgeon's knife' – "cutting out the cancer in us, but also cutting out our creative cells".

Contrary to these few negative instances, the great majority of these metaphors show positive warmth for teachers, an affective dimension of teaching that is combined with cognitive dimensions. There may be several reasons for this. First, the generally positive orientation likely reflects traditional respect for teachers and recognition of their value and contribution to society – a noticeable social feature in modern China and Iran. Second, there is possible reluctance to show negative features to researchers, thus preserving 'face' – a feature of both cultures – but we think this is unlikely in the contexts we know. Third, since our data come from university students, who are successful achievers in education, the metaphors may be unlike those of school students or distinct from those of unsuccessful learners; however, we have other school data which are similarly positive, although we have not sought out data from recognizably unsuccessful learners. Fourth, it seems likely that students have a naïve view of the teaching profession despite years of receiving education; this might be true of any young client view of any profession. This is a limitation, but it is nevertheless an essential angle from which to understand the profession.

This is offset here to some extent by our teacher-generated data in which the metaphors are richer but not noticeably different in kind from those of students. This positivity is seen in a further example from an anonymous teacher in China on Teacher's Day in 2015, who gives the image of teacher as a 'romanticist' whose overall love has negative elements humorously expressed of being unrequited and tortured:

> Teaching is a secret love affair: you try many ways to love a group of people – the result is that you only make yourself emotional. Teaching is a harsh love affair: you use all your effort to love that group of students but they always leave you. Teaching is unrequited love: students have

tortured me thousands of times – but I always treat them as my first love. Teaching is a group love: it connects you through networks and builds up bridges for all members within the group – but the teacher remains unchanged.

(WeChat Internet site, 9 September 2015, trans. Jin)

Conclusions and applications

The insider vision into the teaching profession through metaphor analysis is both broader and deeper than the usual outsider discourse representations. The results of this research challenge a common representation of teachers which, in the West, has recently been dominated by concepts from corporatization and management in such ideas about teachers as 'deliverers of the curriculum', 'managers of learning' and 'marketing and customer service agents'. Striking instances of this challenge are the key notions from China, Iran and elsewhere of teacher devotion, teacher sacrifice and in general the profound appreciation by students of teachers' worth and work in a huge range of metaphors. These metaphor landscapes seem significant counterweights to public pronouncements from British politicians about teachers who 'deliver' a curriculum as 'social engineers', 'producers' and 'providers' of 'future employable economic agents'. The insider representation is a strong counter-melody against some current notions of accountability and assessment of professionals. 'Sacrifice', for example, is widely felt as a deeply worthwhile characteristic, yet it evades measurement or ticking a box in an externally set list of targets.

Students in both Chinese and Iranian datasets generally admire their teachers for their professionalism and – profoundly integrated with this – for their morality, integrity and personal-professional identity, which all help students to develop their own sense of these key attributes of humanity. If teachers are 'engineers of the soul', unpacking this through metaphor analysis shows both the 'engineering' and 'soul' aspects to be finely textured and multidimensional. We can speculate whether this positive multi-dimensional view might be valid for other professions. It is certainly relevant to all professions as a social group, since professionals necessarily undergo schooling, further or higher education and training: this is all realized through teachers in educational institutions. Additionally, in contexts of private or public practice, within legal and health care professions, for instance, experienced practitioners often exercise mentoring roles – they are teachers, too, for the further learning of novices and early career professionals. Teachers in these two spheres therefore influence all other professions: teachers 'engineer the soul' of the professions.

Metaphors for teachers in China have a history of over two thousand years in the Confucian tradition and for not much less in Buddhist and Taoist traditions (not examined here). This longevity implies that such metaphors have been thought relevant for many generations. In modern China metaphors in public discourse reflect changes in education, society, politics and economic policy, yet from a bottom-up perspective metaphors for teachers held by students show both continuity and innovation. Contemporary metaphors for teachers include a 'computer', a 'mobile phone' and 'anti-virus software'; these reflect access to knowledge, connectivity, globalization and student humour: "a teacher is a TV set: it shows you a wonderful world; when you're tired you can turn it off and go to sleep". In China and in Iran the metaphors for a teacher are astonishing in their range, in the details of entailments and, often, their creativity. This is remarkable considering the metaphor elicitation task was completely new to participants and – in English – it reflects confident student expression, which itself is a tribute to their teachers. The metaphors from Iran, as might be expected, reveal a more religious orientation, although this is also occasionally evident in the Chinese data. Both sets show a holistic orientation, an insider view which contrasts with that of many policymakers and researchers.

For practical applications, we have used metaphors in teacher training and in professional development sessions for experienced practitioners: participants generate and discuss their own metaphors, compare them with the kind given here, look at other international examples and reflect on how particular combinations of metaphors relate to their personal-professional identity and contexts of practice. We find these activities are valuable in international and intercultural contexts of teaching and learning in which the cultural experiences of education can vary not only in practices but in images, expectations and interpretations of diverse contexts (Cortazzi and Jin 2013; Jin and Cortazzi 2013). Hence it is vital for teachers (and local students) to be aware of the metaphors of international students, such as those from China or Iran, in order to develop all students' cultures of learning and the professional cultures of teaching.

As the model from China indicates, at least in some contexts the profession of teaching is based on knowledge but also on a rich idea of cultivation and morality. Good teachers in China are expected to sacrifice themselves to cultivate students. But this may not be a virtue in some Western concepts of good teachers. This expectation may have a huge implication for the evaluation of teachers by students with this view when they study internationally. As the holistic model based on metaphors from Iran shows, this implies how at least in some contexts professional development is cognitive, but also affective, aesthetic, moral and spiritual. For professionals elsewhere, these multi-dimensional conceptions surely provide food for thought: they might provide a more positive identity for professions than is seen under the impact of developments like the New Public Management and help to reconstruct a profession through sacrifice for the soul.

References

Cameron, L. (2003) *Metaphor in Educational Discourse*. London: Continuum.
Cleary, J. C. (ed) (1991) *Worldly Wisdom: Confucian Teachings of the Ming Dynasty*. Boston: Shambhala.

Confucius (2007) *The Analects of Confucius.* New York: Columbia University Press.

Cortazzi, M. and Jin, L. (1999) Bridges to learning: Metaphors of teaching, learning and language. In: L. Cameron and G. Low (eds) *Researching and Applying Metaphor.* Cambridge: Cambridge University Press.

Cortazzi, M. and Jin, L. (2012) Journeys of learning: Insights into intercultural adaptation. In: X. Dai and S. Kulich (eds) *Intercultural Adaptation (1): Theoretical Explorations and Empirical Studies.* Shanghai: Shanghai Foreign Language Education Press.

Cortazzi, M. and Jin, L. (eds) (2013) *Researching Cultures of Learning: International Perspectives on Language Learning and Education.* Houndmills: Palgrave Macmillan.

Cortazzi, M. and Jin, L. (2014) Building bridges, using weapons or making music together? Metaphoric (re)framing in intercultural language learning. In: X. Dai and G-M. Chen (eds) *Intercultural Communication Competence: Conceptualization and Its Development in Cultural Contexts and Interactions.* Newcastle: Cambridge Scholars Publishing.

Cortazzi, M., Jin, L., Kaivanpour, S. and Nemati, M. (2015) Candles lighting up the journey of learning: teachers of English in Iran. In: C. Kennedy (ed) *English Language Teaching in the Islamic Republic of Iran: Innovations, Trends and Challenges.* London: British Council.

Cortazzi, M., Jin, L. and Wang, Z. (2009) Cultivators, cows and computers: Chinese learners' metaphors of teachers. In: T. Coverdale-Jones and P. Rastall (eds) *Internationalizing the University: The Chinese Context.* London: Palgrave Macmillan.

Gibbs, R. W. (ed) (2008) *The Cambridge Handbook of Metaphor and Thought.* Cambridge: Cambridge University Press.

Hartman. C. (1986) *Han Yu and the T'ang Search for Unity.* Princeton: Princeton University Press.

Holyoak, K. J. and Thagard, P. (1996) *Mental Leaps, Analogy in Creative Thought.* Cambridge: MIT Press.

Jin, L. and Cortazzi, M. (2008) Images of teachers, learning and questioning in Chinese cultures of learning. In: E. Berendt (ed) *Metaphors We Learn By.* London: Continuum.

Jin, L. and Cortazzi, M. (2011a) The changing landscapes of a journey: Educational metaphors in China. In: J. Ryan (ed) *Education Reform in China, Changing Concepts, Contexts and Practice.* London: Routledge.

Jin, L. and Cortazzi, M. (2011b) More than a journey: 'Learning' in the metaphors of Chinese students and teachers. In: L. Jin and M. Cortazzi (eds) *Researching Chinese Learners, Skills, Perceptions, Adaptations.* London: Palgrave Macmillan.

Jin, L. and Cortazzi, M. (eds) (2013) *Researching Intercultural Learning: Investigations in Language and Education.* Houndmills: Palgrave Macmillan.

Kövecses, Z. (2005) *Metaphor in Culture, Universality and Variation.* Cambridge: Cambridge University Press.

Kövecses, Z. (2006) *Language, Mind, and Culture.* Oxford: Oxford University Press.

Lakoff, G. (1993) The contemporary theory of metaphor. In: A. Ortony (ed) *Metaphor and Thought,* 2nd edition. Cambridge: Cambridge University Press.

Lakoff, G. (2008) The neural theory of metaphor. In: R. W. Gibbs (ed) *The Cambridge Handbook of Metaphor and Thought.* Cambridge: Cambridge University Press.

Lakoff, G. and Johnson, M. (1980) *Metaphors We Live By.* Chicago: Chicago University Press.

Leung, J.Y.M. and Hui, X. (2000) People's Republic of China. In: P. Morris and J. Williamson (eds) *Teacher Education in the Asia Pacific Region: A Comparative Study*. New York: Falmer Press.

Li, L. (2004) *Education for 1.3 Billion*. Beijing: Foreign Language Teaching and Research Press.

Lin, Y. (1938) *The Wisdom of Confucius*. New York: The Modern Library.

Ortony, A. (ed) (1993) *Metaphor and Thought*, 2nd edition. Cambridge: Cambridge University Press.

Pantsov, A. V. and Levine, S. I. (2015) *Deng Xiaoping: A Revolutionary Life*. Oxford: Oxford University Press.

Skvorecky, J. (1984) *The Engineer of Human Souls*. London: Picador.

Wan, W. and Low, G. (eds) (2015) *Elicited Metaphor Analysis in Educational Discourse*. Amsterdam: John Benjamin Publishing.

Westerman, F. (2011) *Engineers of the Human Soul: In the Footsteps of Stalin's Writers*. New York: Vintage.

Xunzi (1961) *The Works of Hsuntze*. Taipei: Confucius Publishing.

10 Metaphors we help by

Socio-cognitive patterns of professionals in social work

Rudolf Schmitt

Introduction

The following chapter discusses metaphors as basic elements of professional knowledge, centred on the example of social work. Social work is particularly suitable for exploring this idea, since it has some special features that make metaphoric thinking a necessary component of professional knowledge. It is both the pivot around which the particular controversy about social work as a profession revolves and its specific subject matter. It can be said that "the content of social work's jurisdiction was . . . a contested, turf-driven matter" (Abbott 1995:552). A large part of the discussion is also about boundary work undertaken both inside and outside of what could be called a profession. This configuration explains the specific semantic networks of professional knowledge in social work, which will be revealed when we compare its metaphors with those of health professions and teachers. In order to avoid arriving at definitive conclusions prematurely, in what follows I shall use a very broad interpretation of the concept of profession which has fuzzy boundaries. It defines the field of social work exercised as paid work and claims a specific knowledge for it (Abbott 1988:8). This chapter considers the ways in which this field can be characterized by the metaphorical knowledge it covers.

Metaphors and professional knowledge

Dewe (2012) assumes that the knowledge of the profession of social work consists mainly in skills or that it employs an implicit or tacit knowledge that is not consciously accessible before an action but can be represented retrospectively. This professional knowledge develops mainly through practising in institutional contexts, while the academic knowledge plays only a preparatory role that allows reflection in the process of acquisition of professional knowledge. However, the knowledge of professional experience can only be verbalized to a limited extent (Schützeichel 2014). Schön (1979) suggests that this knowledge ('knowing how') is condensed in 'generative metaphors'.

On this view, metaphors play a role in the organization, storing and presentation of tacit knowledge. They reduce the complexity of possible perceptions and make it possible to pre-structure and order complexity (Buchholz 1996). According to the most up-to-date theory of metaphors in cognitive linguistics, known as the 'conceptual metaphor theory' (see Johnson 1987; Lakoff 1987; Lakoff and Johnson 1980, 1999), thinking, speech and action are pervaded with unintended metaphors transferred from simple and older experiential patterns to new and abstract issues. Metaphors should therefore be seen as a product not merely of rhetoric, but also, and most importantly, of cognitive research (in the broadest, not psychological, sense). 'Cognitions' are understood as individually acquired patterns of organizing experience that are passed down to us through culture and structured in part by our embodied experience. Lakoff and Johnson (1980) postulate that there is a common cognitive pattern to be found behind several metaphors with a common source and target area (a 'metaphorical concept'). Thus, in interviews with social workers we find metaphors that help 'get people back on track'. When clients encounter the social worker, they are either in a 'tight situation' or 'uprooted'. This is often followed by a 'balancing act' as they teeter between personal needs and institutional demands, finally ending up in a 'place' where they have 'space' for themselves, where they have more freedom. The wealth of metaphors can be subsumed under the heading or concept of 'helping is supporting people on their way'. Black (1983) proposed that all metaphors are the tip of a submerged internal model. Strictly speaking, this actually applies only to metaphorical concepts as defined by Lakoff and Johnson. We can conceive of such metaphorical models as 'patterns of interpretation' as in the terminology of the social sciences (see Schmitt 2011).

The aim of this chapter is to develop the implications of these patterns of interpretation for the knowledge of professionals. To give just a brief description of the method of systematic metaphor analysis: it provides a link between the theory of Lakoff and Johnson (1980, 1999) and the methods of qualitative social research. After gaining the experience of using a five-phase system of data analysis (Schmitt 2005), a seven-phase procedure to provide sufficiently thorough support for a reconstruction is proposed, in order to fulfil the necessary quality criteria for interpretation (Schmitt 2011). The objective of this method is to represent concrete metaphorical concepts as semantic patterns. It does not follow the suggestion by Liljegren (2012) that there are 'key metaphors' that include several metaphorical concepts for two reasons. First, the idea of 'key metaphors' may blur the implicit differences between more concrete concepts. Second, if we do without dominant key metaphors, we can understand a professional field as a specific network of concepts that are heterogeneous (Schmitt 2013). Nevertheless, key metaphors and their elaboration may give fast access to central topics in the field.

Metaphorical concepts of professional knowledge

The following discussion of empirical analyses of metaphors that can provide us with some pointers towards professional knowledge is based on studies conducted by Schmitt (1995) on professionals providing outreach family assistance, which include intensive contact with clients and weaker links with organizational support. Their work thus falls under the heading of 'direct social work practice'. This is then compared with Schmitt (2006) on adult education, Schulze (2007) on family court assistance, and Schröder (2015) on counselling with violent men. A review of metaphors used in the health professions (Schmitt and Böhnke 2009) is added for comparison with an external field. The conclusions drawn are incomplete for a number of reasons: analyses of metaphors do not currently exist for all areas of social work and two of the studies (Schmitt 2006; Schröder 2015) are only single case studies, while the others were conducted using a sampling technique modelled on grounded theory and continued until saturation was reached, in terms of the respective research questions. There are thus limits as to how far the results of these studies can be generalized to the field of social work as a whole.

Abbott (1995:552) distinguishes three functions of profession-specific knowledge, seeing it as "[shaping] these problems into coherent jurisdictions by creating intellectual processes of diagnosis, inference, and treatment." This triad of modes of perceiving and construing problems specific to the profession, causal assumptions peculiar to the profession and profession-specific interventions, brings together the central characteristics of professional activity (see Baier 2015). The empirical study by Schmitt (1995) showed that each metaphorical concept includes a diagnosis, an associated causal attribution and interventions derived from it. Metaphors also generate a normative judgement, assign roles to all parties involved and use these to frame the relationship as a scenic arrangement. Abbott's triad of diagnosis, inference and intervention is not free of medical metaphors. For interventions that are person centred and highly influenced by societal structures, it therefore needs to be complemented by an analysis of these dimensions of normativity and relationship patterns.

The network of metaphorical concepts of social work

The following list of metaphorical concepts of social work therefore applies only to the area of outreach social family assistance and re-interprets the studies from the standpoint of the sociology of professions in order to generate ideas for future research.

Social work is putting people back on track

The diagnosis in the metaphor of a person's 'path through life' sees 'tight' situations, emotional uprootedness or 'dead ends' in which clients are stuck.

In the interviews the relationships are also described in terms of path metaphors, of how one 'gets through to' or 'reaches' the clients, how we 'approach each other' or how they 'evade' relationships. Professional social workers describe their work as 'going through a rough patch' as an attempt to find a new 'way' together and 'move things on' to support clients as they continue on their way in life. This structure composed of a 'tight' starting place, a difficult 'path' and a wider 'space' as an objective constitutes a causal pattern which appears inescapable. According to the logic of the images, it simply seems natural to do things in this order. Thus, in this 'operative' function (Buchholz and von Kleist 1995) the metaphors guide the helpers' definitions of situations, themselves, and the roles of their clients who need to be 'put back on track'. However, we also find statements such that closeness can become threatening because clients do not 'keep much distance'. This shows how these metaphors operate in the management of the professional relationship: it is good to 'find a path that we can follow together', to 'reach' the client, and – if need be – also to try to 'build bridges', but we must not get too 'close'. The relationship is calibrated by finding a level on an imaginary yardstick on which the optimum degree of support is evidently 'not too close' to the client.

Social work is relieving and supporting

Social work is 'supporting' stressed clients who have a 'heavy burden' to carry which needs to be 'lightened'. This diagnosis is shaped by images of the 'heavy burden' that the clients 'carry', which 'weighs them down' because they are so heavily 'overburdened' by fate, their relatives or society that they can no longer 'bear' it and 'break down'. This metaphorical diagnosis is easily internalized because of its spatial up-down dichotomy (Lakoff and Johnson 1980), which is revealed by corresponding prepositional constructions with 'up', 'over', 'down' and 'under'. Examples of expressions used in the interviews are "and it is getting her down", "it weighs her down tremendously", and "she can't bear it any more". Again, there is an implicit causal attribution in these metaphors: help 'lightens their load' and 'pulls clients out of the depths' (or the 'hole' they are in). The corresponding intervention metaphors are (helping to) carry the burden, 'propping up' and providing relief: "she was so relieved herself", "she also needs . . . to be relieved of the burden of her half-sister". This scenario of assistance as relieving the burden shows a distinct asymmetric distribution of the roles between the helper(s) and the helpless person, the helpers assuming some of the life tasks of their clients.

Social work is bonding or freeing from embroilments

Personal relationships are often thought of literally as 'bonds', 'ties' and 'cords' with which one can 'bind', 'shackle' or 'tie' a person to oneself or become 'enmeshed' with them. The words 'to fasten onto someone', 'clingy' and 'dependency' also denote a relationship that has been created by means of a tie. The metaphors of bonding or attachment are found in almost all of the interviews. Children, especially, are 'attached' to their caregivers and older clients often 'withdraw'. Two diagnoses are possible in this line of metaphors: the status of lack of attachment and the status of being 'enmeshed'. The corresponding work metaphors, which have positive connotations, are then expressed as 'linking', 'connecting with' and 'rebinding', when clients are able to 'free' themselves from 'enmeshments', 'involvements' or 'embroilments'. The implicit moral of these metaphors is that it is not desirable for clients to withdraw or 'pull away'. 'Making contacts' is desirable, while, on the other hand, 'ties' must not lead to 'embroilments'. As with the metaphors of support, a linguistic interaction model of 'moderate closeness' is again evoked for the helping relationship.

Social work is opening and closing

Lakoff and Johnson (1980) use the term 'ontological metaphors' to denote the ability to identify complex parts of our experience as simple objects. They distinguish between several forms of linguistic ontologization. The first of these metaphoric mechanisms, the container metaphor, consists in projecting a discrete body image onto mental or social conditions that are not discrete or have no boundaries. The expression 'he opened up' means that someone who was 'closed' and had 'shut himself off' then 'opened up' and 'let something out'. It does not seem possible to describe the idea of 'expressing' concerns and problems without using container metaphors. In this image, human beings are not only units in the physical sense, but also psychologically vessels in which many things collect, accumulate and then stream out again. This unit can also be breakable: one can 'burst with anger'. The helping metaphors often play out at the boundaries of clients who are seen as containers. Some of them were described as highly constricted and had 'closed up'. The work focused mainly on 'getting people to cough up', 'intervening' and 'participating'. The opposite was often more than simply 'open', frequently expressing a lack of awareness of boundaries or violating them. This stimulated the helpers to 'draw boundaries' and keep to a 'line', to 'block' boundary violations and teach the clients to 'restrain themselves'. However, some helpers felt 'drained' by them – a very strong image for the crossing of psychological boundaries. In this metaphorical logic, social work is helping people to 'open up', intervening with 'closed' people and 'drawing boundaries' in the case of clients who are too 'open'. Thus, here again we find a central metaphorical construction, that of the container, which suggests two possible diagnoses and, accordingly, two directions in which interventions can be made. Implicit cultural norms are concerned mainly with the self-control expected of clients in connection with their opening up/closing down of their inner worlds.

Social work is giving (and taking)

In addition to the container structure, Lakoff and Johnson (1980) classify the concept of 'substance' as belonging to the ontological schema. This permits us to label physical and mental experiences as if we were dealing with a physical substance. Someone who has 'a lot of patience' appears to have a measurable – or at least assessable – mass of this characteristic, which can, however, vary widely in quality. In the interviews this ability to quantify feelings and activities is revealed in the helpers' diagnoses in references to clients "hav[ing] so little" of life and "not [being] sufficiently provided for", or to there being a 'lack' of attention or other resources. Real and metaphorical 'losses' of the clients play a large role. The images of giving quantities that are seemingly measurable then become imperative in the metaphorical logic. Accordingly, social work is seen as 'offering' support and attention, within the confines of the cultural norms of helping. It was noticeable that the helpers often saw their giving as a 'substitute' for perceived deficits in socialization within the family. This was indicated by the use of the verbs 'get', 'have', 'be lacking', 'provide for' and 'receive'. If attention were not quantified by the indefinite determinants 'much', 'little', 'more' and 'enough' it would hardly be possible to describe psychosocial assistance. The helpers' descriptions of themselves as 'drained' or 'burnt-out', 'empty' and 'exhausted' corresponded to these metaphors of possession and loss, which not only determine actions, but also structure the helping relationship. It is an empirical question how this metaphorical conceptualization of helping as giving and providing care has connections to the phenomenon of 'burn-out', as 'taking' supervision and 'getting' advice may have a mildly corrective action.

Social work is clarifying

In the interviews the expected polarization and implicit action-guiding effect of the visual metaphors emerged clearly: the history of a case and the motivations involved are usually "[in the] dark" (that is, unclear) and the helpers want to 'clarify' these. The visual metaphors fulfil three functions. The first is that in ambiguous situations, the protagonists and their intentions and insights are very often described in polar epithets, such as 'light' and 'dark' or 'clear' and 'unclear' as metaphoric reductions of complexity. Metaphors of vision are frequently used to present one's own and others' views of a situation. This includes expressions ranging, for instance, from "everything was unclear" at one pole to "there is a perception of the [local] authority" at the other, or the situation was 'unclear' and the helper would have liked to have a 'more expert view' or to 'look through' the situation. The second function relates to the fact that the temporal dimension of cognitive space – that is, the development in the work with the child or family – uses metaphors associated with describing an image or picture: talk about the 'background' stands for the past, while talk about the 'foreground' stands for a current situation and future prospects. The verbs 'clarify' and 'overshadow' transmit the temporal changes of helping work by altering degrees of lightness. Other examples are: "it became so clear to me", "some steps [forward] are evident . . . after four months", or the fact that one could "no longer fail to notice" a change. The third function is that these images also describe the content of the work. To start with, we find 'looking at' the problems together expressed, otherwise an authoritarian dictum of 'making something clear' to someone is uttered, and of course phenomena that have not been understood are 'observed'. The diagnostic process is most strongly emphasized in such metaphors. It follows the cultural norm that Blumenberg (1960) observed in philosophy, namely that since the Enlightenment the truth has no longer been sought in the shadow of darkness, but in control that is rational and visual. Apart from the expression 'looking at something together' with the client, the visual metaphors would seem to be the most distanced descriptions of the relationship.

Social work is tutoring or teaching

Many helpers, particularly those who work with children of school age, often express themselves in images that are modelled on procedures and modes of thought associated with school. Psychosocial assistance thus not only focuses on school problems, but also transfers modes of thought and action associated with school to other areas. Accordingly, reference is made to the work as, for example, 'tutoring'. Life crises are diagnosed as 'tests' or as 'unsolved tasks', or, more generally in the metaphor of being 'behind', which has its own implications. Thus, in metaphors that are typical for school and also used in other phases of life, reference is made to 'exercises', 'the amount of work to be done' and 'regularity' when it comes to practising new behaviours. The goals are 'achievements' and 'successes'. This pattern – 'we learn for life' – implies that the roles follow the teacher-student pattern and the scenic arrangement of school that arises from it.

Social work in the space of speech

That the metaphors of speech belong to an independent spatial and acoustic type of metaphor was inferred by noting the accompanying prepositions such as 'talking to', 'talking about' and 'talking with'. The descriptions of communication touched both on the relationship metaphors of contact on an equal footing like 'initiating conversations' and on the helpers' intervening modes of verbal communication such as 'conducting interviews'. The social workers were confronted with people interfering in their work. On the other side, there were the clients' excuses, and their avoidance of talking about a problem, whereby they were able to sidestep having to fulfil the helpers' demands. Addressing or 'talking to' proved to be a central expression in these intervening metaphors. We thus find all sorts of prepositions such as 'over', 'under', 'into' and 'out of' and 'past'. They constitute an open space which does not entirely fit into the above-mentioned schema and therefore produces a separate class of metaphors, organized in a 'space of speech'. The spatial positions of the schema produce a diagnosis of the social situation which is implicitly addressed by compensatory speech motions. With regard to professional knowledge, this concept appears to be the least specific.

Social work is doing or crafting

One group of metaphors which initially appears to be so 'dead' that it is not noticed can be found in idioms including the verbs 'working', 'making' and 'doing'. We speak of 'youth work' and we have to 'make' house calls. These words seem so natural that they can hardly be seen as images. The image character only becomes more evident when it comes to expressions such as the following: contacts and relationships are 'established', certain conditions are 'productive' or 'counter-productive' and conflicts are 'worked through'. It is only these phrases that alert us to the fact that a process of craftsmanship serves as the background against which helping social interactions are perceived. If one opts for this interpretation, the "making" of house calls and the 'working through' of conflicts no longer seem so literal or real, and these processes are revealed as perceptual patterns: help is also represented as the (joint) production or crafting of objects. It is impossible to list all the things that can be 'made' or 'done': we make fun and meaning, and also make our lives difficult or our work easier, for example, while we do studies, therapy and supervision. The range of this pattern is demonstrated by an abundance of prepositional constructions involving the word 'work': we work together, that is, col-labor-ate with clients, first re-appraising conflicts, then working them through, and finally processing them so that we can work towards certain goals. The conceptual metaphor behind this pattern is 'life is work'. The diagnostic elements of this metaphor consist in identifying what is to be considered unfinished work, which leads to the conclusion that this state needs to be changed by work. The relationship between professionals and clients can consist in working together on an (imaginary) object, but also in professionals working on clients without their collaboration.

All metaphorical concepts contain an implicit diagnosis of the clients, a figurative and cognitive core and recommendations for action that are normatively loaded. They assign roles, provide a normative background and suggest certain forms of relationship. These functions are melded with the social scene imagined in the metaphor and can only be separated out by analysis. Each concept highlights different ways of shaping the relationship and contains alternative frames. In the individual analyses these metaphorical patterns of interpretation associated with helping were linked to each other in individualized combinations or were unavailable to individual helpers in characteristic ways. This knowledge that is structured in narratives and metaphors is tacit and thus cannot be represented in propositions: these are the 'metaphors we help by'.

Dark holes in the network of concepts – or boundaries of the profession?

The field of outreach social family assistance is thus characterized in the patterns of its professional knowledge – but the field and its boundaries become more evident when we look at which metaphors are not used or look at metaphors used in other professional fields. For comparison, some other studies from neighbouring professions, education and the health professions are therefore presented.

In the studies conducted by de Guerrero and Villamil (2000, 2002) which employed a sentence completion test, English teachers in Puerto Rico were first asked to complete sentences such as 'A teacher is like . . .' with a metaphor. In the course of the workshop the metaphor was then further differentiated in discussions. The group discussion was recorded and evaluated using the method described by Cameron and Low (1999). The following complementary metaphoric constructs emerged of teachers and students:

- Artists and raw material
- Challengers and objects of transformation
- Co-operative leaders and active participants
- Providers and recipients of knowledge
- Providers of nourishment and developing organisms
- Providers of tools and builders
- Reformers and resisters
- Repairers and defective individuals
- Trainers and sportsmen

In Germany, Marsch (2009) has collected metaphors of teaching and learning used by biology teachers. She sees four main patterns of metaphors, in which teaching and learning respectively are depicted as walking and travelling, drumming in and internalizing, building and constructing, and connecting and linking. Less frequently used concepts for teaching and learning were planting and gardening, seeing and uncovering, working and performing, educating and leaving an imprint, saving and storing, and fighting and training. Even this initial comparison with the metaphors of social work shows that the semantic networks that characterize the distinctiveness of the profession are completely different from those of teachers. Before going on to draw conclusions, reference will be made to two further studies on the health professions.

Van Rijn-van Tongeren (1997) analyzed thirty-three papers from two major works on oncology. She identified the following source areas of medical thinking and notable metaphoric concepts: tumour cells are understood as acting like persons who disregard the rules of their society, in that they do not bother about the rules of their tissue but act autonomously. When their spread is described metaphorically as 'invading' healthy tissues and 'colonizing', discussions of the various cell mechanisms are unavoidably couched in images of defence and attack: cancer becomes a war. In this context, we often find attributions of a causal agency. Other metaphors are the representation of the reproduction of DNA and other types of cells using the metaphor of a text that is copied or translated. The malignant process is also portrayed in spatial terms as steps or stages, in a variation on the path metaphor. In addition, the author draws attention to medical theories formulated in these metaphorical concepts. Here the metaphor of disorderly, deviant cells as the 'enemy' obscures other factors such as the social influences on cancer. In treatment, conceived as a 'war' against these cells, all radical means become appropriate – consequently, the side effects of treatments such as chemotherapy and radiotherapy may not be very explicitly addressed.

Schiefer (2006) investigated the metaphors contained in hospital discharge reports and doctors' referral letters and reconstructed the following metaphorical concepts: sickness as a subject that can be captured, located and quantified; sickness and therapy as a course or path; health as the exclusion of sickness; diagnosis as an isolated space; treatment as a position in space; examination results as a scale; understanding and diagnosis as seeing; sickness and diagnosis as a heavy or light weight; sickness as a burden to be borne; and diagnosis as a riddle or puzzle, where the doctor is a detective. In this study the metaphor of the 'fight' against illness is missing, which evidently did not fit the special communicative situation of the doctor's referral letter, which can be seen as a controlled or controlling transfer of knowledge.

What, then, are the overarching commonalities and variances between the metaphoric networks of professional knowledge? First, there are similarities over the path metaphor, albeit with nuanced differences. Like Schiefer (2006) for doctors, both de Guerrero and Villami (2000, 2002) and Marsch (2009) demonstrate the employment of path metaphors by teachers. However, each of these metaphors has different field-specific connotations. In social work the concern is to put clients back on track; in education it is to tread the path systematically, each stage developing after another; and in medicine the interest is in developing a path and, where there is evidence-based knowledge, in prescribing a path. Second, metaphors that conceive of life as organic growth and compare professional activities to the tasks of a gardener – from watering and fertilizing to pruning and destroying weeds – are also partly shared in common. They go back to a group of pedagogical metaphors from the Renaissance (Bilstein 1996) and are also found in humanistic forms of therapy, as well as teaching in adult education (Schmitt 2006), and in counselling (Schröder 2015). However, in contexts of crisis in outreach social work, helpers find it more difficult to frame their work in terms of naturally occurring processes. Third, there are also similarities and differences between professions in the use of metaphors of 'fighting'. Schulze (2007) found that metaphors of 'battle' were used by helpers working as court-appointed special advocates to describe proceedings in contentious custody cases. The social work professionals also mostly see themselves as 'peace strategists' or 'peacemakers'. Here the 'battle' is either located outside of the profession or the profession is defined in opposition to it, in parallel with the more systemic use of this metaphor in the health professions in relation to life-threatening illnesses (see, for example, Schmitt and Böhnke 2009).

Given the current incomplete state of the empirical analysis of metaphors, we cannot exclude the possibility that there may be other important metaphors used in social work. Nevertheless, the comparison with the semantic networks of education and the health professions demonstrates that each of these networks is different and that the metaphors of social work are simpler, but more existentially central in addressing tasks in this area, such as giving and taking, attachment and freedom, providing clarity of vision, and opening up and closing. The professional knowledge of social workers should therefore be characterized as a network of cognitive constructs, in which certain aspects like self-definition and diagnosis are largely missing. Metaphorical concepts leave room for differentiation. However, each metaphor not only generates possibilities, but also leaves alternative modes of thinking out of the picture. Lakoff and Johnson discuss this in terms of 'highlighting' and 'hiding' (Lakoff and Johnson 1980).

Conclusion: the development of professional knowledge in social work

In light of the aforementioned nine models of metaphors of social work and the two contrasting professions, we can arrive at a more specific characterization of professional knowledge in social work. For example, we already know from pre-theoretical and everyday language what the goals of successful social work are. Psychological and social flexibility are associated with well-being. This does not imply a lack of connection, but being connected in many ways and to many people. We want 'clear', predictable life situations rather than 'dark times' and must try to be not too 'burdened, but 'relieved'. Procedural or flow models, as well as goals, are generated on the basis of metaphoric concepts, as illustrated by starting in a 'tight' situation and moving through 'balancing acts' to reach a 'free space for oneself', beginning with 'embroilments' and moving through 'development' to 'attachments' – progressing from the 'dark' to the 'clear', from the 'burden' to 'relief'. The normative potential of metaphors for the success of helping interventions is obvious; they reveal cultural schemas and judgements, as it may not be true in all cultures that movement is preferred to rest and light to dark. Metaphors therefore constitute an 'unintended learning paradigm' (Oevermann et al. 1976:376) into which we are socialized. They are patterns of experience and categorical frames which guide our future experiences.

In addition, in developing the categorization of social work, the metaphorical expressions used by social workers may seem to border on banality. However, in the accentuated form shown by the metaphor analysis they reveal implicit rules and patterns of professional knowledge. Thus, for instance, the model of 'moderate closeness' in the helping relationship that is suggested by the metaphors of path/pathway and bond/attachment presents a view of successful interaction that needs to be re-learned again and again during training. Where assistance is unsuccessful, this can be both anticipated and interpreted in terms of a 'relapse', 'embroilment' or 'overload'. Overall, the metaphorical models constitute a system of action that is both contradictory and mutually corrective. Thus, if social workers were to act only by giving support and providing relief, allowing themselves to be guided by the metaphors of burden alone without observing the recommended metaphorical distance in the helping relationship, this would be more likely ultimately to lead to unsatisfactory resolutions of the dilemmas of their clients.

Moreover, the social work profession is organized on the basis of pre-theoretical patterns of interpretation. None of the metaphorical concepts has a strong relation to theories learned during the interviewees' professional education. That practitioners make little reference to academic knowledge is a frequent criticism in studies on the theory of the professions (Dewe 2012). This criticism, though, fails to take note that professional knowledge draws on other sources. The metaphorical cores described above are doubly determined. They spring from collective commonsense knowledge and are rooted in the individuals' personal histories (Schachtner 1999; Schmitt 2006). While life history studies are carried out in research on the social work profession, they do not link the schema of interpretation of the world built up over the life span with the reservoir of collective patterns of thought (Jakob 2010). Only these blends of cultural and personal patterns produce the cognitive core in which theories and methods can be assimilated. In the literature, students' patterns of interpretation are often described as dark matter that repulses more scientific formulations. Such texts tend to teach students to distance themselves from, and be critical of, their own personal histories (Graßhoff and Schweppe 2012). They do not draw attention to the importance of common sense and the helper's personal life history as a source of professional knowledge. Studies using metaphor analysis suggest that it is such prior understanding gained in the individual's life world that is central to professional knowledge. Following this line of argument, Schachtner (1999) has linked *habitus* and metaphorical concepts of professional practice with personal history in relation to general practitioners, but no corresponding study has yet been carried out in social work.

A further aspect of the characterization of social work arising from this chapter is that the metaphorical schema that are present in the respective cultures and have been individually acquired can be modified by several processes in the course of theoretical and practical training. Concepts such as those invoking war or organic conceptions are either not supported or negatively sanctioned and are thus used less and less. Other concepts such as metaphors of learning reminiscent of school become more differentiated as students become acquainted with more complex metaphors. Theories often cannot be reduced to a single metaphor, as they are all complex architectures of linguistic images (Buchholz 1993). Blumenberg (1960) has reconstructed the metaphors central to philosophy, while Kuhn (1993) has described metaphors as the core of scientific paradigms. However, there are as yet no studies on metaphors in theories of social work. It is also possible that new metaphorical patterns can be learned, even if they have not previously been relevant in a person's life. From the standpoint of cognitive linguistics, learning is an interaction between the metaphorical schema that students already employ and the metaphors of the target material to be learned (Gropengießer 1998). In a study by Schmitt (2014), first year students' seminar papers were analyzed for their metaphors of 'society'. The majority of these revealed a critical view of society. Apart from the metaphors of the division into 'lower' and 'upper' social classes, the classical sociological metaphors for society, from Durkheim and Marx to Bourdieu and Goffman (see López 2003; Rigney 2001), were not systematically found in students' texts. Nonetheless, despite the limited nature of the students' metaphors, they had a clear normative content relevant to how social work defines itself. Far from adjusting students' thinking to the metaphors of scientific theories, it is essential in terms of cognitive linguistics that academic and practical training links up with students' patterns of thinking. Didactic methods are therefore needed that allow further differentiation of existing patterns of learning to encompass new metaphorical models and the critical appraisal of both old and new patterns with a view to finding blind spots.

Finally, it is precisely when they fall back on everyday patterns of interpretation that social workers can bridge the boundaries between professional systems and institutions and act as brokers for their clients (Abbott 1995). While this everyday knowledge enables us to transcend boundaries, it profits little from being upgraded by knowledge at a higher symbolic level in terms of science. Perhaps this is the reason why social work has a lower social status than the classical professions. In view of the metaphors taken from everyday language, incursions that extend into the 'jurisdictional claims' of social work from the theoretically homogeneous linguistic worlds of other disciplines are difficult to defend. This can also be seen as a paradox for social work as a profession, for on the one hand using simplistic metaphors can provide a good position for understanding and helping clients, but on the other these simple metaphors might stand in the way of professionalization in terms of a defensible jurisdiction, discretion and status in relation to the public and other professions. Müller (2008) was using a metaphor that upgrades the profession when he spoke of the 'polyglot' communication in social work that transcends the boundaries of the systems and likewise the exclusions to which the systems lead. As such, this chapter, in reviewing the metaphors we help by, has important lessons for the future of social work as a profession.

References

Abbott, A. (1988) *The System of Professions: An Essay on the Division of Expert Labor*. Chicago: University of Chicago Press.

Abbott, A. (1995) Boundaries of social work or social work of boundaries? *The Social Service Review* 69(4): 545–62.

Baier, F. (2015) Bedrohungen und systemische kontexte sozialarbeiterischer professionalität in schulen. In: R. Becker-Lenz, S. Busse, G. Ehlert and S. Müller-Hermann (eds) *Bedrohte Professionalität: Einschränkungen und Aktuelle Herausforderungen für die Soziale Arbeit*. Wiesbaden: Springer.

Bilstein, J. (1996) Zur metaphorik des generationenverhältnisses. In: E. Liebau and C. Wulf (eds) *Generation: Versuche über eine Pädagogisch-anthropologische Grundbedingung*. Weinheim: Deutscher Studien Verlag.

Black, M. (1983) Mehr über die metapher. In: A. Haverkamp (eds) *Theorie der Metapher*. Darmstadt: Wissenschaftliche Buchgesellschaft.

Blumenberg, H. (1960) Paradigmen zu einer metaphorologie, *Archiv für Begriffsgeschichte* 6: 7–142.

Buchholz, M. B. (ed) (1993) *Metaphernanalyse*. Göttingen: Vandenhoeck & Ruprecht.

Buchholz, M. B. (1996) *Metaphern der 'Kur'. Eine Qualitative Studie zum Psychotherapeutischen Prozess*. Opladen: Westdeutscher Verlag.

Buchholz, M. B. and von Kleist, C. (1995) Metaphernanalyse eines therapiegespräches. In: Buchholz, M. B. (ed) *Psychotherapeutische Interaktion: Qualitative Studien zu Konversation und Metapher, Geste und Plan*. Opladen: Westdeutscher Verlag.

Cameron, L. and Low, G. (eds) (1999) *Researching and Applying Metaphor*. Cambridge: Cambridge University Press.

de Guerrero, M. C. M. and Villamil, O. S. (2000) Exploring ESL teachers' roles through metaphor analysis, *TESOL Quarterly* 34(2): 341–51.

de Guerrero, M. C. M. and Villamil, O. S. (2002) Metaphorical conceptualizations of ESL teaching and learning, *Language Teaching Research* 6(2): 95–120.

Dewe, B. (2012) Akademische ausbildung in der sozialen arbeit – Vermittlung von theorie und praxis oder relationierung von wissen und können im spektrum von wissenschaft, organisation und profession. In: R. Becker-Lenz, S. Busse, G. Ehlert and S. Müller-Hermann (eds) *Professionalität Sozialer Arbeit und Hochschule: Wissen, Kompetenz, Habitus und Identität im Studium Sozialer Arbeit*. Wiesbaden: Springer.

Graßhoff, G. and Schweppe, C. (2012) Fallarbeit – Studium – Biographie. In: R. Becker-Lenz, S. Busse, G. Ehlert and S. Müller-Hermann (eds) *Professionalität Sozialer Arbeit und Hochschule*. Wiesbaden: Springer.

Gropengießer, H. (1998) *Didaktische Rekonstruktion des Sehens: Wissenschaftliche Theorien und die Sicht der Schüler in der Perspektive der Vermittlung*. Oldenburg: Carl von Ossietzky-Universität.

Jakob, G. (2010) Analyse professionellen handelns. In: K. Bock and I. Miethe (eds) *Handbuch Qualitative Methoden in der Sozialen Arbeit.* Opladen: Barbara Budrich.

Johnson, M. (1987) *The Body in the Mind: The Bodily Basis of Meaning, Imagination and Reason.* Chicago: University of Chicago Press.

Kuhn, T. (1993) Metaphor in science. In: A. Ortony (ed) *Metaphor and Thought.* New York: Cambridge University Press.

Lakoff, G. (1987) *Women, Fire and Dangerous Things: What Categories Reveal about the Mind.* Chicago: University of Chicago Press.

Lakoff, G. and Johnson, M. (1980) *Metaphors We Live By.* Chicago: University of Chicago Press.

Lakoff, G. and Johnson, M. (1999) *Philosophy in the Flesh: The Embodied Mind and Its Challenge to Western Thought.* New York: Basic Books.

Liljegren, A. (2012) Key metaphors in the sociology of professions: Occupations as hierarchies and landscapes, *Comparative Sociology* 11: 88–112.

López, J. (2003) *Society and Its Metaphors: Language, Social Theory and Social Structure.* London: Continuum.

Marsch, S. (2009) *Metaphern des Lehrens und Lernens. Vom Denken, Reden und Handeln bei Biologielehrern.* Dissertation zur Erlangung des akademischen Grades eines Doktors der Naturwissenschaften Eingereicht im Fachbereich Biologie, Chemie, Pharmazie der Freien Universität Berlin.

Müller, M. (2008) *Polyglotte Kommunikation Sozialer Arbeit: Eine Sozialarbeiterische Kommunikationstheorie der Praxis.* Heidelberg: Carl Auer.

Oevermann, U., Gripp, H., Allert, T., Konau, E., Krambeck, J., Schroeder-Caesar, E. and Schütze, Y. (1976) Beobachtungen zur struktur der sozialisatorischen interaktion. In: M. Auwärter, E. Kirsch and K. Schröter (eds) *Seminar: Kommunikation, Interaktion, Identität.* Frankfurt am Main: Suhrkamp.

Rigney, D. (2001) *The Metaphorical Society: An Invitation to Social Theory.* Boston: Rowman & Littlefield.

Schachtner, C. (1999) *Ärztliche Praxis: Die Gestaltende Kraft der Metapher.* Frankfurt am Main: Suhrkamp.

Schiefer, M. (2006) *Die Metaphorische Sprache in der Medizin: Metaphorische Konzeptualisierungen in der Medizin und Ihre Ethischen Implikationen Untersucht Anhand von Arztbriefanalysen.* Berlin: LIT-Verlag.

Schmitt, R. (1995) *Metaphern des Helfens.* Weinheim: Psychologie Verlags Union.

Schmitt, R. (2005) Systematic metaphor analysis as a method of qualitative research, *The Qualitative Report* 10(2): 358–94.

Schmitt, R. (2006) "Was ihr einmal gelernt habt, kann euch keiner mehr wegnehmen". Metaphern in biographien der erwachsenenbildung. In: D. Nittel and C. Maier (eds) *Persönliche Erinnerung und Kulturelles Gedächtnis: Einblicke in das Lebensgeschichtliche Archiv der Hessischen Erwachsenenbildung.* Opladen: Barbara Budrich.

Schmitt, R. (2011) Systematische metaphernanalyse als qualitative sozialwissenschaftliche forschungsmethode, *Metaphorik* 21: 47–82.

Schmitt, R. (2013) Zuwendung zum menschen und andere bilder sozialer Interaktion. Metaphernanalyse als forschungsmethode in der sozialen arbeit. In: W.-R. Wendt (ed) *Zuwendung zum Menschen in der Sozialen Arbeit: Festschrift für Albert Mühlum.* Lage: Jacobs.

Schmitt, R. (2014) Bilder der gesellschaft von studierenden der sozialen arbeit: Das eltern-modell und andere herausforderungen für soziologisches wissen. In: U.

Unterkofler and E. Oestreicher (eds) *Theorie-Praxis-Bezüge in Professionellen Feldern. Wissensentwicklung und Verwendung als Herausforderung*. Opladen: Budrich UniPress.

Schmitt, R. and Böhnke, U. (2009) Detailfunde, überdeutungen und einige lichtblicke: Metaphern in pflegewissenschaftlichen analysen. In: I. Darmann-Finck, U. Böhnke and K. Straß (eds) *Fallrekonstruktives Lernen: Ein Beitrag zur Professionalisierung in den Berufsfeldern Pflege und Gesundheit*. Frankfurt am Main: Mabuse.

Schön, D. A. (1979) Generative metaphor: A perspective on problem-setting in social policy. In: A. Ortony (ed) *Metaphor and Thought*. Cambridge: Cambridge University Press.

Schröder, J. (2015) *"Ich könnt ihr eine donnern": Metaphern in der Beratung von Männern mit Gewalterfahrungen*. Weinheim: Beltz-Juventa.

Schulze, H. (2007) *Handeln im Konflikt: Eine Qualitativ-empirische Studie zu Kindesinteressen und Professionellem Handeln in Familiengericht und Jugendhilfe*. Würzburg: Ergon.

Schützeichel, R. (2014) Professionshandeln und professionswissen – eine soziologische skizze. In: U. Unterkofler and E. Oestreicher (eds) *Theorie-Praxis-Bezüge in Professionellen Feldern*. Opladen: Budrich UniPress.

van Rijn-van Tongeren, G. (1997) *Metaphors in Medical Texts*. Amsterdam and Atlanta: Editions Rodopi.

11 Metaphors in medical practice
A jurisdictional tool

Inge Kryger Pedersen

Introduction

Metaphor is a common way to describe life and death as well as symptoms and health. Sontag (1991) has shown in her book *Illness as Metaphors* how metaphors perform basic functions in doctor–patient encounters and communication. An understanding of metaphor is as important for doctors as for patients, and indeed for the sociology of professions. Metaphor analyses can allow us to develop new and interesting insights about how professions can and might work. As metaphors interact not only with our understanding, but also with our actions and practice, metaphor studies of professional work itself are important. Metaphors reveal underlying assumptions, and through metaphor we generate an image of data (Morgan 1980). In line with this knowledge, the thesis for this chapter is that medical doctors' metaphorical projections are drawn from their profession's resources of images and symbols attached to their work tasks, jurisdiction, and the issues available in their professional culture. The chapter will illustrate that doctors and patients use different kinds of metaphors – and metaphors shared by both. Different kinds of metaphors illuminate different cultures (Lakoff and Johnson 1980). Mutual metaphors illuminate where they meet.

Suffering, pain, many symptoms and ailments can meaningfully be represented only in metaphor. Most metaphor studies are found within how patients embody medical explanations (Mabeck and Olesen 1997; Webster, Douglas and Lewis 2009) and sick people describe and perceive their illness (Fleischman 1999; Gwyn 1999; McMullen 1989; Reventlow et al. 2008). How metaphors are used in medical practice as a kind of tool for the practitioner to either fashion meaning as a listener (Kirmayer 1993) or use as illustrating or conceptualizing knowledge in the act of speaking to the patient is less investigated (Skelton, Wearn and Hobbs 2002). This chapter builds on empirical studies to examine which metaphors come into being in the encounter between medical doctors and their patients in order to locate metaphor as part of professional culture. Indeed, there are complex ways that metaphor arises from such encounters and this is not the only way to understand metaphors. For example, metaphor is also part of mind and bodily experience. However, the focus here is to demonstrate how students and scholars within the sociology of professions can use metaphor studies to examine the tasks of professions. The chapter seeks to provide awareness of doing metaphor research that "requires scholars to be explicit about underlying mechanisms of thought and language central to metaphor theory" (Gibbs 2008:10).

As it is emphasized in the literature on metaphor (Fitzgerald 1993; Geertz 1973; Keesing 1987), metaphorical domains are influenced by values and norms in the social and cultural context. In this chapter it is assumed – although they can be surface analogies for the sake of lucidity (Skelton, Wearn and Hobbs 2002) – that metaphors are the embodiment of experience, as well as anchored in shared worlds of experience. Gibbs (2008:3) has noted: "Metaphor is not simply an ornamental aspect of language, but a fundamental scheme by which people conceptualize the world and their own activities." However, there are also a variety of types of metaphor and hierarchies – for example: deep, surface, conceptual, poetic, scientific, idiosyncratic, conventionalized, live, dead and many other metaphorical concepts (Morgan 1996). In this chapter, I will focus on conceptual metaphors in order to explore how medical doctors apply their knowledge in practice. Drawing on the notions of jurisdiction and boundary work (Abbott 1988, 1995), I will discuss the use of conceptual metaphors as a reassuring signal of expertise. In particular, the focus is on which conceptual metaphors of the body are used in medical practice. The human body is the core object of medical science and practice and is wracked by complexity as a concept. Thus, the use of bodily metaphors seems to help communication in medical practice.

Through a search of literature on medical practice and metaphor, I have selected a few studies that are not necessarily representative but are proposed to draw attention to how conceptual metaphors used by doctors in the encounters with their patients might be indicators of professional culture. In what follows, I begin by defining the concept of metaphor used in this chapter. I address how 'culture', here professional knowledge and encounter culture, is a filter for emerging metaphors. Following this, I examine metaphor use in medical practice and the role that metaphors can play in the doctor–patient encounter. Tensions inherent in the doctor's role are examined by analyzing the use of conceptual metaphors as a reassuring signal of expertise. It is shown how metaphors are epistemological in contributing specific frames for viewing, in this case the human body. Before concluding the chapter, how the metaphorical system of the doctor may be regarded is discussed, as an "appropriate way of imposing ordered calm on a disparate mass of expressive data" (Skelton, Wearn and Hobbs 2002:117). It is argued that engagement with professional metaphors can facilitate understanding of authorized expertise and implicit jurisdictional claims.

Conceptual metaphors as indicators of professional culture

In their book *Metaphors We Live By*, Lakoff and Johnson (1980) demonstrate how metaphors are not just talk – or poetical or rhetorical embellishments. We can be conscious of using metaphors or we employ so-called dead metaphors of which we are not consciously aware. In both cases, metaphors condition the ways we conceptualize the world. 'Dead' metaphors also have the power to influence. As Kövecses (2002:ix) has emphasized, 'dead' metaphors that have become so conventional that they have ceased to be metaphors are, indeed, "metaphors we live by". Lakoff and Johnson (1980) write about 'conceptual metaphors' as covering profound truths about the way we perceive the world. A well-known conceptual metaphor is 'argument is war' as structuring a cultural way of thinking, experiencing, functioning and acting when we argue. This metaphor is reflected in a wide variety of expressions. They mention, for example: 'Your claims are indefensible', 'He attacked every weak point in my argument', 'His criticisms were right on target', 'I've never *won* an argument with him' (Lakoff and Johnson 1980:4). Argument and war are different kinds of things – this is essential about metaphor – but 'argument' is partially understood and talked about in terms of 'war' and this metaphor structures the actions we perform in arguing.

In many metaphor analyses, similes are distinguished from metaphors only by the presence of the word 'like', or its equivalent. Here this distinction is not relevant, and 'metaphor' covers both similes and metaphors. However, too much similarity might be of no use. Brown (1976:173) notes that a good metaphor "offers us a new awareness" and is an appropriate mix of difference and similarity. A common definition is that a metaphor is the act or process of denoting one concept or idea with a sign conventionally tied to another field, context or domain. However, there are gradations, for example, between metaphor and metonymy. As Morgan (1996) has noted, metaphor opens a domain of understanding, metonymy ties down the detail. In other words: "metonymy is the process whereby the name of an element or characteristic of a phenomenon is used to represent the total phenomenon" (Morgan 1996:230). He refers to the well-known example of 'the Monarchy' (the total phenomenon) being described as 'the Crown' (metonymy). Another example is 'intelligent people' being described by the metonymy 'good heads'.

Morgan (1996) observes that metonymy is dependent on metaphor, since it draws on a prefigured image, and identification of metaphors is controversial. He addresses organization studies as an example, when illustrating the different roles of metaphor and metonymy. For example, if 'organization' is studied through a mechanical metaphor, an organization will likely be represented as 'a structure of parts' (metonymies), whereas if it is viewed through a cultural metaphor, it might be represented by different rituals or beliefs as metonymies. This means that when analyzing metonymies it is possible to indicate a metaphorical image. Giving proper acknowledgment to metaphor and metonymy is important for the work of many professions. Using metaphor is not just 'loose talk' or necessarily unscientific. But when science seeks to achieve an objective form of knowledge, the tendency is, as Morgan (1996:231) has noted, "to try to tame, moderate, deny or deride the metaphorical, while implicitly asserting the importance and superiority of the metonymical".

Yu (2008) argues, in line with Lakoff and Johnson, that 'culture' is a filter for emerging metaphors. This might explain why within science we see examples on 'taming' metaphors. Yu has shown how some expressions are closely equivalent across the Chinese and English languages, but he has also found that some are not. Many bodily experiences, such as making a mistake or forgiving, are commonly shared by all human beings. However, they may not pass the 'filter of culture' for metaphorical mappings. As Lakoff and Johnson (1980:14–21) have shown, our physical and cultural experience provides many possible bases for spatialization, orientational and other metaphors. As Yu (2008:253) says: "Which ones are chosen and which ones are major may vary from culture to culture". The cultural basis for metaphors is also emphasized by Gibbs (1999:155) when he notes that:

. . . embodied metaphor arises not from within the body alone, and is then represented in the minds of individuals, but emerges from bodily interactions that are to a large extent defined by the cultural world. . . . [B]odily experiences that form the source domains for conceptual metaphors are themselves complex social and cultural constructions.

Indeed, as Yu (2008:254) observes, there is a bodily basis of metaphors, but this is only part of the whole experiential basis: "The actual selection of a metaphor depends to an important extent on its cultural basis". Likewise, Lakoff and Johnson (1980, 1999) argue that conceptual metaphors structure our conceptual systems, not arbitrarily but grounded in our physical *and* cultural experience. When I highlight 'and' in italics, it is because Lakoff and Johnson (1980:57) emphasize that physical or embodied experience "is never merely a matter of having a body of a certain sort; rather, *every* [their emphasis] experience takes place within a vast background of cultural presuppositions". They continue:

Cultural assumptions, values, and attitudes are not a conceptual overlay which we may or may not place upon experience as we choose. It would be more correct to say that all experience is cultural through and through, that we experience our 'world' in such a way that our culture is already present in the very experience itself.

However, not all metaphors are necessarily culture specific. Some might be potentially universal or widespread, but I will not dwell on that discussion in this chapter (see Kövecses 2002, 2005; Yu 2008). A lot more could be said about the complexity of metaphor (see, for example, Lakoff and Johnson 1999), but the important issue is that these theoretical and analytical considerations stress that metaphor emerges from the interaction between body and culture – or rather between the cultural body and the cultural and social world. This issue is a point of departure for this chapter that is too short for undertaking a decompositional analysis (see Yu 2008). Metaphor use in professional work will be illustrated in a bodily, cultural and sociological perspective assuming that metaphors are not only a 'heuristic' rule for simplifying reality but fundamental to knowledge. Metaphor shapes the thinking and language we use to talk about things (Brown 1976), but also creates the social world. This means that scientific thinking and studies are also guided by – and create – metaphors. As Morgan has noted (1980:611), science may be seen:

> . . . as a creative process in which scientists view the world metaphorically through the language and concepts which filter and structure their perceptions of their subject of study and through the specific metaphors which they implicitly or explicitly choose to develop their framework for analysis.

The sections that follow are positioned to illustrate how and which metaphors are used within the practice of medicine and will only be exemplified with words or statements which are clearly metaphors (for identifying metaphors, see Cameron and Low 1999). From a bird's eye view, the remainder of this chapter will observe and discuss examples of metaphors used in medical work to strengthen our attention on what engagement practitioners might be trying to evoke in the encounter with their patients. Metaphors do more than "just add a little extra rhetorical spice. They also help to increase our communicative capacities" (Alvesson and Spicer 2011:38). Human bodies are successively represented by machine metaphors, without asserting that they are these things. Patients are thrust back on their own interpretations in making sense of their bodies' 'reality'. The assumption here is that metaphor captures and creates features of our world. Metaphor shapes but can also darken our thinking, practice and perceiving. We should be open but also alert to the partiality and sometimes arbitrariness of how metaphor is used. In what follows, we shall see that critical scrutiny is important in use and analysis of metaphor because certain metaphors in specific contexts can be dangerous and counteract compliance.

Metaphors in medical practice

Why do metaphor and the medical profession matter to each other? In this section, I will demonstrate how studies of conceptual metaphors can disclose a way of thinking and seeing within professional work. The assumption is that as within law and legal reasoning (Winter 2008) as well as mathematics (Núñes 2008), metaphors used by practitioners within the medical field as another 'exact' professional area will demonstrate important aspects of medical reasoning. Very little empirical research has been conducted within this area, so this section should not be taken as showing how medical reasoning and practice is always performed. Empirical studies of conceptual metaphors that are used in doctor–patient encounters are particular examples of verbal metaphor and might not be representative. Which metaphors are used in tasks by the medical profession will be illustrated and discussed as a precursor to future metaphor studies on the medical profession in defending a metaphorical view of how professional work is enacted.

How does a bladder work? What is a urinary tract infection? These questions posed by patients might be dependent on metaphor for their answers. Skelton, Wearn and Hobbs (2002) have found that doctors use mechanical metaphors to explain disease – for example, the urinary tract was depicted as the 'waterworks'. Based on transcriptions of 373 consultations with 40 doctors from 21 UK general practices, a central difference between doctors and patients appeared to be a greater frequency in use of metaphors to do with machines among doctors. Back pains could be 'mechanical' and the body was 'a machine' or 'a system' that could be 'repaired' (Skelton, Wearn and Hobbs 2002:116). Among the patients the body was 'a container for the self' – for example '[her temper's] like Satan's got into her' or 'my body seems full of nerves'. On several occasions, patients used metaphors when apologizing for their inability to describe their sensations. In describing their symptoms they employed a wide spectrum of vivid metaphors, less mechanical and problem- or solution-oriented and more sensitive when, for instance, describing pains by 'torture'. It is striking in the study by Skelton, Wearn and Hobbs that patients had a lot of different metaphorical descriptors for aches and pains, whereas doctors had only few and mostly literal terms, such as 'severity'.

However, as Skelton, Wearn and Hobbs (2002) recount, doctors and patients also had several metaphors they shared. For example illness is an 'attack', 'battle', 'defense', 'fight' or 'fire' and pains can be 'burning'. In line with these metaphors, doctors spoke of themselves as 'problem solvers' and 'controllers of disease'. They were most likely to talk of 'controlling' and not curing disease. Illness was 'a puzzle' and a problem that they as doctors should solve. Skelton, Wearn and Hobbs (2002:117) note that doctors used metaphors which "hint at knowledge and power in obvious ways" – reinterpreting patients' explanations as "emotionally neutral problems of a general, depersonalized type". The authors suggest that patients might be reassured "by having their images reinterpreted into recognizable disease states that enable categorization and alleviation", and they might regard their doctor's metaphors "as an appropriate way of imposing ordered calm on a disparate mass of expressive data". Thus, this study on the whole shows how the doctor's metaphorical system signals expertise within solving and controlling illness problems which are a kind of mechanical attack. Skelton, Wearn and Hobbs emphasize, though, that it might not be a bad thing if doctors would make a few attempts to enter the patients' metaphorical world. They argue that knowing how their patients perceive their bodies might further the doctors' abilities to communicate in the encounter.

This point is supported by the metaphor study of Reventlow et al. (2008) on women's perception of risk related to osteoporosis. Their study illustrates how knowledge about patients' perceptions is important for professional practice. When patients perceive their body as a 'building' and perceptions of osteoporosis are framed by imagery of brittle bone, frail skeleton and a collapsing backbone in this 'building' it might be difficult for practitioners to get patients to be compliant if they recommend physical exercises as a tool to prevent the potential consequences of the risk condition. Without knowing how their patients perceive their bodies, practitioners might not be able to communicate with them. By obtaining information about the patients' conception of their ill-health – for example, knowing that their patients are not able to trust their bodies – the professional work would be likely to be more qualified.

Reventlow et al. (2008:112) emphasize that the "way language is used is crucial for the perception of the risk in lay people". In particular, when the illnesses or bodily risk factors, such as the case of osteoporosis, share the feature of invisibility, it can be difficult for people to connect the risk information with their own experiences. If their images of their bodies are 'buildings' and osteoporosis destroys the 'foundations' and 'bricks', it might be an important professional task to construct new images of more dynamic bone mass as a living material to change patients accounts of the destruction of bones. Thus, the challenge for the clinician/practitioner is, as Reventlow et al. (2008:113) put it: "to discover what metaphors best serve the patients' healing process and conception of the general health", in this case to "convey images of bones as living tissue that can benefit from exercise and that can be reconstructed during life". Here metaphor can become a tool in medical practice for the practitioner to fashion new meaning (see Kirmayer 1993).

We have shown how patients and doctors use different frameworks of knowledge and how doctors relate to more concrete domains in order to make explanations more comprehensible to their patients (see also Calnan 1984), as well as how their use of conceptual metaphors are a reassuring signal of expertise. A common metaphor medical doctors employ to talk about their patients' bodies is that of a machine or an engine. It may seem paradoxical to use a mechanical metaphor to designate the body that is a living entity. As a researcher with an active interest in the sociology of the body, health and illness and as a former researcher in the sociology of sport, I have been struck by the observation that the metaphors of the human body – and mind as well, for example in psychiatry and sport psychology – very often draw on a mechanical vocabulary (see also Gleyse 2013). The use of conceptual metaphor such as 'the body as a machine' or 'the body as an engine' might seem awkward from a sociologist's point of view and create – or confirm – some myths about a profession's view on humanity. In the next section, I shall, however, from a theoretical perspective discuss – and defend – such conceptual metaphors in a discussion about what a 'good' metaphor is when used conceptually in a professional context.

Jurisdictional work within metaphorical domains

Metaphors used about medicine help us in our search for professional culture and practice and practitioners' professional identity. Life and death are recurrent themes within medicine, and these themes are so broad and important that they can be represented meaningfully only in metaphor. By using certain kinds of metaphor, I will argue that medical doctors are practising jurisdictional work. Jurisdiction – that is "the more or less exclusive right to dominate a particular area of work" (Abbott 1995:551) – can be demonstrated in the use of metaphor. The core of a profession is to create the boundaries of the professional field. In the core or heart of the field, professionals may deal with pure professional knowledge and talking to other professionals in such a way as they would never speak to patients. To speak to patients directly or when acting as brokers, however, implies that doctors sometimes are doing some kind of 'boundary work'; they want to protect and legitimate their work within a medical scientific field. Therefore, they use a 'tamed' metaphor that is not subjective or expressive but clarifies their jurisdiction and not their temper or personal opinion.

The metaphor 'body as a machine' follows a long tradition going back to Descartes (1971:104), who wrote about the body, for example, as this "whole machine made up of flesh and bones". The machine metaphor is well suited to capturing an idea that the body needs to be kept in perfect running order. What store of meanings medical doctors draw on to construct and convey the notion of the body as a machine refers probably to occupational morality and professional ethics. Within the domain of machine metaphors, doctors figure as kinds of mechanics or repairers; this underpins their authority. In line with this, Abbott (1995:561) has stated that doctors, like most other professions, since the nineteenth century have changed their manner of justifying themselves as authorities from "trusted health advisors to technological sorcerers". Beisecker and Beisecker (1993) also discuss conflicts in doctor–patient relationships between paternalistic and consumeristic roles.

General practitioners might have a specific role compared with medical specialists such as surgeons or psychiatrists when they communicate with their patients about more general health problems. They are generalists and regularly act as brokers between such institutions as hospitals and families, as well as the social work profession. In bringing forces together in order to articulate their resources, we have seen that general practitioners and patients sometimes share metaphors. Likely, doctors want to deal only with patients' medical problems and they will have a higher status if they can remain separate from other kinds of complications. However, dealing with professional knowledge and practice is for general practitioners also a matter of communicating with patients and patients' relatives, and they may need to share understandings of the illness. Metaphors shared by doctors and patients in managing illness are, as we have seen, often military metaphors. Illness is described as an 'attack' and as something the doctor as well as the patient want to 'fight' and 'struggle with' or 'kill'. Treatments and the patient's body itself are seen as 'weapons'. The doctor as well as the patient are 'warriors' and 'fighters' who engage in the 'war'. Disease is endemic and should be 'combated'. These are mutual metaphors, which can also be shared with relatives or other third parties.

Within polar extremes ranging from paternalism to consumerism in terms of the autonomy of doctors and patients, doctors doing boundary work might behave paternalistically or consumeristically. As Beisecker and Beisecker (1993) have noted, paternalism was traditionally advocated within the medical profession as a metaphor for the doctor–patient relationship, where the role of the patient was to obey and cooperate and the role of the doctor was to direct and prescribe (see also Parsons 1951). Consumerism focuses not on obligations for both parties but on each side's right and is as a metaphor employed to characterize the doctor–patient relationship in the context of free-market competitive forces (Beisecker and Beisecker 1993). Due to the professional ethic that 'doctoring together' should always be in the best interests of the patient (Freidson 1975), doctor and patient may agree on different relationships depending on the patient's condition. When the patient is healthy or has a chronic illness, a consumeristic relationship involving patient decision might be preferred, whereas when a patient's health status is severe, he or she may prefer the doctor to behave paternalistically (Beisecker and Beisecker 1993). These polar extremes are about patients' as well as doctors' obligations and rights, and patients and doctors might use and create appropriate metaphors for viewing their relationship as well as their different tasks in the encounter.

Among others, Martin (1997) has suggested that metaphors used in science differ from those employed in expressive language. This has been illustrated by patients' use of different kinds of metaphors than those of doctors. Metaphors used in science are often well defined and validated by a number of correct inferences. Doctors' metaphorical system may be regarded – as we previously have seen from Skelton, Wearn and Hobbs (2002) – as a way of ordering a disparate mass of data. Although many metaphors are used in science, they are sometimes hidden behind a veil of 'objectivity'. Metaphor might present a threat to this objectivity on which science seeks to build, as Morgan (1996) has also noted. He argues, though, that science is influenced by and creates metaphor, but this does not make science less objective. Metaphor can create 'truths'; however, he emphasizes that these are 'partial truths'. For example, Morgan (1996:232–33), taking the scientific question of whether light is a wave or a particle, says:

If scientists study light as a wave, it reveals itself as a wave. If it is studied as a particle, it reveals itself as a particle. Each image or way of seeing generates distinctive insights; distinctive 'truths'.

When creating partial truths, it is clear that metaphor has both strengths and limitations. Metaphors can create and express meaning but also blind spots as well as misunderstanding, or surface rather than in-depth understanding. From a sociological point of view, the 'body as a machine' metaphor might appear as surface rather than in-depth understanding of the human body. However, from a medical point of view, this metaphor may underpin medical doctors' jurisdictional task – that the patient's body needs to be kept in perfect running order.

From a scientific viewpoint, the use of metaphor may be seen as having unfortunate consequences in terms of its relativity and lack of rigour, bringing potential ideological bias (Alvesson 1993). These are not reasons not to use metaphor in scientific or professional work, since doing metaphorical work can open up and advance research as well. Among others, Morgan (1993, 2006) has demonstrated this in his books *Imaginization: The Art of Creative Management* and *Images of Organization*. Indeed, it is important to address use of metaphor critically and understand how and why certain metaphors come into prominence. In this chapter, I have tried to highlight this by indicating how metaphors work epistemologically by contributing with specific frames of perception and judgement, in relation, for example, to the human body. By using different metaphors, we can gain different kinds of knowledge and relationships. Therefore, some metaphors are more relevant and useful than others. Conversely, under certain circumstances, they might be misleading and create non-compliant patients.

The study by Reventlow et al. (2008) of osteoporosis patients' perceiving their body as a 'building' has illustrated such a problem. The body as a building is a metaphor in line with our definition that it denotes one concept or idea with a sign conventionally tied to another field, context or domain. Moreover, it is covered by the definition presented previously of a 'good' metaphor, namely a metaphor that "offers us a new awareness" (Brown 1976:173). However, in a clinical perspective the machine or engine metaphor might be better, if it is of importance that the patient is physical active. Reventlow et al. (2008:113) point out the challenge for the practitioner to "discover metaphors which convey images of bones as living tissue". Maybe the authors, hereby, indicate that the 'body as a machine' is not the best conceptual metaphor either. However, they present the 'discovery' of metaphor as a professional task. This is an important point, since metaphor also comprises 'meaning' – or involves a transfer, as Brown (1976) puts it. As Brown (1976:172–73) says, our understanding of metaphor "involves more than the ability to recognize its referent, or even to use it correctly". Using a metaphor involves understandings of implicit connotations of both sets of referents – 'the body' and 'a machine', the two systems or levels of discourse, the literal and pretended. Therefore, the 'meaning' of a metaphor is not only situational and contextual, but also professional. For example, 'the body' as well as 'a machine' can change meaning as a metaphor in a clinical setting compared with a sociological, philosophical or poetic context. The criteria for judging what makes a 'good' metaphor are therefore not just that it offers us a 'new awareness', but also a relevant awareness in a professional context, such that it is not misunderstood.

Brown (1976) emphasizes the importance of metaphor retaining its consciously 'as if' quality. Here I will refer to Descartes (1971) again, since he used the machine metaphor several times, not least in writing: "I have described the Earth and the whole visible universe as if it were a machine, having regard only to the shape and movement of its parts" (cited in Brown 1976:175–76). This metaphorical awareness – 'as if' and not 'is' – is essential. Metaphor is exactly defined as being not a direct representation of 'the fact'. Metaphor can make 'facts' visualizable. Therefore, to use metaphor in professions is not about discovering or creating correspondence to some directly knowable referent. Rather 'good' professional metaphors are about being attentive towards what is not available in the language, which can emerge in the tension between and interplay of different referential systems. This means that the keyword in the use of metaphor is translation – not identity. As Brown notes (1976:185): "Metaphors lose vivacity as they gain veracity".

In line with this approach transferred to professional tasks, metaphors should provide a new way of understanding that which professionals already know. In this way, a metaphorical use of language is not 'bad' science, nor 'bad' practice. On the contrary, metaphor makes it possible to speak about phenomena not already observed and thereby develop science or practice. The elaboration of metaphor – for example, the 'body as a machine' – may be furthered if we ask, as Brown (1976) suggests, in what respect? In a medical context, we will learn what medicine can teach us about the body, in a philosophical way. If 'machine' is still a metaphor and not a positivist correspondence to experimental evidence, we might also learn about the body what is not like a machine. In this way, we can obtain knowledge of professions' more implicit claims of jurisdiction (Abbott 1988) by studying metaphor. Depending on the metaphors chosen to describe professional work, there will be differing ramifications for the aspects of the task that are perceived by professionals as being relevant. In analyses of professional work, we should discover metaphor as a way of experiencing facts rather than suggesting the use of terms for facts.

Conclusion: using conceptual metaphors as a reassuring signal of expertise

This chapter has studied conceptual metaphors used by medical doctors in their practice, based on the assumption that such metaphors emerge from the interaction between medical science, the doctors' professional knowledge and the experiences and imaginations of their patients' everyday culture. I have drawn on metaphor studies of the very act of professional work itself, presuming that metaphors are indicators of professional culture. How doctors and patients use different but also mutual metaphors (shared by both) has demonstrated that different kinds of metaphors illuminate different cultures, but also where they sometimes fuse. The professional culture is not constituted only by scientific knowledge and evidence, but also in the clinic by the doctor–patient relationship. In this encounter, use of scientific concepts probably make no sense, at least not for all patients. Empirical studies indicate that medical doctors do not use patients' metaphors either. Doctors are 'problem solvers' and 'controllers of disease' and they are doing boundary work within the polar extremes, paternalism and consumerism. The metaphors used in medical practice might illustrate where in this spectrum they act. Acting in sometimes paternalistic, sometimes consumeristic, ways, they – and their patients – can use metaphors to conceptualize relationships. Medical doctors use specific conceptual metaphors as a reassuring signal of expertise, whether it is paternalistic or consumeristic, or within these polar extremes.

Exactly which metaphors are used in professional practice might vary. The use of conceptual metaphors also changes historically. For example, as Abbott (1988) has noted, the physicians who handled the fever and the surgeons who fixed a broken thumb had little to do with one another before the nineteenth or twentieth century. At that time the surgeons were closer to engineers building a bridge, both involving the science of mechanics, or they were barbers, closer to craftsmen, both using tools such as sharp knives. The body is not an objective entity but culturally treated and enacted, sometimes as a machine or an engine, other times as a building or a tool – or as energy or craft. Of course, as Morgan (1996:228) has stated, 'old metaphor' is used "to negotiate what we already know, or think we know". But metaphors have also a constitutive, generative force – being part of the craft and therefore also a process. This chapter has demonstrated that engagement with professional metaphors can facilitate an understanding about not only professional practice and jurisdictional work, but also authorized expertise that is linked to the clinical changing culture and the clinics' plurality of clients. Metaphor is the process of experiencing one domain through another and it stretches reality. Therefore, metaphor use might be fruitful in a learning process and we need more studies to explore how professionals use metaphor, which kinds of metaphor they use, when and why.

References

Abbott, A. (1988) *The System of Professions: An Essay on the Division of Expert Labor*. Chicago: University of Chicago Press.
Abbott, A. (1995) Boundaries of social work or social work of boundaries? *The Social Service Review* 69(4): 545–62.

Alvesson, M. (1993) The play of metaphors. In: J. Hassard and M. Perker (eds) *Postmodernism and Organizations*. London: Sage.

Alvesson, M. and Spicer, A. (eds) (2011) *Metaphors We Lead By. Understanding Leadership in the Real World*. London: Routledge.

Beisecker, A. E. and Beisecker, T. D. (1993) Using metaphors to characterize doctor-patient relationships: Paternalism versus consumerism, *Health Communication* 5(1): 41–58.

Brown, H. R. (1976) Social theory as metaphor: On the logic of discovery for the sciences of conduct, *Theory and Society* 3(2): 169–97.

Calnan, M. (1984) Clinical uncertainty: Is it a problem in the doctor-patient relationship? *Sociology of Health and Illness* 6(1): 74–85.

Cameron, L. and Low, G. (eds) (1999) *Researching and Applying Metaphor*. Cambridge: Cambridge University Press.

Descartes, R. (1971) *Discourse on Method and the Meditations*. Harmondsworth: Penguin.

Fitzgerald, T. K. (1993) *Metaphors of Identity: A Culture-Communication Dialogue*. Albany: SUNY Press.

Fleischman, S. (1999) I am . . . , I have . . . , I suffer from . . . : A linguist reflects on the language of illness and disease, *Journal of Medical Humanities* 20: 3–32.

Freidson, E. (1975) *Doctoring Together: A Study of Professional Social Control*. New York: Elsevier.

Geertz, C. (1973) *The Interpretation of Cultures*. New York: Basic Books.

Gibbs, R. W. (1999) Taking metaphor out of our heads and putting it into the cultural world. In: R. W. Gibbs and G. Steen (eds) *Metaphor in Cognitive Linguistics*. Amsterdam: John Benjamin.

Gibbs, R. W. (ed) (2008) *The Cambridge Handbook of Metaphor and Thought*. Cambridge: Cambridge University Press.

Gleyse, J. (2013) The machine body metaphor: From science and technology to physical education and sport in France (1825–1935), *Scandinavian Journal of Medicine and Science in Sports* 23: 758–65.

Gwyn, R. (1999) 'Captain of my own ship': Metaphor and the discourse of chronic illness. In: L. Cameron and G. Low (eds) *Researching and Applying Metaphor*. Cambridge: Cambridge University Press.

Keesing, R. M. (1987) Models, 'folk' and 'cultural' – paradigms regained? In: D. Holland and N. Quinn (eds) *Cultural Models in Language and Thought*. Cambridge: Cambridge University Press.

Kirmayer, L. J. (1993) Healing and the invention of metaphors: The effectiveness of symbols revisited, *Culture, Medicine and Psychiatry* 17: 277–99.

Kövecses, Z. (2002) *Metaphor: A Practical Introduction*. New York: Oxford University Press.

Kövecses, Z. (2005) *Metaphor in Culture: Universality and Variation*. Cambridge: Cambridge University Press.

Lakoff, G. and Johnson, M. (1980) *Metaphors We Live By*. Chicago: University of Chicago Press.

Lakoff, G. and Johnson, M. (1999) *Philosophy in the Flesh: The Embodied Mind and Its Challenge to Western Thought*. New York: Basic Books.

Mabeck, C. E. and Olesen, F. (1997) Metaphorically transmitted diseases. How do patients embody medical explanations? *Family Practice* 14(4): 271–78.

Martin, P. (1997) *The Healing Mind: The Vital Links between Brain and Behavior, Immunity and Disease*. New York: St Martin's Press.

McMullen, L. M. (1989) Uses of figurative language in successful and unsuccessful cases of psychotherapy: Three comparisons, *Metaphor and Symbolic Activity* 4(4): 203–26.

Morgan, G. (1980) Paradigms, metaphors, and puzzle solving in organization theory, *Administrative Science Quarterly* 25(4): 605–22.

Morgan, G. (1993) *Imaginization: The Art of Creative Management*. London: Sage.

Morgan, G. (1996) An afterword: Is there anything more to be said about metaphor? In: D. Grant and C. Oswick (eds) *Metaphor and Organizations*. London: Sage.

Morgan, G. (2006) *Images of Organization*. London: Sage.

Núñes, R. (2008) Conceptual metaphor, human cognition, and the nature of mathematics. In: R. W. Gibbs (ed) *The Cambridge Handbook of Metaphor and Thought*. Cambridge: Cambridge University Press.

Parsons, T. (1951) *The Social System*. Glencoe: Free Press.

Reventlow, S. D., Overgaard, I. S., Hvas, L. and Malterud, K. (2008) Metaphorical mediation in women's perceptions of risk related to osteoporosis: A qualitative interview study, *Health, Risk and Society* 10(2): 103–15.

Skelton, J. R., Wearn, A. M. and Hobbs, F. D. R. (2002) A concordance-based study of metaphoric expressions used by general practitioners and patients in consultation, *British Journal of General Practice* 52: 114–18.

Sontag, S. (1991) Illness as metaphor. In: S. Sontag *Illness as Metaphor and AIDS and Its Metaphors*. London: Penguin.

Webster, A., Douglas, C. and Lewis, G. (2009) Making sense of medicines: 'Lay pharmacology' and narratives of safety and efficacy, *Science as Culture* 18(2): 233–47.

Winter, S. L. (2008) What is the 'color' of law? In: R. W. Gibbs (ed) *The Cambridge Handbook of Metaphor and Thought*. Cambridge: Cambridge University Press.

Yu, N. (2008) Metaphor from body and culture. In: R. W. Gibbs (ed) *The Cambridge Handbook of Metaphor and Thought*. Cambridge: Cambridge University Press.

Index

2, 5, 6, 15, 21, 23–4, 49–59, 63–75, 77–93, 98–113; zoos, circuses and safari parks metaphors 77–93
Nietzche, Friedrich 3

organism metaphor: ecological metaphor 31, 38; hierarchies and landscape metaphors 3, 25; Justice-as-a-Woman metaphor 126–7
organizational theory 1, 80

paternalism 171, 174
Portugal: professions and public welfare 58
professional knowledge in social work: back on track metaphor 149–50; bonding or freeing from embroilments metaphor 150–1; boundaries metaphor 151, 159–60; clarifying or visual metaphors 152–3; development 157–60; diagnosis concept 149–55; doing or crafting metaphors 154–5; giving and taking metaphors 152; inference or causation concepts 149–55; intervention or treatment concepts 149–55; metaphorical concepts 149–57; metaphors 47–8; opening and closing metaphors 151; overview 6, 147; quantifiable measures 152; relieving and supporting metaphor 150; socio-cognitive patterns in 147–60; space of speech or communication metaphors 153–4; teaching and health care metaphors 155–7
professions: health and medical professions 5–6, 20, 41, 52, 53–7, 77, 79–82, 86–93, 155–7, 163–4, 167–74; introduction to 1–7; legal profession 6, 78–9, 81–4, 114–28; social work 4, 6, 54, 98–113, 147–60; teaching profession 6, 71, 72–5, 130–44, 155, 156–7; *see also* sociology of professions

race relations 103–4
Redfield, Robert 33
Reflexivity of Mirrors metaphor 125

Research Excellence Framework 58
Russia: health and medical professions 55–6; INTAS project 55–6; Soviet Realism literary movement 132

safari parks metaphor *see* zoos, circuses and safari parks metaphors
Salic Law 120–1
Selden, John 121
Shipman, Harold 54, 87, 89
similes 165
Smith, Adam 36, 40, 42, 69
social closure: boa constrictor metaphor 5, 64, 71–5; boundaries metaphor 23, 24, 66; conceptual refinement 65; exclusionary 15–17, 23, 24, 64–5, 66, 67, 70, 82–3, 87; expansion 71, 72–5; external closure 70, 71, 73–5; Greek mythology metaphors 51–2; hierarchies metaphor 14–17, 23, 24; internal closure 70, 71, 73–5; overview 5, 64, 75; Frank Parkin 65–7, 69–70; sociology of professions 5, 14–17, 23, 24, 51–2, 63–75, 82–3, 87; spatial analogy 64, 65, 66, 67, 68, 70; teaching profession 71, 72–5; tragedy of metaphors 63; usurpatory 15–16, 66, 70; Max Weber 5, 14, 64–5, 66, 67–71, 72–3; zoos, circuses and safari parks metaphors 82–3, 87
social work: altruism 112–13; back on track metaphor 149–50; bonding or freeing from embroilments metaphor 150–1; boundaries metaphor 6, 98–113, 151, 159–60; capitalist metaphor 4; clarifying or visual metaphors 152–3; doing or crafting metaphors 154–5; evolution 98–9, 107–13; functionalist perspective 99–102, 104, 110; funding 111–12; gender issues 109; giving and taking metaphors 152; Greek mythology metaphors 54; heroine metaphor 4; home economics 99, 107, 109; kindergarten 99, 105, 107, 108–9; legitimacy 112; opening and closing metaphors 151; privatization 4; probation 98, 99, 105–6, 107, 108–9; professional knowledge

For Product Safety Concerns and Information please contact our EU
representative GPSR@taylorandfrancis.com
Taylor & Francis Verlag GmbH, Kaufingerstraße 24, 80331 München, Germany

www.ingramcontent.com/pod-product-compliance
Ingram Content Group UK Ltd.
Pitfield, Milton Keynes, MK11 3LW, UK
UKHW020951180425
457613UK00019B/630